SAECULUM: HISTORY AND SOCIETY IN THE THEOLOGY OF ST AUGUSTINE

SAECULUM: HISTORY AND SOCIETY IN THE THEOLOGY OF ST AUGUSTINE

R. A. MARKUS

Senior Lecturer in Medieval History
in the University of Liverpool

CAMBRIDGE

AT THE UNIVERSITY PRESS

1970

Published by the Syndics of the Cambridge University Press
Bentley House, 200 Euston Road, London N.W.1
American Branch: 32 East 57th Street, New York, N.Y.10022

Library of Congress Catalogue Card Number: 71–87136

Standard Book Number: 521 07621 8

Printed in Great Britain
at the University Printing House, Cambridge
(Brooke Crutchley, University Printer)

44060

CONTENTS

PREFACE

This book is, in the first place, a historical study. It seeks to discover and to understand a slice of the past: the particular slice being the thought of St Augustine of Hippo on a particular cluster of themes. Its object is not to cover ground already adequately covered. Even in English alone, there are several good expositions of Augustine's political thought. Accordingly, much that falls within the field generally recognised as 'political theory' is here not dealt with at all, or only touched on lightly. I have, for instance, allowed myself only the briefest of discussions of law, and not considered such cognate themes of Augustine's reflection as property, justice or war. On the forms of government and on the right way to exercise its functions even the little that Augustine has to say has fallen outside my scope. On the other hand, much of the book is concerned with subjects which would not normally be found in an exposition of Augustine's political thought. My purpose has been to consider the fundamentals of the way in which Augustine conceived the social dimension of human, especially Christian, existence. This is why much of the book is concerned with themes such as Augustine's vision of history and of God's work in human history. Such discussions have at times landed me in considering even more distant topics, such as, for instance, Augustine's views on prophetic inspiration, or on youth and age. I have, of course, had to take into account Augustine's attitude to Roman history, and especially to Roman history in his own times; and one could not claim to have come to grips with Augustine's fundamental ideas on the social dimension of human living without entering into some account of the Church in his theology. Here too I have had to draw a somewhat arbitrary line between the topics I thought it necessary to discuss, and the vast riches of Augustinian ecclesiology which it is not my purpose to tap.

I have excluded a great deal in order to keep to the central line of my enquiry: how did Augustine conceive the purpose of human society, in relation to his conception of man's ultimate destiny? How did he think of actual, historical societies—particularly of the 'state' of his own day, the Roman Empire—in relation to the whole history of human societies? What, in the end, did he consider to be man's right posture in the *saeculum*: the world of men and of time? Questions like these form the kernel of my enquiry. In trying to answer them, I have always sought to relate Augustine's ideas to a living context of thought: a living context, in the first place, in his own mind. I have tried to follow ideas in their sometimes tangled ramifications and to achieve some insight into Augustine's thought as a developing and changing complex. The most significant aspects of Augustine's reflection often turn out to be his changes of mind rather than the vast body of *idées reçues* which he simply took over as part of a contemporary stock of ideas, often without devoting very much thought to them. And to trace his changes of mind more is usually required than a reading of his *Retractationes*. In the second place I have tried to relate Augustine's ideas to a further context: that of contemporary debate, and, in so far as older alignments entered into the terms of contemporary debate, to older traditions. In this way it has often been possible to sharpen the issues before Augustine's mind, to distinguish in his writings what he was content to accept of his intellectual environment from that which he was urgently addressing to his hearers and readers, and especially what he had come to think for himself, often after sustained anguish and interior debate.

To gain some insight into a living though past body of thought has been my first aim, and it is in this sense that my enquiry is a historical one. It will, however, be clear to the reader that at many points my interest in the past merges into a present concern. Any sustained historical enquiry ought to do something to the mind of the historian who undertakes it. It should force him to scrutinise his own assumptions, to question some of his own values, to challenge some of the stock responses of his own age. Prolonged contact with a mind of the stature of Augustine's is inevitably a two-way commerce between the past and the present. To read

Augustine for fifteen years or more would have been intolerably tedious had it not in some way given insight into problems such as that of a 'Christian society' or a 'secular city'. At this point my enquiry merges into theology. Augustine once wrote, quoting Cyprian, that we must return to the sources—they were both thinking of the Apostolic tradition—and 'carve a channel from them to our own times'.[1] To go back to Augustine merely with a view to finding in his work warrant for some particular theological position would be suspect; certainly suspect as historical scholarship, but also suspect as sound theology. But to return to Augustine and to 'carve a channel' from him to our own times, to find oneself, willing or unwilling, involved in a dialogue with him on questions agitating theology today, cannot be condemned as unsound, either in historical or in theological procedure. I have therefore allowed myself to 'carve a channel' from Augustine to our own day; and it would have been dishonest not to indicate the direction that its course insisted on taking. I have confined myself to the barest of explicit indications of this direction in an epilogue, the last chapter of the book. It may be that some day I shall be able to follow the signposts.

The appendixes, even those previously published, were all originally written for this book. Their object is to substantiate parts of the argument where the necessary detail or rigour required for this purpose would have constituted a large disparate block in the text. Their conclusions are incorporated in the text and form essential stages of the argument. But the details of the evidence and the arguments from it to the conclusions have been confined to the appendixes. The first three have been previously published, and are reprinted here in a slightly abbreviated and revised form. I am grateful to the Editors of *Augustinus* (Appendix A) and of the *Journal of theological studies* (Appendixes B and C) for permission to reprint material first published in their journals.

[1] Augustine, *De bapt.* v, 26.37; Cyprian, *Ep.* 74, 10.3. On them, see Bakhuizen van den Brink, 'Tradition and authority', 22.

References are given in an abbreviated form in the footnotes. Recourse to the list of works referred to (pp. 235–48) will provide the necessary details. This list has been compiled as an aid to convenience, not as a bibliography. To provide anything like a complete bibliography to the subject of this book, extending, as it does, into history, theology, political theory, would have been an immense task which I have not attempted. With the aid of the bibliographical note (pp. 233–4) the reader should find himself in a position to survey the relevant literature.

A great body of irredeemable debts is inevitably contracted in the writing of a book over a period of more than a decade. Among those of which I am conscious I must put first what I owe to the University of Liverpool, and especially to my colleagues and pupils in the School of History. I am deeply grateful for the congenial environment, the intellectual stimulus and the friendship which I have found here to sustain me in my work. What I owe to individual scholars, I have acknowledged in the appropriate place, whenever I was conscious of relying on their work. One exception of which I am aware is Walter Stein, from whom I have learnt more than from anyone else about the fundamental problems in the middle distance and the background of my study. Another exception is Peter Brown. What my understanding of Augustine owes to his work is more than I can easily estimate. At the time when his book *Augustine of Hippo: a biography* (1967) was published, more than half my book had been written. Through his kindness I had, however, seen parts of the typescript before publication. Peter Brown and Henry Mayr-Harting have generously read much of the book in typescript. To their criticism and encouragement I owe much. I have followed many of their suggestions and would probably have done better to follow more.

R. A. MARKUS

Liverpool, 1969

In Augustine's day Christians, conscious of a debt to their spouses which they could not pin-point at all closely, were content to record their gratitude in simple inscriptions:

CONIUGI BENEMERENTI

Their words I borrow to record here my gratitude for something I can specify as little as could they

ABBREVIATIONS

Aug. mag.	*Augustinus magister* (Congrès International Augustinien, Paris, 1954), 3 vols.
CC	*Corpus Christianorum.*
CQR	*Church quarterly review.*
CSEL	*Corpus scriptorum ecclesiasticorum latinorum.*
GCS	*Die griechischen christlichen Schriftsteller.*
HTR	*Harvard theological review.*
HZ	*Historische Zeitschrift.*
JRS	*Journal of Roman studies.*
JTS	*Journal of theological studies.*
MGH. AA	*Monumenta Germaniae historica. Auctores antiquissimi.*
NS	New series.
OCT	Oxford Classical texts.
PG	*Patrologia graeca,* ed. J. P. Migne.
PL	*Patrologia latina,* ed. J. P. Migne.
Rech. aug.	*Recherches augustiniennes.*
RB	*Revue Bénédictine.*
REAug	*Revue des études augustiniennes.*
Ric. rel.	*Ricerche religiose.*
SSLAug	Schilling, *Die Staats- und Soziallehre des hl. Augustinus.*
SSLThom	Schilling, *Die Staats- und Soziallehre des hl. Thomas von Aquin.*
T. & S.	*Texts and studies.*
T. & U.	*Texte und Untersuchungen.*
VC	*Vigiliae christianae.*
ZKG	*Zeitschrift für Kirchengeschichte.*
ZNTW	*Zeitschrift für neutestamentliche Wissenschaft.*

See also the list of works referred to, pp. 235–48.

Augustine's reflections on history owed much both to the development of Christian historiography during the fourth century, and to the challenge of his own troubled times. With Orosius he had little in common;[1] with Ammianus and the classical tradition of historiography even less. With this tradition he took care to dissociate himself expressly. In an early chapter of his *City of God*[2] he goes out of his way to say that he does not wish to enter the sphere of the historian: if he were to recount the details of the calamities that had afflicted Rome in the course of the Punic wars, he says, 'I too should become no more than a writer of history'. This was not his purpose; and throughout the fourth century, history conceived in this traditional sense had been the preserve of pagan writers.[3] It was pagans like Eutropius and Festus whom the Emperor Valens commissioned to prepare short summaries of the Roman past for a new class of reader to whom these were not familiar. Pagans also were responsible for works of more advanced historical enterprise, and for historical romance such as the *Historia Augusta*.[4] When, on rare occasions, such writers touched on the great religious issues of their day, they did so in cautious and reserved terms; or they took care to disguise their controversial intent. There was little about their work that could give offence to Christians, and their short epitomes of Roman history could without any difficulty be incorporated by Christian writers in their own works. History as traditionally practised and understood remained a pagan preserve. Its characteristic reticence and even neutrality in religious matters helped to avoid conflict between pagans and Christians in this sphere. The years after Theodosius brought with them new political crises, and, in their train, a new kind of polemical history. But the bitterness of theological controversy was absent from the

---

[1] On Orosius, cf. below, Ch. 7, pp. 161–2.   [2] III, 18.1.

[3] On this and what follows, see the brilliant study by Momigliano, 'Pagan and Christian historiography'.

[4] An increasing consensus is taking shape on the dating of this to the later Theodosian or not too remote post-Theodosian years. Cf. most recently, Syme, *Ammianus and the Historia Augusta*. Its *Geschichtsapologetik* might be equally at home in the somewhat later setting to which it is assigned by Straub, *Heidnische Geschichtsapologetik*.

CHAPTER I

HISTORY: SACRED AND SECULAR

IF historiography is to be divided—as history used to be—into 'periods', the years of Saint Augustine's episcopate would mark an important watershed among them. Little more than twenty years lie between the publication of the last great work of classical historiography, that of Ammianus Marcellinus, and the *Seven books of histories against the pagans* by Orosius. In 395, when Ammianus, in all probability, had just completed his work, Augustine became bishop of Hippo. Orosius, the Spanish priest who had found his way to Hippo in his flight from the barbarian upheavals in his home province, wrote his work at Augustine's bidding, in the years 416–17. Ten books of his master's great work of historical apologetics, the *City of God*, were by now completed. Ammianus was not much read during the middle ages; Orosius, though he found few imitators, became one of the standard textbooks. To contrast these two authors as 'classical' and 'medieval' or as 'pagan' and 'Christian' does not take us far. They share scarcely any assumptions about how history is to be written and what it is about. Ammianus wrote towards the end of a century of profound changes in the life of the Roman Empire, political, economic and social, as well as religious. The rate of change quickened towards the end of the century. A further crisis lay between the publication of his book and the writing of Orosius's. These were the years following the death of Theodosius I, the years which saw the division of the Empire between his young sons and the political troubles attendant on the eclipse of imperial power. They were the years of the great barbarian break-through on the Rhine (406–7) and of the sacking of Rome by the Goths (410). Behind Ammianus lay the development of the Christian Empire between Constantine and Theodosius; behind Orosius the more recent crises of the early fifth century.

atmosphere of fourth-century historiography. Pagan and Christian historians had almost entirely different interests, and there could be no conflict between them because their concerns met at scarcely any point.

If Christians during the fourth century were content to leave history as generally understood to pagans, they were by no means uninterested in the past. From the beginning they based their faith on a particular group of historical events, in which they saw God's mighty acts for the salvation of men accomplished among his chosen people and brought to a consummation in Jesus Christ, who was born under Augustus and suffered under Pontius Pilate. They read and re-read the narratives of this redemption history as contained in the books which had slowly crystallised into the canon of the Bible. But they did not only read them, meditate on them, comment on them; they could scarcely avoid reflecting on the question: if the things told in these stories really happened, where did they fit into the past? Already Luke, especially, among the evangelists, had felt the need to give his narrative a firm anchorage in contemporary secular history. The need to make room for Abraham and Moses and the rest among Ninus, Hercules and the less remote figures of ancient history became more strongly felt as the contacts between Christianity and pagan culture grew more extensive. The Christian chronographers who catered for this need did so almost incidentally. Their concern had been, in the first place, to vindicate the claims of the biblical revelation to greater antiquity and thus to priority over the wisdom of the Greeks. In catering for this whim, they did, nevertheless, perform a task of wider significance. Their work made it possible to trace the contours of the biblical landscape on a historical map familiar to educated Romans. They thus introduced the pagan convert to Christianity to a redemptive history for which the history he learnt at school had no place; and at the same time they provided their Christian readers with a framework, derived from the redemptive history on which their faith was founded, into which they could fit other historical information as

1-2

it became familiar to them. Both for the pagan convert to Christianity and for the uninstructed Christian, such works helped to map out the course of human history with the aid of the fixed points in the story of redemption. They compelled the pagan convert to 'enlarge his historical horizon'.[1] They introduced him, as well as the Christian believer, to universal history, and, at the same time, furnished the clues with the aid of which it could be read as bound up with man's destiny. This kind of chronography was well developed before the time of Eusebius,[2] but it can scarcely be called 'history'. It was a way of meeting a need for elementary Christian orientation in a predominantly pagan world, rather than of catering for a desire to know the past.

An interest in the past was not entirely lacking in Christian circles. The fourth century did see the development of a major new form of historiography, that of ecclesiastical history;[3] but Augustine was not very much more interested in this than in the kind of history that Ammianus and others had written for a pagan reading public. His attitude to ecclesiastical history was far from simple, and, as we shall see (especially in Ch. 2), it underwent profound changes. As for political and military history as it would have been understood among the sort of people who read Ammianus, this held little interest for Augustine. Until his own days, this kind of history could safely be left to its pagan practitioners. In the years following 410 Augustine became conscious of a need for a new kind of Christian historical apologetic. In 416 he commissioned Orosius, a refugee from Spain who had placed himself under Augustine's patronage, to carry out this task.

That Augustine himself did not consider it to be for him to carry out the work he assigned to Orosius can be explained in several ways. He was a busy bishop, in the centre of conflicts extending well beyond the bounds not only of his own diocese, but of the African Church of which he had rapidly become one

[1] I quote the phrase from Momigliano, 'Pagan and Christian historiography', 83. I lean heavily on his treatment of this topic on pp. 82–5.
[2] Cf. Von den Brincken, *Studien*, 43–60.
[3] I shall not discuss here the third *genre* enumerated by Momigliano, that of hagiography.

of the acknowledged leaders. His complaints about the lack of time for study and writing, of the *episcopalis sarcina*, are a recurrent commonplace in his correspondence. But beyond such immediate reasons for his assigning the task to someone else, we may also discern obstacles to his performing it himself which lay deeper in his mind. Notwithstanding his realisation of a need for a new Christian historiography, his own attitudes to history were very like those of most fourth-century Christians. It is unlikely that he read Ammianus Marcellinus. History of this kind held little interest for him, and in so far as the pagan opposition with which he set himself to deal in the *City of God* had historical roots, they lay elsewhere. The sort of history Ammianus wrote had not even the distinction in his eyes of standing in need of refutation.

Augustine could, on occasion, undertake sustained historical research, as he did, for instance, in the course of supplementing Optatus's dossier on the history of the Donatist schism by his own enquiries. But this is exceptional in his work, and in any case it scarcely amounts to an interest in history for its own sake. It is part of a running debate, in which the history of relatively recent times was among the issues at stake. Augustine could show meticulous care in accumulating relevant material from official archives when this served his purpose. In general, however, this kind of work was foreign to his interests. It is in the educational scheme drawn up in his *De doctrina christiana* that he came most closely to grips with the place that history ought to occupy in the Christian curriculum of studies. Like other educational disciplines, history gains admission to the Christian round of studies in so far—and only in so far—as it can serve as an aid to the understanding of the scriptures.[1] The whole educational programme of the *De doctrina christiana* is narrowly conceived. We may concede that its narrowness is linked with a clear vision of purpose, a vision lacking from much of the contemporary educational tradition. It is, nevertheless, almost inhumanly rigid in its determination to outlaw any field of study which does not contribute to an

---

[1] II, 27.42–28.44.

'understanding of the faith'. Whatever its merits,[1] this exclusive orientation to the *intellectus fidei* did not encourage the study of history as it would have been understood by most of Augustine's contemporaries. It is not difficult to guess what kind of history Augustine had in mind when he considered its usefulness to the understanding of the scriptures. It was certainly not the kind of history which Ammianus had just completed. This, like its classical model, the work of Tacitus, and the other classics of Greek and Roman historiography, would have had little or no contribution to make to an understanding of the biblical revelation. The kind of history Augustine must have had in mind was primarily that of the Christian chronographers, and especially Jerome's extended translation of Eusebius's work in this *genre*. It is clearly to works of this type he is referring when he speaks of their helping us to date the events of the redemption history 'by Olympiads and the names of the Consuls'. Information of this kind could extend the range of our knowledge by being collated with scriptural data, or it could serve to determine claims to priority among Greek philosophers and Hebrew prophets. These are precisely the purposes served by Christian chronography. Its compilers may thus usefully draw on extra-biblical material such as can be learnt *puerili eruditione* outside the Church. The secular history contained in Book XVIII of the *City of God*, itself no more than a perfunctory repetition of the material from the handful of sources utilised in it by Augustine, falls entirely within the scope defined in the *De doctrina christiana*. The narratives of secular history are co-ordinated with the sequence of the biblical history; some attempt is made—following, of course, Eusebius and Jerome—to anchor the biblical story in the general history of antiquity. Even in this book, as we shall see, Augustine shows much creative originality; but it does not lie in his use of historical material. In this sphere he was an heir to the pioneers and the fourth-century masters of the craft. His interest in extra-biblical history, like theirs, had

---

[1] An eloquent and persuasive defence of its value and originality is to be found in Marrou, *Saint Augustin*, 352–6.

arisen from the need to think of world history as including the biblical history, and it remained confined within this perspective. This incorporation of biblical in world history certainly had a part to play in leading Augustine to meditate, supremely among Christian thinkers, on the unity of world history; but not counting, for the present, his theological interpretation of the historical process, he was following well-trodden paths.[1] Behind his remarks on 'history' it is easy to discern the familiar outlines of Christian chronography in the fourth century. There is no mention of or allusion to ecclesiastical history in this passage of the *De doctrina christiana*. The complexities of Augustine's attitude to this subject will engage our attention in due course.

The distinction between the *historia gentium* taught outside the Church, of which he speaks in the *De doctrina christiana*, and the history contained in the scriptures, the *temporaliter praeterita...quae pro salute gessit...aeternitas divinae providentiae*, as he puts it elsewhere,[2] is an inherited commonplace. It is simply the distinction between the biblical redemption history and all other history, and was familiar to any Christian, even of the less well-educated kind. Augustine took it over as it stood. In the course of time, however, he devoted much thought to the theological grounds for this distinction.

Some fourteen years after his conversion to Christianity Augustine wrote a memorable account of the process that had led to it. In a famous chapter of the *Confessions* he recounts his passage from the intellectual world of neo-Platonism to Christianity. It had been easy, in the heady atmosphere of Milan in the mid 380s, to pass from the world of Plotinus and Porphyry to that of Saint Paul and the Fourth Gospel. Looking back upon his reading of the 'books of the Platonists', Augustine could, in retrospect, see many of the central doctrines of Christianity contained in them. There, he tells us,[3] he had read of God and his Word and of the human soul, which, though not itself the Light,

---

[1] This seems to be overlooked by Marrou, who devotes some pregnant paragraphs to this topic: *Saint Augustin*, 466–7.   [2] *De agone chr.* 13.15.
[3] *Conf.* VII, 9.13–14.

gave testimony to it; there he had read of the unchangeable eternity of God and his Son. But he had not read in these books that the Word became flesh and dwelt among men. The events of the Incarnation and the earthly life, death and resurrection of Jesus Christ are the beliefs which defined the gulf between Christianity and the *praeparatio evangelica* in the works of the philosophers. Even the 'Platonists', the *praecipui gentium philosophi*,[1] had not been able to anticipate these truths in their teaching. The reason for this failure is that these truths were contingent, historical facts and as such were inaccessible to the abstract, general method of argumentation appropriate to philosophy. They belong to the 'course of changing things and the fabric of temporal history'[2] on which the philosopher cannot but be silent: this is the province of the historian and the prophet. Augustine's sense of a gulf fixed between Christianity and pagan philosophy grew sharper with age and episcopal office. With it grew the stress he came to lay on the historical and eschatological elements in Christian teaching.[3] But there is no reason to call in doubt his appreciation, even at the time of his conversion, of the essential historical substance of the Christian Gospel. As early as in his *De vera religione*, written in Africa soon after his return, he could assert unambiguously that the head and substance of the Christian religion was contained in 'the history and prophecy of the temporal dispensations of divine providence for the salvation of the human race';[4] and there is much about the place of reason and of authority in Christian teaching in his earliest dialogues which points in the same direction.[5] He knew that the claim to truth of Christian teaching stood or fell with the historicity of the events on which it rests.

---

[1] *De Trin.* XIII, 19.24. This is the central theme of *De civ. Dei* VIII.

[2] *De Trin.* IV, 16.21. In *De agone christiano* 13.15 Augustine says that the faith of the Church refers both to eternity and to *temporalia praeterita et futura quae pro salute hominum gessit et gestura est aeternitas divinae providentiae*. Cf. *ibid.* 16.19. Augustine had to widen his conception of *scientia* to accommodate the *cognitio historica* to which the *temporaliter gesta* of the redemption history are known; cf. *De Trin.* XIII, 1.2.

[3] For one aspect of Augustine's thought which illustrates this generalisation cf. Markus, 'Alienatio'.

[4] 7.13.   [5] Cf. Holte, *Béatitude et sagesse*, 73 f., 303 f.

There was, then, a privileged strand of history in which Augustine could not, as a Christian, fail to take an interest. This was the biblical narrative of God's saving work among his chosen people, the promise and preparation in the Old Testament and the fulfilment in the New. This privileged strand of history commanded Augustine's assent as a matter of faith. For the Christian, the biblical books supersede all other authorities. They provide a yardstick, endowed with divine authority, whereby to measure all other beliefs.[1] For the people of God, the biblical authors are 'their philosophers, that is, their lovers of wisdom, they are their wise men, their theologians, their prophets, they are their teachers of righteousness and of holiness'.[2] This is an example of the kind of transposition of pagan language into the Christian vocabulary of which Augustine was notoriously fond. It served him well in his rhetorical exploitation of the contrast between Christians, their works and their institutions, and their pagan counterparts.[3] In an early letter Augustine had spoken of the pagans' *historia sacra*.[4] Here, the expression refers to the pagan myths about the gods. It is by no means impossible that when he used the phrase in reference to the Christian scriptures[5] Augustine was indulging his liking for this kind of transposition in the interests of a more dramatic confrontation. We shall follow Augustine in adopting the phrase 'sacred history' to distinguish the biblical narratives from other, 'secular', historical narratives. The distinction is thoroughly Augustinian, even though the expression 'secular history' does not form part of his vocabulary.

All history, sacred and secular, has its origin in God's creation of the world.[6] The full exposition of the faith (*plena narratio*)

---

[1] Cf. *De civ. Dei*, XVIII, 40: *nos vero in nostrae religionis historia, fulti auctoritate divina...*; *nostra religionis historia* is the Bible. Cf. *ibid.* XI, 3 on the *eminentissima auctoritas* of the scriptures, and XII, 10.2 (= 11 in D & K) on its use as a criterion for selecting the least discordant account among the pagan 'fables' masquerading as true accounts of antiquity; cf. *De Trin.* III, 11.22: *auctoritas divinarum scripturarum unde mens nostra deviare non debet...*   [2] *De civ. Dei*, XVIII, 41.3.

[3] Cf. Kamlah's remarks on Augustine's fondness for referring to the Church's institutions etc. as 'ours' in contrast with their Roman counterparts as 'theirs'.—*Christentum und Geschichtlichkeit*, 167–8.   [4] *Ep.* 17.1.   [5] *De civ. Dei*, XV, 8.1.

[6] On this subject I may refer to the excellent discussion by Wachtel, *Beiträge*, Ch. 4.

which he recommends to the deacon Deogratias is to embrace the whole story from the creation to the present state of the Church.[1] The creation is the beginning of all things. Time itself only came into being with the creation of temporal things.[2] In a strict sense, however, man's condition between the creation and Adam's fall, though temporal, can be described as not fully historical. But for man's primal sin and fall from the condition of grace there would have been no need for God's saving work. Nor would man's existence in that state, had he continued in it, have been fully historical. Both sacred history in particular and history itself as experienced by men arise from this primal tragedy. This is the source of the 'river of human history',[3] the *series calamitatis*,[4] the *res humana* which flows like a river.[5] Allusions to the impermanence of human things and the transitoriness of human achievement in the *ordo rerum labentium*[6] are scattered through Augustine's writings. The image of the river of human history is sometimes replaced by that of the bitter sea, 'with the depths of curiosity, the swelling of pride and the restless tossing of instability'.[7] History in the full sense, as the troubled past of the human race, is the consequence of a world plunged into the ambivalence of time;[8] time as the vehicle of sin and tragedy as well as the medium of redemption. History in general, the troubled careers of men, societies and their institutions, as well as sacred history, the unfolding of God's plan for healing man's fallen condition, both arise from this primordial strain in the human situation. Temporality itself is involved in being created; but temporality falls short of historicity. Historicity is the mark of a world in which there is *nihil solidum, nihil stabile*.[9] Man therefore creates a historical situation for himself in the very same act in

---

[1] *De cat. rud.* 3.5. On this I shall have more to say below, Ch. 2.
[2] The most complete treatment of this is in *Conf.* XI. On it, see the analysis in Markus, 'Marius Victorinus and Augustine', 376–9 and *idem*, 'Augustine', 94–5.
[3] *De Trin.* IV, 16.21.   [4] *De civ. Dei*, XIII, 14.
[5] *Sermo* 25.6.   [6] *Enarr. in Ps.* 65.11.
[7] *Conf.* XIII, 20.28; cf. *Enarr. in Ps.* 65.11, where the sea- and river-imagery are brought together. On this cf. Rondet, 'Le symbolisme de la mer'.
[8] The allusion is, of course, to the title of Marrou's *L'ambivalence du temps de l'histoire chez saint Augustin*.   [9] *De civ. Dei*, XX, 3.

which he provides God with an opportunity to exercise within human history his saving work. As a first rough approach to the distinction between sacred and secular history we may define sacred history as the story of God's saving work, secular history as all the rest, all that is left, so to speak, when we subtract from history the strand singled out as 'sacred'.

Few Christian theologians can equal the inwardness of Augustine's sense of the *mutabilitas rerum humanarum*[1] and the poetic imagery in which it finds expression in his work. For all that, his vision of human history in general and of the sacred history of the divine work of redemption had nothing novel about it. He stood in the central tradition of Christian theology, at least from Justin and Irenaeus onwards, in his reading the biblical stories as the history of God's mighty acts done for the salvation of his people. Like them, and like even the least instructed of Christians, he endowed the biblical history with a privileged status, which I have, for convenience, labelled as 'sacred'. Nor was there anything more original about his belief that 'there is nothing that is not subject to the administration of divine providence'.[2] It appears in his earliest works, and later he devoted much thought to the problem of God's continuing activity in everything that happens at any time.[3] The vilest and least significant of things as well as the destinies of nations; the crimes of men no less than their finest achievements are in the hands of the Lord of history.[4] In them all he is at work, though his purposes remain inscrutable.[5] It was above all in his great commentary on the early chapters of Genesis that Augustine came to grips with the problem of God's continuing activity in time. Written between 401 and 414, this collection of miscellaneous but searching explorations allows us to glimpse the first and fullest working out of many ideas more sketchily presented, or alluded to only in passing, in other works written during the same period or later. It is in this work that we

[1] *De civ. Dei*, XVII, 13.   [2] *De lib. arb.* I, 5.13.
[3] E.g. *De Gen. ad litt.* V, 21.42; *Ep.* 205.3.17; *De civ. Dei*, XXII, 2.
[4] E.g. *De civ. Dei*, V, 11; IV, 33.
[5] *De civ. Dei*, XX, 2; *De cons. Ev.* I, 12.19.

find his most penetrating analysis of the ultimate theological grounds for the distinction between what we have called 'sacred' and 'secular' history respectively.

Borrowing the language Augustine uses in a letter written during this period, we may state his problem in this way: men can convey their meaning by means of words and their like; but it is in God's power to speak not only with words but also with events (*facta*).[1] But how does God speak with events? If all events are, in effect, his doing—as they are on Augustine's premises —what distinguishes those which 'speak' from those which do not? Alternatively, if all events 'speak' equally, what entitles us to distinguish a particular series of them and regard this series as revelatory? What gives some events a distinctive divine voice? To answer questions of this kind we shall have to look deeper than Augustine's more polemical statements on secular history and its writers, such as those contained in the eighteenth book of the *City of God*, where he contrasts the muddles and contradictions of secular writers with the harmony and order of the canonical scriptures,[2] or their polytheism with the biblical authors' unanimous summons to the worship of the one true God.[3] What we need to enquire into is the sense which Augustine attached to this special strand of history, the way in which he construed its privileged status when he singled it out as that history 'which excels the rest by divine authority'.[4]

The traditional answer of the Church to this question was the insistence that the scriptures were divinely inspired, that they were, in some sense, the work of divine authorship. Augustine adhered to this common Christian insistence, and often spoke of the purposes of the Holy Spirit acting through the human authors of particular biblical passages.[5] A 'theory of inspiration', in our modern sense, he never took the trouble to work out. The nearest

[1] *Ep.* 102. vi. 33; the discussion of *res* and *signa* in the *De doctrina christiana*, I, 1–2 is relevant.   [2] XVIII, 40.
[3] Cf. *De vera rel.* 25.46–7. Cf. *Ep.* 101.2.
[4] *De lib. arb.* I, 3.7.
[5] For a good example see *De civ. Dei*, XV, 8.1.

he comes to formulating anything of this kind is in his remarks on the nature of prophetic insight.

His account of prophecy forms part of an elaborate account of the processes of perception, imagination and judgement, most fully sketched in the twelfth book of his long commentary on Genesis.[1] Taking his cue from Paul's rhetorical question 'Now, brethren, if I come to you speaking in tongues, how shall I benefit you unless I bring you some revelation or knowledge of prophecy or teaching?', Augustine remarks that the seeing of images and visions does not by itself constitute prophecy, unless accompanied by the requisite activity of mind. This activity is that of understanding, insight into the meaning of the images presented, and is the distinctive activity of the prophet. Hence we should rather call Joseph the prophet, who understood the meaning of Pharaoh's dreams, than Pharaoh himself, the dreamer to whom the meaning of the images in his mind remained opaque. Insight into meaning rather than mere perception of what is hidden constitutes true prophecy. Augustine goes on to draw a distinction between the prophet who discerns the meaning of public facts, open to anybody's perception, and the prophet who discerns the hidden meaning of what is itself hidden and accessible only to his own mind in the images surging up within it. Thus Daniel's ability to tell the king both his dream and its meaning is an example of a kind of prophecy superior to Joseph's. In terms derived from his theory of 'vision' Augustine here states the distinction between what we might call a 'prophet' in a narrow sense—one to whom a private vision of hidden or future realities is vouchsafed—and a 'prophet' in a wider sense, one to whom a hidden meaning is revealed in publicly accessible facts, present or past. What constitutes a 'prophet' is a special quality of judgement or of understanding.

A biblical author, whether he be a 'prophet' in the narrow (and usual) sense or not, will on this theory rank as a prophet

[1] On what follows, cf. Appendix A, in which I have argued this case in greater detail and given the necessary references.

in the wider sense; he is a man to whom divine inspiration discloses the significance of the historical facts which he recounts. The form and content of his narrative may be historical; it is his judgement, his interpretation of them in terms of the pattern of the redemptive history into which divine inspiration vouchsafes him insight, that differentiate his history from history as it might be written by a non-inspired writer. Inspiration, the gift of prophecy (in this wide sense) is the constitutive difference between 'sacred' and 'secular' history.

This difference is thus not a difference between what is God's work and what is man's.[1] Augustine had no doubt that all history was in a sense God's doing and, conversely, that the redemptive history told in the Bible is in fact carried out through human agency. His distinction between 'sacred' and 'secular' history only makes sense if 'history' is understood not as a series of past events but as statements about the past, recording events. 'History', in this sense, *tells* of what happened; it *is* not what happened, but its record. 'History', so understood, carries with it the complexities of interpretation and selection, of emphasis and omission involved in presenting an integrated narrative. If 'history' is recorded, recounted and interpreted events, 'sacred history' is history to the recording, recounting and interpreting of which some special quality is attached. In calling a strand of history 'sacred', no special claim is made on behalf of the mode of divine action in the events narrated and no special quality is attached to these events. The special quality resides in the narrative. The difference between 'sacred' and 'secular' history is therefore to be defined by distinguishing between two different kinds of narrative: the

---

[1] The recent survey by Schmölz, '*Historia sacra et profana*', illustrates the fact that this distinction cannot be construed on these lines. Schmölz admits the possibility of a distinction between *historia sacra* and *historia profana* in so far as these concepts refer only to the *narratio rerum gestarum* (p. 37). But when he seeks to distinguish them on the level of 'the objective course of world history' he can find nothing within the total course of history as directed and ruled by God—and in this sense ranking as *historia sacra*—that could be called *historia profana*, except with qualifications such as lead, in the end, to an obliteration of the distinction. I should prefer not to speak of *historia sacra* and *profana* at all in this context, and to restrict the applicability of these concepts to the realm of historiography.

one prophetically inspired, the other not. The privileged status of sacred history derives from the privileged status of the biblical authors and hence of their stories, rather than from the nature of the events they tell of.

The interpretations and judgements of significance, the very selection from the material and the omissions, are part of the revelatory purpose of the Spirit whose inspiration moves the author of the *sacra historia*.[1] The writer's inspired insight presents the past events he tells of in a pattern of significance, a significance which may not be disclosed by the immediate context but only in its full unfolding in a possibly remote future.[2] Only the Lord of history can bring this about. Only he can vouchsafe an insight to a 'prophet' into his story such that this insight will link it within a single redemptive pattern with far-distant, future—or past—events, recounted by other authors inspired by the same sovereign Lord.[3] In this way, for instance, the psalmist's laments over his own troubles become prophetic of the sufferings of Christ.[4]

Augustine, to be sure, does not expressly extend his theory of prophetic insight to cover biblical inspiration in general. Indeed in some passages in his earlier writings he thought of prophecy and history as mutually exclusive categories, both exemplified in the Bible: the one referred to the future, the other to the past. But by the time he wrote the *City of God*, Augustine had come to abandon this way of speaking. The contrast of 'history' and 'prophecy' is softened, even rejected. The theory of prophetic insight on which I have expounded Augustine's views on the inspiration of the scriptures was first worked out by him fully in the last book of his *De Genesi ad litteram*, written probably around 414. He had by this time embarked on the vast enterprise of the *City of God*; and it is not surprising that in this work he seems often to assimilate scriptural authors in general to 'prophets'. *Divina historia, nostrae religionis historia,*[5] *sacra historia,*[6]

---

[1] *De civ. Dei*, XV, 8.1.   [2] *De civ. Dei*, XVII, I.
[3] On this theme, cf. Markus, 'Presuppositions'.
[4] *De civ. Dei*, XVII, 15–19.
[5] *De civ. Dei*, XVIII, 40.   [6] *De civ. Dei*, XV, 8.1.

prophetica historia[1] are used almost interchangeably, and are, of course, all identified with the canonical scriptures and contrasted with the historical books of pagan authors.[2] This is the fruit of Augustine's reflection on prophetic insight, and the application of his conclusions to scriptural inspiration in general. Sacred history is simply what is in the scriptural canon. It is history written under divine inspiration and endowed with divine authority, presenting, under this inspiration, its historical material within a perspective which transcends that of the secular historian, for it is throughout conceived as part of the pattern of God's redemptive work. All other history, even where it casts its light directly on the economy of salvation, is 'secular', since only God-given insight can possess the prophetic quality required by 'sacred history'. Such 'secular' history may, as we have seen,[3] be a useful constituent of the cycle of disciplines which can contribute to a Christian's understanding of the Bible. For all that it remains 'secular' in so far as it is extra-biblical.

Augustine had begun with a simple, unreflective acceptance of the Bible as containing a privileged strand of history; in his theory of prophetic insight he had evolved the categories in terms of which this privileged status could be given a theological explanation. In the course of his searching meditations on the ways of providence in the *City of God* he came, gradually and not without hesitation, to see the applicability of these categories to scriptural inspiration in general. He was certainly never without a deep sense of God's ever-present activity in each and every moment of time, as in every part of space.[4] He often thought of the whole vast fabric of human history as a majestically ordered whole, an extended song or symphony,[5] in which each moment has its unique, if impenetrably mysterious significance.[6] In this sense all

---

[1] *De civ. Dei*, XVI, 2.3.

[2] *auctores eorum*—*De civ. Dei*, IV, 1. For the contrast, see especially *ibid.* XVIII, 40; cf. also above, p. 9 and n. 3.

[3] Cf. above, pp. 6–7.   [4] E.g. *Conf.* VII, 15.21.

[5] *Ep.* 138.5; *De civ. Dei*, XI, 18 etc.

[6] Cf. *De civ. Dei*, IV, 17: *cuius consilium occultum esse potest, iniquum non potest*; on the distinction between *kairos* and *chronos*, cf. *Ep.* 197.2.

history displays the working of God's providence. But in another sense only 'sacred history' tells us what God *really* has done, what meaning events have within the economy of salvation. The difference is analogous to two ways of describing the same series of actions, for example, the actions involved in buying a house. What we refer to as 'buying a house' is a fairly complicated and protracted sequence of activity, activity which, in the nature of the case, is bound to be only one strand in the rich variety of actions which constitute daily living. An uninitiated spectator is not in possession of the principle of selection which would enable him to choose among them all those actions which belong to 'house-buying': the negotiation, the instructing of solicitors, the signing of cheques and deeds of conveyance and so forth. In his description these acts will be lost among endless reports of telephone calls, signing of bits of paper, eating meals and much other relevant and irrelevant material. The house-buyer, or the initiated spectator, will be able to omit all the irrelevance of daily living and describe the stages of 'house-buying' in a coherent way which will make explicit their total meaning: buying a house. It is on some such model that Augustine appears to have conceived the difference between profane and sacred history. Only 'sacred history' will furnish the clues to what God has *really* done—apart from such insight as he may grant to individuals *privatim* into his dealings with them personally.[1]

The significant divisions in human history are, for Augustine, the turning-points in the sacred history. His divisions of history into 'ages' are all primarily ways of dividing the sacred history, and only derivatively applicable to universal history. The landmarks of the sacred history are the fixed points in universal history; universal history is articulated in a meaningful structure in so far as its course is projected on to a map defined by the co-ordinates of the sacred history. The scheme which Augustine expounds in his earliest exposition of the 'six ages' of human history[2] is founded on the notion that the unfolding of human

[1] Cf. *De vera rel.* 25.46; cf. *De civ. Dei*, xvii, 3.2.   [2] *De Gen. c. Man.* 23.35–24.42.

history is foreshadowed in the work of the six days of the Creation followed by a seventh day of rest. In one or other variant form it was an old scheme and a commonplace of patristic literature.[1] The landmarks which divide the six 'ages' of human history are all taken from the biblical narrative. The details of the division are of no interest for our purpose. In this scheme the 'sixth age' is that inaugurated by the preaching of the Gospel and the coming of Jesus Christ, the second Adam, corresponding to the crowning of the work of the six days in the making of man. In this sixth age appears the new man, reborn to new life according to the Spirit. The new life appears in the last, extreme old age of unregenerate humanity. The sixth age ends with the return of the Son of Man in glory, and is followed by the seventh 'day', the eternal rest of the just. This classical Christian periodisation is brought into relation with another scheme: a map of human history drawn on the analogy of man's progress from infancy through childhood, adolescence, manhood and senescence to death. The division of history according to the stages of human growth, too, was an old commonplace, and one used in pagan circles as well as Christian.[2] It was easy for Christians to take it over, to relate it to the sixfold scheme based on the creation story, and to introduce into it the theme of rejuvenation in that last age, the age of the Incarnation.[3] The decisive event of the Incarnation tends to eclipse the sixfold division by casting its shadow backwards. The Incarnation reduces the previous five ages to one. They tend to merge into what we may call the prehistory of Christ: 'the whole duration of history comprises six ages...in five he was announced by the prophets, in the sixth proclaimed by the Gospel'.[4] Behind the traditional six periods Augustine saw a more fundamental duality between the period of promise and that of fulfilment. On occasion

[1] Cf. the somewhat sketchy survey by Schmidt, 'Aetates mundi'; Daniélou, 'La typologie millénariste' and his Bible et liturgie, 303–28; now, above all, the full study by Luneau, L'histoire du salut.

[2] On the interpretation of contemporary history in terms of a mundus senescens I shall have more to say in Ch. 2, below.

[3] Cf. the very closely parallel treatment in De div. qu. LXXXIII, 58.2.

[4] C. Faust. XII, 14. This is discussed with insight by Wachtel, Beiträge, 59–60.

he displays history as articulated in the threefold Pauline (and Rabbinic) scheme: before the law, under the law, under grace.[1] In all these representations of the course of human history, one thing stands out: the divisions are drawn from the biblical narrative. The meaning and structure of history derive from sacred history.

Augustine used schemes that lay ready to hand. Both the threefold and the sixfold division were old by this time, reaching beyond the work of Christian writers into Jewish traditions. Augustine drew on these as it suited his purpose, sometimes turning from one to the other scheme within a single paragraph.[2] Many of the earlier writers who had utilised the sixfold division of history, with the verse 'with the Lord one day is a thousand years and a thousand years as one day' (2 Pet. 3:8; cf. Ps. 90:4) in their minds, thought of each of the six periods as of a thousand years' duration. With this kind of mathematical literalism Augustine, for all his fondness for numerical speculations, had little sympathy even in his earliest works. Repeatedly, he goes out of his way to dissociate himself with the idea that each age necessarily lasts 1,000 years:[3] not only do earlier 'ages' comprise a varying number of generations, but just as a man may continue to live for an indefinite number of years after passing the flower of his manhood, so the time when the last 'age' shall come to an end has been kept hidden. Nevertheless, there are traces in Augustine's early work of the older millenaristic ideas.[4] In some of his writings before the *Confessions* (c. 400) one may catch an occasional echo of the apocalyptic expectations to be found in the writings of earlier Christian authors, such as Irenaeus, Hippolytus,

[1] References in Wachtel, *Beiträge*, 55, n. 26.

[2] E.g. *De Trin.* IV, 4.7. According to Luneau, *L'histoire du salut*, 291–2, Augustine's originality in this matter lies in the fact that he was the first to bring together the idea of the seven ages of man and the allegory of the seven days of the creation story in his account of world history.

[3] E.g. in the passages discussed above, *De Gen. c. Man.* I, 25.42 and *De div. qu. LXXXIII*, 58.2.

[4] This has been shown in an important article by Folliet, 'La typologie du Sabbat'. The passages in question are here analysed in detail, and I need only refer to Père Folliet's paper where references to them will be found.

Tertullian and others. We hear, on occasion, of a period during which the saints shall rule in glory with the returned Lord, of a sabbath rest in a seventh age on earth, preceding the heavenly rest of an 'eighth day'. But even when voicing ideas of this kind, Augustine is very far from the primitive literal millenaristic dreams which were haunting some of his contemporaries. In a sermon on Psalm 6, preached probably in the year 392, he alludes to speculations to the effect that after seven thousand years shall have passed the Lord will return in glory.[1] He denounces the temerity of those who wish to calculate the time of his returning, paying no heed to the Lord's own warning that it is not for us to know the times which the Father has fixed by his own authority (Acts 1:7). Even at a time when Augustine is prepared to envisage a period in which Christ will rule with his saints before the final consummation of history, he repudiates naïve millenaristic speculations such as those of Bishop Hilarian, who calculated in the year 397 that another 101 years were to pass before the coming of Antichrist and the subsequent resurrection of the saints.[2] At a time when the old millenaristic dreams were again being dreamt, at the end of the fourth century, Augustine was moving ever further from the conceptions which lay behind them. After c. 400, even the residual echoes of millenaristic ideas which have been detected in his earlier writings finally disappear. Some famous chapters of his *De civitate Dei*[3] contain a frontal attack on chiliasm.

Augustine's thought moved with increasing certainty towards the rejection of any attempt to introduce any division derived from sacred history into the history of the age after Christ. Despite the revival, here and there, of chiliastic ideas towards the end of the fourth century, chiliasm can scarcely have been a live force in Augustine's day. All the same, his attack on it displays one of the fundamental themes of his reflection on history: that since the coming of Christ, until the end of the world, all

---

[1] *Enarr. in Ps.* 6.1–2.
[2] *Libellus de mundi duratione* (or *De cursu temporum*), 16–17, *PL* 13.1104–5.
[3] *De civ. Dei*, xx, 7 and 9.

history is homogeneous, that it cannot be mapped out in terms
of a pattern drawn from sacred history, that it can no longer
contain decisive turning-points endowed with a significance in
sacred history. Every moment may have its unique and mysterious
significance in the ultimate divine *tableau* of men's doings and
sufferings; but it is a significance to which God's revelation does
not supply the clues.

CHAPTER 2

TEMPORA CHRISTIANA: AUGUSTINE'S HISTORICAL EXPERIENCE

WE look upon the past in the light of our experience of the present. The fears and hopes we find disclosed in our own world evoke their echoes from the past as it appears to us. In a mind that is historically conscious there is necessarily some relation between its experience of the present and its evaluation of the past. The dynamic rapport between past and present in such a mind is a two-way affair. The perspectives within which it grasps the past also help to determine the shape imposed upon the present. If there is any sense in speaking of a man's 'historical experience', it is his total experience in relation to the way he sees the past and the future.

Augustine saw past, present and future within the theological schemes we have noticed in the last chapter. According to his favourite sixfold division of history, the world was now in its old age. This is the 'sixth age', stretching from the coming of the Lord in the flesh to his return in glory at the end. This is the age in which 'the exterior man—also referred to as the old man—is undergoing the decay of old age, while the interior man is renewed from day to day'.[1] Senescence and renewal are the two poles of Augustine's representation of the present epoch. In this chapter we shall examine the extent to which this representation prompted Augustine to take up any specific attitude to his own time. Did the notion of a *mundus senescens* crystallise any sense of a world in full decay, tired of life and only waiting for its end? Did the notion of *renovatio* suggest to Augustine any consciousness that he was witnessing a renaissance? Could the idea of an old pagan world rejuvenated by Christ be translated in political terms

---

[1] *De div. qu. LXXXIII*, 58.2; cf. *De Trin.* IV, 4.7: *in quo tempore* [i.e. *sub gratia*] *sacramentum renovationis accepimus...*

as the christianised Roman Empire of the fourth century, particularly of the Theodosian 'establishment'? What, in general, are
the relations between the abstract, theological schematisations of
the course of history, and Augustine's personal response to his
experience of the present and his understanding of the past? These
are the questions with which we shall be concerned in this chapter.

Whether Augustine is displaying world history within a sixfold or a threefold structure, the time since the Incarnation is
identical with the last age. It is the old age of the world, *senectus
mundi*. There is no other decisive phase to look forward to, no
turning-point to fear or to hope for; only the end. On the map of
sacred history the time between Incarnation and Parousia is a
blank; a blank of unknown duration, capable of being filled with
an infinite variety of happenings, of happenings all equally at
home in the pattern of sacred history. None are privileged above
others, God's hand and God's purposes are equally present and
equally hidden in them all. On them all the old prophecies are silent,
for their reference is to the Incarnation and to the final fulfilment. The interim is dark in its ambivalence. There is no sacred
history *of* the last age: there is only a gap for it *in* the sacred history.

What is uppermost in Augustine's mind when he refers to the
world's 'old age' is invariably to be understood in terms of the
structure of the redemption history. The first and direct reference
is always[1] to the age inaugurated by the coming of Christ, the
age of the Church, the age of the preaching of the Gospel, or, as
he expressed it in one of his sermons, the age of man's reformation:
this is the age in which 'we are reformed to the image of God'.[2]
Conventional feelings of horror of senility are generally far from
his mind. On occasion Augustine is capable of thinking of old age
as something men look forward to, though they are apt to find it
disappointing when attained.[3] Nor is it necessarily an immediate

---

[1] For a list cf. Wachtel, *Beiträge*, 58, n. 39, and above, pp. 17 f.

[2] *Sermo* 125.4.

[3] *In Joh. Ev. Tr.* 32.9; *Enarr. in Ps.* 36.9. In contrast with Cicero, for whom bodily
infirmity was one of the miseries of age, Augustine speaks of a righteous old age as
spiritual youth: *senecta ista iuvenilis est, senecta ista virilis est, semper virebit*—*Enarr. in Ps.*
91.11. On the comparison with Cicero cf. Sizoo, 'Augustinus de senectute'.

prelude to death: a man may well have as much as half of his life still before him when he enters upon his old age.[1] On the 'cold friction of expiring sense' and the accompanying disillusions of age revealed to the poet of *Little Gidding* by his ghostly mentor, Augustine dwells rarely: and when he does, it is always in order to throw into sharper relief the hope of rejuvenation: 'Old age has many complaints—coughs, rheums, sore eyes, anxiety, weariness'; but, he goes on, 'fear not: your youth shall be renewed like the eagle's'.[2] The decrepitude associated with old age appears to have been a matter of little concern to Augustine. He alludes to it only when he wishes to heighten the contrast between the oldness of the first creation and the newness of the re-creation in Christ. In the absence of this rhetorical pressure his mind turned more naturally to childhood and infancy as the epitome of the wretchedness of the human condition. It was in them that he saw the misery of man's lot on earth most fully concentrated. 'Who would not tremble and wish rather to die than to be an infant again, if the choice were put before him?'[3] Once, preaching to the young, he addressed them as *flos aetatis*; but immediately he adds: *periculum mentis*, and the phrase launches him on the theme of his sermon, the deflation of all romantic idealisation of youth.[4] There was nothing in Augustine's theology of original sin that would have allowed him to extol the virtues and attractiveness of youth, still less its innocence. In his *Confessions*[5] he dwells rather on the helplessness, ignorance and frustration of infancy and childhood, not to mention the sinful inclinations to anger and selfishness which already show their power in the child. Youth carries with it the seeds of death.[6] Childhood rather than old age ranks, for Augustine, as the chief *locus* of the miseries of life.

Growing old did not mean decline for Augustine. The analogy

[1] *De div. qu. LXXXIII*, 58.2.
[2] *Sermo* 81.8; cf. *De vera rel.* 26.48; *Enarr. in Ps.* 38.9.
[3] *De civ. Dei, XXI*, 14.   [4] *Sermo* 391.1–2.
[5] I, 6.7–7.12; cf. also *De civ. Dei*, XXI, 16; *De Trin.* XIV, 5.7; *Ep.* 166, 6.16–7.18; *De lib. arb.* III, 23.68.
[6] *Sermo* 391.1; cf. *De civ. Dei*, XXII, 22.1–2.

of stages in a man's life-span, when applied to history, has no
implications with regard to the quality of the world's 'old age'.
There is nothing inherently pessimistic about this way of representing the course of history; nor was there anything inherently
optimistic about the idea of rebirth and rejuvenation associated
with the sixth age. The whole scheme is an entirely formal
expression of the theological conviction that the decisive event
of history has already taken place, in the coming of Christ. In
Augustine's hands it is altogether devoid of any direct contemporary reference, of any emotional colouring, of any note
of fear or hope of what the future may be expected to bring. As
we shall see, there was certainly a phase in his thinking when he
was prepared to look upon the Christian Roman Empire as a
decisive stage in the fulfilment of the Old Testament prophecies
and of God's promises. But there was nothing in the conventional
map of redemption history, or in Augustine's use of it, that
implied any special significance attaching to the period of the
Empire's christianisation. Indeed, in so much as these schemes for
dividing the sacred history treated the whole period since the
Incarnation as homogeneous, they could be said to be inimical
to any attempt to give special theological significance to any
period since Christ, to any strand of history, such as, say, Roman
history, or to any slice of it, such as the period of the Christian
Empire.[1]

The thought of the world in its old age had not always been
quite so neutral in its contemporary reference. For centuries
Christian writers had used these expressions, and behind their
language stood one or other of the traditional schemes for arti-
culating the history of redemption. Often their views had strong
millenaristic colouring; sometimes one may catch an echo of
urgent anxiety about an imminent end to the existing order. The
image of a *mundus senescens* could serve as the poignant expression
of a sense of the ebbing away of life or the fear of a final

---

[1] Some scholars are puzzled by the absence of any mention of the Roman Empire in
this scheme; for a recent example of such a misunderstanding, cf. Archambault, 'The
ages of man', 204–5.

catastrophe. But this need not necessarily be its implication. The same image could nourish attitudes of a very different kind, such as Augustine's.

It is curious that at no time do men seem to have been as ready to speak of an ageing world, or of Rome in her old age, as in the last decades of the fourth century and the early years of the fifth.[1] Neither among Christian nor among pagan Romans was there any sense of a radical transition between speaking of 'Rome' and of the 'world'. 'Rome' was the head, centre and sum of the 'world'; the 'world' was only the expanded version of the City. Christians were led to speaking of their 'old age' by the very framework in which they articulated the history of salvation. But Christians were not alone in thus designating their own time. Roman historians like Florus had long ago divided the history of Rome into periods corresponding to the stages in a man's life. According to Lactantius[2] the idea goes back at least to Seneca. The notion that Rome—or the world—had reached her old age had become a commonplace by Augustine's time. Among pagan writers this did not mean—any more than it meant to Augustine —that the Empire was undergoing senile decay. The poet Claudian, for instance, once described Rome during the Gildonic rebellion as an aged figure exhausted with hunger and weakness; but in less than two hundred lines he could restore her *meliore iuventa*.[3] More generally, the image of a venerable, grey-haired Rome could focus the loyalties of a Symmachus;[4] to his friend, Naucellius, the idea of old age summed up a sense of achievement, ripeness, repose;[5] Ammianus Marcellinus may, on occasion, complain of declining standards of virtue, of the arrogance of wealthy Romans to their provincial clients; but in his work, too, the image of a Rome *vergens in senium* is an image of achievement: the venerable city has entered upon a time of tranquil enjoyment

[1] Cf. Vittinghof's penetrating article 'Zum geschichtlichen Selbstverständnis', especially 561.
[2] *Div. inst.* VII, 15.14–16. The reference is probably to the elder Seneca.
[3] *De bello Gild.* I, 17 f., 208; cf. *ibid.* 50 f. [4] *Rel.* 3.9.
[5] Cf. especially Epigram 5: *vivere sic placidamque proferre senectam, docta revolventem scripta virum veterum*, in W. Speyer, *Naucellius und sein Kreis*, 51. Cf. also Epigram 9, p. 68.

of the fruits of the arduous labours of the past.[1] Even after the sack of the City by the Visigoths in 410, the image of Rome's hoary old age prompts Rutilius Namatianus to voice his faith in the future: though the City was in her 1,169th year, there are no bounds to the span of life left to her, so long as earth and heaven remain; for the things which destroy other kingdoms serve to restore Rome—*ordo renascendi est crescere posse malis*.[2] None of these pagan writers drew the inference from the image of a *Roma senescens* that Rome was destined for a speedy end. In their work the image of old age expresses a sense of achievement, of venerable maturity, of the well-founded claims of her traditions on men's loyalties. Nowhere is this more succinctly expressed than in Macrobius's lines *vetustas quidem nobis semper, si sapimus, adoranda est*.[3]

This is the very claim which Christian writers are concerned to undermine in the course of the polemics of the late fourth and early fifth centuries. Both the mood and the point of the conflict emerge very clearly in the debate over the Altar of Victory. Symmachus's appeal to *vetustas* in his plea for toleration of the *instituta maiorum*, the *mores parentum*[4] voices the aspirations of the class above all dedicated to their preservation. Ambrose's sharp rejoinder sees in the antique what is also antiquated: 'why bring up the model of the ancients?. . .let old age that cannot amend its ways be ashamed. Not the maturity of years, but of manners, is what we should praise.'[5] Ambrose saw the new world of the Christian Empire coming into being, and he wished to hasten the completion of this process. He spoke with the accents of a man who knew that in the transformations that were taking place he was on the side of triumphant novelty.

The confidence engendered by this conviction appears with the utmost clarity in Prudentius's poem on the same theme. The assurance of this poem is perhaps one of the most disturbing

[1] XIV, 6.3–6.
[2] *De red.* I, 115–40; the line quoted is 140.   [3] *Sat.* III, 14.2.
[4] *Rel.* 3.2–4; cf. *Rel.* 4.3: *illud maluimus cuius usus antiquior.*
[5] *Ep.* 18.7–8; cf. *ibid.* 28–30. Cf. Prudentius, *C. Symm.* II, 309–23; and Ambrosiaster, *Q. Vet. & Nov. Test.*, 114, 24 f.

symptoms of Theodosian Christianity. The establishment of Christianity and the christianisation of the Roman Empire emerge here as definite, fully achieved realities. Taught by the edicts of Theodosius I,

Rome fled from her old errors and shook the dark mist from her wrinkled face; her nobility now ready to enter on the ways of eternity and to follow Christ at the calling of her great leader...

Then, for the first time, in her old age, Rome would learn, and blush with shame; ashamed of her past, turning with revulsion from the years passed in foul superstition. (*C. Symm.* I, 506–13)

All the best families are now turning to Christ, and duly the populace follow the lead of their betters to the Vatican or the Lateran:

and shall we then doubt that Rome, dedicated to thee, O Christ, has placed herself under thy rule? (*Ibid.* 587–8)

For Prudentius a new era had begun in the history of the Empire. In her old age Rome had at last 'passed with entire love to faith in Christ'.[1] Jupiter's promise of unending empire to Rome in Vergil's *Aeneid* has become transmuted in the achievement of Theodosius. With deliberate allusion to Vergil's famous lines Prudentius affirms his belief that Rome's empire is to last, her power and glory shall know no age.[2] He takes up an old Christian theme in endorsing the idealised *pax Romana*:

The world receives you now, O Christ, the world which is held in bonds of harmony by peace and by Rome. These you have appointed to be the chief and highest powers in the world.

Nor does Rome please thee without peace; and it is only Roman excellence that ensures a lasting peace. Her supremacy keeps order, awe of her power checks disorder. She has not lost the strength of her former valour in growing old, nor felt the burden of the years...
(*C. Symm.* II, 635–41)

Prudentius writes as if Rome had come to the achievement of her destiny under his very eyes. Under Theodosius I and—odd as it

---

[1] *C. Symm.* I, 523.   [2] *Ibid.* I, 541–3.

may seem in retrospect—under his sons[1] Rome had at last fulfilled her historic mission. Through her supremacy the world was now united under the rule of Christ. Now fit and proper reverence is paid to her years, now she is rightly called venerable and *caput orbis*.[2]

Almost twenty years before this, in Ambrose's answer to Symmachus's arguments, we hear the confidence of aggressive enterprise. In Prudentius's treatment of the same themes the confidence is born of a sense of achieved success. Symmachus's subdued plea for tolerance, by the side of Ambrose's impatient 'do not let me hear of the wisdom of old men', becomes a poignant expression of a world which is passing. Ambrose belongs to the new world for which he is striving. Even the striving is now gone from Prudentius's poem: the world for which Ambrose had fought was achieved. This sense of achievement engendered a boundless confidence in the future. The victory over the Goths at Pollentia is interpreted as a divine guarantee of Rome's survival:

> timor omnis abesto;
> vicimus, exultare libet. (*Ibid.* 737-8)

Prudentius did not live to experience the shattering of this post-Theodosian euphoria in the course of the years following Pollentia. Though he was not alone in shutting out any threat to this sense of security,[3] his poem *Against Symmachus* is the finest example of one common way in which Christians could view the *senectus mundi*.

Prudentius's way owed much to a long tradition of thought about the Roman Empire in the perspective of Christian salvation history. This tradition, and Augustine's standpoint in its regard, will occupy us in the next chapter. For the present we need to enquire into Augustine's attitude, more specifically, to the Theodosian age—the age of achievement, as it seemed to Prudentius. At the time of Theodosius's death Augustine was forty-one and just

---

[1] *Ibid.* II, 655-6, under them *senium omne renascens/deposui vidique meam flavescere rursus/ canitiem: nam cum mortalia cuncta vetustas/imminuat, mihi longa dies aliud parit aevum,/quae vivendo diu didici contemnere finem.—Ibid.* 656-60.

[2] *Ibid.* II, 661-2.

[3] Cf. Claudian on Pollentia in *De bello Goth.* 544-647.

entering on his episcopate. There can be no doubt that the vision of the triumphant progress of Christianity, assisted by the coercive measures of the emperors, had some fascination for his mind. As early as 392, commenting on Psalm 6, he interpreted it with half an eye on its contemporary fulfilment:

> Let all my enemies be ashamed and very much troubled;
> let them be turned back and confounded very speedily (v. 11)

—*valde velociter:* the prospect of a sudden collapse of paganism induced a mood of optimism. Augustine's mind turned naturally to thoughts of the power of Christ, 'who turned the idolatrous persecutors of the Church to the faith of the Gospel within so brief a period of time'.[1] This is a recurrent theme in Augustine's works of this time. In the sermons and polemical writings of the 390s and the early years of the fifth century the extinction of paganism is frequently represented as God's work, fulfilling the ancient prophecies. His viewpoint has aptly been called 'the prophetic viewpoint';[2] what was happening around him was happening *secundum propheticam veritatem.*[3] In a remarkable passage written about the year 400 Augustine allows us to see the way his mind worked: 'The few pagans that remain fail to realise the wonder of what is happening...Now the God of Israel himself is destroying the idols of the heathen... Through Christ the king he has subjugated the Roman Empire to the worship of his name; and he has converted it to the defence and service of the Christian faith, so that the idols, on account of whose cult his sacred mysteries had previously been rejected, should now be destroyed.'[4] The idols have gone, or are going; Christianity has spread to the four corners of the world: 'the whole world has become a choir praising Christ'.[5] In our own day, *temporibus christianis,* God has brought to a fulfilment the prophetic promises. He is uprooting the idols of the nations from the face of the earth, he is calling kings to serve his name.[6] Augus-

[1] *Enarr. in Ps.* 6.13.   [2] Cf. Brown, 'St Augustine's attitude', 110.
[3] On this cf. Mandouze, 'Saint Augustin et la religion romaine', 218–21. The paper gives a multitude of references to Augustine's writings on this point.
[4] *De cons. Ev.* I, 14.21.   [5] *Enarr. in Ps.* 149.7.
[6] *De cons. Ev.* I, 34.52; cf. *Enarr. in Ps.* 62.1.

tine's jubilation could scarcely be defended against the charge of intolerable arrogance[1] were it not for its purpose: to proclaim solemnly the triumph of a God faithful to his promises.

The establishment of the Christian Empire and the repression of paganism have entered the sacred history. They have become part of God's saving work and are described in the categories of the biblical prophecies. The *tempora christiana* have become a distinct phase in the history not only of the Roman Empire, but of salvation. Augustine appears to have been oblivious here of the implications of his views on sacred history, such as we discovered them to be in the last chapter. His sixfold scheme for the division of history, too, insisted on the homogeneity of the period between Incarnation and Parousia. The fundamental structures in which he articulated his notion of sacred history allowed no further decisive divisions or turning-points in this last epoch. Far-reaching changes could, of course, always take place; momentous upheavals in the framework of society, of institutions, and in the shape of human living could not be ruled out. But any such transformations, if they took place, would not appear on the map of sacred history. From this point of view the whole period, whatever its vicissitudes, is homogeneous, and characterised by the features of the 'last times': it is at once the time of the building up of the Church and of the persecution of the saints of God, for these are the two facets of the preaching of the Gospel. But now, from the 390s for some ten or fifteen years, Augustine appears to have joined the chorus of his contemporaries in their triumphant jubilation over the victory of Christianity.[2] Like others, he saw here the hand of God, the fulfilment of prophecies like those of Ps. 72:11 ('And all the kings of the earth shall adore him, and all the nations shall serve him'), Jer. 16:19 and Isa. 2:11.[3] Augustine's theology of scriptural inspiration and of sacred history is plainly not hospitable to ideas of this kind. The

---

[1] Cf. Mandouze, 'Saint Augustin et la religion romaine', 218.

[2] In addition to Prudentius, cf. Rufinus' interpretation of the battle of the River Frigidus as a divine victory over paganism, *HE*, II, 33. Cf. Orosius, *Hist.* VII, 35. For Augustine's view on this, cf. below, Ch. 6, p. 149, n. 2.

[3] Cf. e.g. *C. Faust.* XIII, 7; 9; XXII, 76; *De cons. Ev.* I, 26.40.

divergence—it would perhaps be hasty to speak of contradiction—calls for comment.[1]

It was no mere passing infatuation with the Theodosian achievement that found expression in Augustine's jubilant endorsement of the *tempora christiana*. For a decade or more his historical thinking was dominated by this motif. In the instructions written to Deogratias, the Carthaginian deacon, on the way to instruct catechumens, Augustine asserts specifically that the *plena narratio* of the history of salvation, beginning with the creation, should end with 'the present times of the Church'.[2] Nothing could be more deliberate than his insistence in this work, dated 399–400, and in works written at about this time, that the triumphant spread of Christianity, assisted by the kings of the earth, is part of God's work for the salvation of his people and the fulfilment of the ancient prophecies.[3] Looked at in this light, it quite properly formed a part of sacred history: the interpretation of the events Augustine has witnessed is derived straight from the scriptures. The clue to what is going on under his eyes is contained in the inspired prophetic books. The events seen in these terms are as much part of the history of salvation as the other phases of God's action fulfilling the Old Testament prophecies and promises. They form not an optional extra, but an essential component of the basic catechesis of converts; they are theology, as we might say, rather than Church history. Around the turn of the century, Augustine was clear enough about the implications of his view of the *tempora christiana*. He had allowed the Theodosian establishment to drive a wedge into the single, blank stretch of the 'last age' of history. The full history

---

[1] It is curious that, so far as I know, it has not so far received any. Many writers such as Erik Peterson and others (cf. below, Ch. 3, p. 47, n. 4) have studied Augustine's concern to withdraw the history of the Roman Empire from the dimension of sacred history and to render it theologically neutral. Others, for instance Brown, 'St Augustine's attitude', have drawn attention to the reverse tendency in Augustine's mind: to his readiness to assimilate the christianisation of the Empire to the *prophetica veritas* of sacred history and to his use of this view as a theological justification for the coercive measures of the emperors. In this context Augustine spoke the language of the *Reichstheologie* which Peterson and others have amply shown he rejected. I know of no study which has attempted to reconcile or to account for this divergence.

[2] *De cat. rud.* 3.5; cf. on this above, Ch. 1, p. 10, n. 1.

[3] *Ibid.* 27.53.

of salvation could not be told without recounting recent, indeed contemporary, history.

For all the seriousness, however, with which Augustine held and expressed these views, he held them little longer than some ten or fifteen years. In 398 the Roman armies had crushed the African revolt of Gildo; the following year, the imperial commissioners arrived in Carthage to 'destroy the temples and overturn the idols'.[1] These events may have loomed large in Augustine's mind in the years 399–400: at any rate, it is in his writings of these years that Augustine was most emphatic in his identification of the Roman with a Christian order. It is about this time that he refers repeatedly to the fulfilment of the prophecies *temporibus christianis: ecce nunc fit*—now, under our very eyes, the nations are coming to Christ from the ends of the earth; they sing Jeremiah's verses, 'O Lord, my strength and my stronghold, my refuge in the day of trouble, to thee shall the nations come from the ends of the earth, saying: "Our fathers have inherited nought but lies, worthless things in which there is no profit"' (Jer. 16:19), and breaking their idols.[2] This kind of language is not found in Augustine's later work. The tone seems to change. The official christianisation of the Empire seems to lose much of its significance to Augustine. A prophetic text, such as that of Ps. 72:11,[3] which in the late 390s had served as one of the chief props for Augustine's prophetic interpretation of the Empire's christianisation, receives much more reserved treatment some fifteen years later. In a commentary written actually on this Psalm, one of the latest in the collection and one of the few known to have been specially composed, Augustine can be seen in the act, almost, of correcting himself:

[1] *De civ. Dei*, XVIII, 54.1.
[2] *De cons. Ev.* I, 26.40. The works in which thoughts like this occur most frequently are *De consensu evangelistarum, Contra Faustum* and *De catechizandis rudibus*, all of 398–400. The relevant passages referred to by Mandouze and others, such as e.g. *Ep.* 232.3, *Sermo* 24.6, spread over an only slightly longer period, and are concentrated in these years. Apart from a few scattered distant echoes in polemical contexts, I have come across only one isolated late example of this theme, in *Ep.* 185.5.20 (417). It is also voiced by Jerome in the year 400: *Ep.* 107.1.
[3] Cf. above, p. 31, n. 3.

The kings of Tharsis and the isles render him tribute,
the kings of the Arabs and Seba bring him gifts;
and all the kings of the earth shall adore him, and all the nations shall
    serve him.   (Ps. 72:10–11)

Augustine does not reject the reference he had seen in these verses
to his own time; this had become too much of an exegetical *topos*
under his pen. The gifts brought by the kings are 'men—the men
who are brought within the communion of Christ's Church by the
authority of kings'. But the reference of the verses to contemporary history is forthwith evacuated of its significance: 'not
as if the persecuting kings had not also brought their gifts, without
knowing what they were doing, in immolating the holy martyrs'.[1]
This is a wholly gratuitous afterthought, added by Augustine
without any *point d'appui* in the text he was commenting on. It
indicates the need he now felt to loosen the links between the
prophecies and their fulfilment specifically in the Christian Empire.
One could scarcely wish for a clearer disavowal of his previous
'prophetic' interpretation of the *tempora christiana*. Spreading the
Gospel and immolating its witnesses are now both brought within
the prophetic perspective. The legal enforcement of orthodoxy has
lost much of its special significance for Augustine. It has become
one of the many and varied historical events characteristic of the
'last times'.[2] No longer separated from the period of persecutions,
it no longer defines a particular phase of the sacred history. The
reading of contemporary history in terms of fulfilling the prophecies—apart from the literary reminiscence of earlier writings—
has become no more than an assertion that God is at work in all
events, whatever they are. Contemporary history has been quietly
removed from the perspective of sacred history. The scripture
imposes no pattern upon it; or, if it does, the pattern is so open in
its texture that anything—the 'established Church' of the Theodosian age no less than the age of the martyrs—will fit.

    Along with this change in Augustine's views the very notion of

[1] *Enarr. in Ps.* 71.13.
[2] For a striking and succinct statement of the 'last times' as a homogeneous epoch
stretching from Apostolic times to Parousia, cf. *Ep.* 199.8.24.

tempora christiana undergoes a drastic devaluation. It is not easy to give this vague phrase any chronological precision; but it is plain that whatever meaning it did possess for Augustine around the year 400 underwent a profound change in his writings of the years which follow. Around 400, *tempora christiana* served to designate the period of the legal repression of paganism: the destruction of the temples, the banning of sacrifices and the breaking of idols predicted of old took place *temporibus christianis.*[1] Augustine gives some hints that he is thinking, above all, of his own times when he speaks in these terms. The coming of the peoples from the ends of the earth to worship Christ, the uprooting of the idols prophesied by Jeremiah—all this is happening now: *ecce nunc fit.*[2] Augustine sometimes speaks like a man surprised by the success he has witnessed. But whether he is thinking of the christianisation of the Empire since Constantine, or of the increased impetus given to this process in the last two decades of the fourth century, he is thinking of a specific, limited period of Roman history. The 'Christian times' are not the age inaugurated by the Incarnation, but a more restricted period with its own significance in the redemption history.

Sometimes Augustine lays special stress on the distinction between this restricted period of time and all earlier periods of Christian history. Christians had read the prophecies about the uprooting of idols and the extension of the Church over the world before our time, Augustine says in a sermon; only a few years ago—*ante paucos annos*—they read and believed these things, without seeing them accomplished. What they entertained as a future hope, or believed while persecuted, that we have seen accomplished.[3] As late as the year 417, in his notorious letter to Boniface, Augustine invoked the idea of a changing *ordo temporum* to justify the use of coercive power against the Donatists: to the Donatists' plea that the Apostles would not have wished to resort to such powers, Augustine replies that the time of the Apostles

---

[1] *De cons. Ev.* I, 16.24.
[2] *Ibid.* I, 26.40; cf. *C. Faust.* XIII, 7; *Enarr. in Ps.* 71.13.
[3] *Sermo* 22.4; cf. *Enarr. iii in Ps.* 32.9.

reflected a very different stage in the gradual realisation of the prophecies from the present time, now that the Church has acquired the power to coerce by means of the faith and devotion of kings; and everything is to be done in its season. In Apostolic times the wedding-guests were invited; in these times they are rightly compelled to 'come in'.[1] In passages such as these one can almost sense a gulf opening between the *tempora apostolorum* and the *tempora christiana*.

Augustine's prophetic interpretation of the Theodosian age equipped him with a powerful theological justification for religious coercion.[2] The way was now prepared for an ever further retreat from the unitary conception of the post-Incarnation period of history; and in the course of his debate with Donatism Augustine travelled far along the way. Optatus had long ago accused the Donatists[3] of wishing to 'separate the times'; they opposed the old and the new dispensations in respect of the place given in them respectively to the role of force. The Law may have condoned force; the Gospel left no room for it, for the coming of Christ has inaugurated the age of *mansuetudo*.[4] Against this neat division of history into B.C. and A.D. Augustine came to lay increasing weight on 'distinguishing the times' within the Christian era. The old schemes in which he mapped the course of the salvation history, whether in three or in six ages, were eclipsed by the increasing importance he came to attribute to the profound changes within the last age: the change from the apostolic age and the age of the martyrs to the age of the Christian rulers and of the Church with coercive power at its disposal. These were among the ideas which nourished Augustine's assent to religious coercion. His assent, tragically, survived the repudiation, later in his career, of the ideas which had provided his justification of religious coercion.

---

[1] *Ep.* 185.5.19–20; 6.24.   [2] Cf. Brown, 'St Augustine's attitude' and Ch. 6 below.
[3] *De schism.* III, 7. Cf. the young Augustine's views on moral advance since the Old Testament, in *De div. qu. LXXXIII*, 53.4.
[4] Cf. Augustine, *C. Cresc.* IV, 46.56. I owe this reference to Peter Brown. When pleading with officials to proceed with leniency against schismatics, Augustine could, however, urge the claims of *mansuetudo*. E.g. *Ep.* 134.3: *alia est causa provinciae, alia est ecclesiae. illius terribiliter gerenda est administratio, huius commendanda est mansuetudo.* Cf. *Ep.* 133.3.

But around the year 400 he had not yet come to question the mirage of his generation about its own significance. Together with his contemporaries, he was quite prepared to endow it with a real importance in the sacred history of salvation. At this time he was prepared, even, to speak of an *imperium Christianum*.[1] The period of the Christian Empire is a definite phase in the history of salvation, with only slightly blurred chronological edges.

Augustine continued to speak of *tempora christiana* long after this time. The *City of God*, in particular, is full of talk about *tempora christiana*. The whole work, especially its earlier part, is a running argument with the *mentes amentes* who will not acknowledge the evil they do but impute the evil they suffer to the 'Christian times'.[2] The argument is, of course, one of the *topoi* of the debate between pagans and Christians. Long before the Sack of Rome in 410 we hear of people complaining about a decline in the felicity of human affairs in 'Christian times', and in the year 400 Augustine, reporting such complaints, asserts that they derive from the polemical writings of the philosophers.[3] There can be little doubt that the reference is to Porphyry, and that some of the arguments summarised by Augustine in his set replies to the queries of Deogratias represent part of the background of this debate.[4] In the years immediately after 410 'the Christian times' move into the focus of the debate between pagan and Christian.[5] Augustine's sermons preached on the morrow of the Sack of Rome reveal the bitterness of the pagan charges: 'in Christian times there is so much tribulation,[6] the world is derelict';[7] in Christian times Rome is fallen;[8]

---

[1] *C. Faust.* XXII, 60.

[2] *De civ. Dei*, I, 33; cf. ibid. I, 1; 7; 15.1, 2; 30; V. 22; *Enarr. in Ps.* 136.9; *De cura*, 2.3.

[3] *De cons. Ev.* I, 33.51. Cf. O'Meara, *Porphyry's Philosophy from Oracles*, 85 f., on the Porphyrean reference of *De cons. Ev.* I, 11 f. Cf. also P. Courcelle, *Les lettres grecques*, 163 f.

[4] *Ep.* 102.ii. The title given to this section by Possidius in his *Indiculus*, *De tempore christianae religionis*, has, however, no relevance to our problem. It concerns the question: why was Christianity so late in coming? It shows, if anything, that by his time the old usage re-established in Augustine's later work (cf. below, p. 38 n. 3) has become general currency.   [5] Cf. Courcelle, 'Propos anti-chrétiens'.

[6] *pressura* is Augustine's favourite word for this; cf. *Sermo Denis*, 24.11 (Morin, 151).

[7] *Sermo* 81.7. Bad Christians are here said to echo the complaint—*ibid.* 8. Cf. also *Sermo Frangip.* II, 9 (Morin, 200.13).

[8] *Sermo* 81.9; cf. *Sermo bibl. Casin.* I, 133 (Morin, 407.1–3).

in Christian times everything is going to the dogs.[1] *Mala, dura molesta, laboriosa tempora:*[2] such were the pagan synonyms for *christiana tempora.* The very phrase *christiana tempora* is now part of the pagan vocabulary of abuse of the Theodosian establishment and its defenders. After 410, Christians were very much less ready to boast of the achievements of the *tempora christiana.* When they use the phrase at all, as Augustine does in his apologetic sermons and in the *City of God,* they use an expression supplied by their opponents, and in the sense given it by their opponents. It is abundantly clear that what pagan public opinion had in mind in its attack on the 'Christian times' was the period of the Empire's christianisation, and above all the most recent period of the legal establishment of Christianity and repression of paganism. But by this time the idea of *tempora christiana* had lost its appeal to Augustine. Even though he continued to use the phrase, as supplied by his adversaries in the debate, he had ceased to attach any positive meaning to the Theodosian settlement.

It is significant that the one occasion on which Augustine speaks of *tempora christiana* in the *City of God* without reference to the pagan polemic, the phrase in fact refers to something different: it refers to the whole period since the Incarnation.[3] Here is a linguistic pointer to the fact that the perspective established in this work, as we shall see in the next chapter, leaves no room for 'Christian times' understood in any other sense. But even before Augustine had come to re-think the place of the Roman Empire in God's providence in the *City of God,* there are signs that he had come to see the mirage of the Theodosian *tempora christiana* for what it was. He is, for instance, very much less ready to speak of a Christian Empire, or of the conversion of *regna* to Christianity.[4]

[1] *pereunt omnia—Sermo,* 105.6.8.

[2] *Sermo* 80.8; *Sermo Caillau,* II, 19.7–8 and II, 92.1 (*Morin,* 270 and 272.14 f.).

[3] *In De civ. Dei,* XVIII, 47. The phrase occurs in the title. On the question of the chapter headings in the *City of God* and the *Breviculus,* cf. Lambot, 'Lettre inédite', and Marrou, 'La division en chapitres'. Another context in which the phrase may bear this wider sense is that in which Augustine speaks of pagan philosophy and its errors surviving *temporibus christianis,* e.g. *De cons. Ev.* I, 23.35; *Ep.* 118.20–1; cf. *De vera rel.* 3.3.

[4] This is ably shown by Lohse, 'Augustins Wandlung', where the contrary view argued by Maier in *Augustin und das antike Rom,* 37 f., is decisively refuted.

Around 400 he had been prepared to think of conversion to Christianity in institutional terms,[1] and of a Christian Empire;[2] in the course of the second decade of the fifth century he became much more reserved. The change is already apparent in one of the sermons preached soon after the Gothic sack of Rome. He was comforting his flock in their perplexity over the calamities allowed by God to take place *temporibus christianis*. Did God promise permanence to things such as social institutions and political arrangements? Are we to praise God when things go well and blaspheme him in adversity?[3] He joins issue in this sermon with the pagan belief in Rome's eternal destiny and its expression in Vergil's *Aeneid*;[4] but it is more than a pagan myth that is being repudiated. The idea of a Christian Empire, as an achieved institutional reality such as he had envisaged ten years earlier, now vanishes: 'The City which begat us according to the flesh still remains; thanks be to God! If only it would also be spiritually reborn, and go over with us into eternity!'[5] Augustine is still speaking of the *civitas* as—perhaps—capable of spiritual rebirth; but this is a hope, dubiously realisable, if at all. The whole myth of the christianisation of the Empire is blown away in this optative sigh of Augustine's. The legal, institutional enforcement of Christianity has now lost its importance; what is needed is spiritual regeneration. What ten years ago had seemed to Augustine achieved is now a hope, perhaps a forlorn hope, for the future.

Others were still living in the honeymoon period of the Empire's marriage with the Christian Church. As late as 418 the Dalmatian bishop Hesychius would draw from the spreading of the Christian faith to the ends of the earth, assisted by the measures of the Christian emperors, an argument for the imminent end of the world:[6] for was this not one of the signs of the 'last days'? Augustine's

---

[1] Cf. *De cons. Ev.* I, 14.21 (cf. above, p. 30, n. 4) and *De cat. rud.* 24.44, referred to by Lohse, 'Augustins Wandlung', 452.

[2] *C. Faust.* XXII, 60, referred to above, p. 37, n. 1.

[3] *Sermo* 105.6.8.   [4] *Ibid.* 10, quoting *Aen.* I, 278 f.

[5] *Ibid.* 9: *manet civitas quae nos carnaliter genuit. Deo gratias. Utinam et spiritaliter generetur et nobiscum transeat ad aeternitatem.*

[6] *Ep.* 198.6.

reply to his letter is perhaps the sharpest rejection of the whole theology of *tempora christiana* to be found in his writings. Almost ten years later, finishing, as an old man, his *City of God*, he will refer to this letter as his last word on the subject of eschatology.[1] The substance of his argument is that the 'last days' began with the Apostolic period and will end with the return of the Lord in glory. As for that, he would rather not try to calculate the times and the seasons, and one by one he disposes of his correspondent's arguments: it might be near or far off, it could be any time. As for the spreading of the Gospel under the Christian emperors, let us not make too much of that. For there are still, Augustine recalls, plenty of barbarian tribes beyond the imperial frontiers whom the Gospel has not yet reached,[2] and was the Gospel intended only for Romans, or for all nations?[3] Not only was there still plenty of scope for the Christian faith 'to grow and fructify',[4] but even within the Roman boundaries Augustine had his reservations on this imperial evangelisation: the Church may now be held in honour and may be exalted; the kings of the earth and the nations may serve Christ—but what does it all add up to? Augustine disposes of the question with a single devastating comment: 'The very same people who fill the churches on the festivals of Jerusalem fill the theatres for the festivities of Babylon.'[5] The kings' service of Christ, far from securing the Church's glory, is dismissed as constituting a 'greater and more dangerous temptation'.[6]

Augustine changed his mind on many things, and few of them are noted in his *Retractationes*. His deflation of the myth of the Empire's *tempora christiana*, too, is passed over in silence; but it appears time and again in his writings of these years. In another sermon preached soon after the fall of the City the very possibility of the concept of *tempora christiana* is called into question and the collective, institutional christianisation of the Empire derided as illusory: 'Bad times, hard times—this is what people keep saying; but let us live well,

---

[1] *De civ. Dei*, xx, 5.4.   [2] *Ep.* 199.12.46.
[3] *Ibid.* 47. Cf. *De civ. Dei*, xviii, 32; *Enarr. in Ps.* 95.2; Prosper, *De voc.* ii, 16; for contrast cf. Optatus, *De schism.* iii, 3.   [4] *Ibid.*
[5] *Enarr. in Ps.* 61.10.   [6] *De perf. iust.* 15.35.

and times shall be good. We are the times: such as we are, such are the times.'[1] The whole idea of *tempora christiana* is here rejected, as an invalid objectification of the attitudes of a multitude of individuals. In a letter, also of this time, written to a priest who had apparently been a witness to the affliction suffered in Italy in consequence of the barbarian invasions, Augustine once more exposed the illusion: those who complain about these disasters taking place in these 'Christian times', Augustine writes, 'take note of the energy which is devoted to spreading the Gospel; but they fail to take note of the perversity with which it is despised'.[2] So much for the mirage of the fulfilment of the prophecies *temporibus christianis*.

The fact that Augustine's reflection on his own times underwent such profound changes is of more importance for our enquiry than the reasons for them. We may, however, conclude this chapter with some conjectures as to the reasons for his changes of attitude, and some suggestions on the inner coherence of Augustine's thinking as it took shape in the course of the years following 410.

The old divisions of world history in terms of biblical schemes and the main landmarks of the redemption history appear in Augustine's writings very early. The division of history into six ages, in particular, remained a recurrent theme in his writings from 388 onwards. We have already noted[3] that in the course of the 390s Augustine's use of this scheme was progressively purified of millenaristic ideas. At no time could this scheme itself have led Augustine to a position in which he would find it necessary to give any special significance to the period of the Christian Roman Empire. This period would always have formed a part of the sixth age. There was no subdivision within this sixth age which could serve to define the Christian Empire as a significant phase of the sacred history. The scheme simply had no landmarks to serve as clues. In its final form the scheme, as Augustine used it, came to insist with uncompromising clarity on the homogeneity of

---

[1] *Sermo* 80.8.   [2] *Ep.* 111.2.
[3] Cf. above, Ch. i, p. 19 and n. 4.

41

the redemption history in the epoch between Incarnation and Parousia. *Senectus mundi* was a phrase capable of only one meaning in this context, the whole period since Christ. If we seek reasons for Augustine's changes of view about the significance of the Christian Empire, we must seek them elsewhere.

Why, then, did Augustine give such special significance to the *tempora christiana* of the Empire in his writings of the 390s and the turn of the century? Attempts have been made to trace the 'influences' working on Augustine's mind in this respect and to identify the sources in previous Christian writers from which Augustine might have drawn his ideas on the Christian Empire.[1] That individual Christian writers, such as Optatus, the African historian of the Donatist schism, with whose work Augustine was undoubtedly acquainted, or ecclesiastical statesmen like Ambrose whom Augustine knew, had something to contribute to Augustine's thinking on this subject we need not doubt. The search for particular sources may, however, obscure the fact that the whole intellectual climate of the late fourth century was deeply permeated with ideas of this kind. In Christian circles the Empire had become quite generally represented as a vehicle of salvation, with a divine mission in history.[2] Among pagans, too, looking from the other side at the progressive legal enforcement of Christianity, the *tempora christiana* were becoming a no less definite and recognisable slice of history. The principal issues at stake in the controversies between pagans and Christians during the aftermath of the reign of Theodosius combined to push the notion of *tempora christiana* into the foreground of men's consciousness. It was not easy in the *fin de siècle* mood to escape the spell which the collapse of paganism cast over Christian minds. What we need to enquire into is the question why Augustine, almost alone among his contemporaries, managed, in the end, to break the spell, rather than why he succumbed to it in the first place.

---

[1] A particularly interesting discussion of the case for Optatus rather than Ambrose is to be found in Lohse, 'Augustins Wandlung', 470 f.

[2] This is discussed in Ch. 3, below.

If, then, we pose the question in this way, there are several considerations which help to explain why Augustine came to abandon his earlier views on this subject. One will occupy us in a later chapter: the course of his reflection on human society in general. Another formed the subject-matter of the enquiry pursued in the last chapter: the development of his theology of prophetic inspiration and its implications for his theology of history. It was not much before 414 that Augustine had worked out the foundations for his mature views on sacred and profane history. It is difficult to say how long these ideas took to crystallise in his mind, and impossible to date with any precision their first appearance in his writings. The nearest we can get to dating the emergence of his theology of prophetic inspiration is to the early years of the second decade of the fifth century. By 414 they were fully worked out in Book XII of his great Genesis commentary, and they left their mark on the *City of God*, and on the understanding of history to be found especially in its later books.[1] As a result of this development in his thinking, Augustine had come to see 'sacred history' as confined to the history to be found within the scriptural canon, and he came to deny this status to any other interpretations of historical events. Beyond this, all history is starkly secular, that is to say, it is incapable of being treated in terms of its place in the history of salvation. Now plainly the development of Augustine's views about the Christian Roman Empire which we have traced in this chapter is entirely in line with the development of his ideas about sacred history as we traced them in the last chapter. We shall not be far wrong if we think of the years immediately after 410 as the phase in his intellectual life at which these changes gathered momentum. The obscurities of intellectual chronology and the nature of the inevitably gradual and piecemeal crystallisation of concepts prevent us from saying what was cause and what was effect in this development. It is, at any rate, clear that on both fronts Augustine's reflection was advancing rapidly in these years, and that both developments point

[1] Cf. above, Ch. 1, pp. 13 f., and Appendix A.

in the same direction. The theory of prophecy and the theology of history bound up with it made it increasingly difficult to speak of any episode of post-Incarnation history in terms of any *heilsgeschichtlich* significance; the disillusion with the Theodosian mirage of a Christian Empire removed the urge to do so.

That the change in Augustine's thinking on these subjects should have gathered momentum in the years immediately following 410 cannot be accidental. The Gothic sack of Rome in the summer of that year for the first time made the Roman state into a problem for Augustine. His ideas on it before this time have to be reconstructed from scattered utterances, most of them concerned, primarily, with other things. It is scarcely unexpected that they show themselves to a very large extent to be in line with the *idées reçues* of the time. It is only in his mature work we should expect to encounter not what Augustine accepted and took for granted, but what he had come to think after sustained reflection. The fall of the City in 410 and the controversies provoked by this event moved the Roman state from the periphery to the centre of his mind. Some of the conceptual materials which went into the construction of Augustine's reappraisal of the meaning of Rome were ready to hand. But much had to be worked out anew, and, perhaps most important, the pressure behind the thought was now more urgent. The new directions in which Augustine was moving can be discerned in their first beginnings in some of the sermons preached and letters written under the impact of the news and in the atmosphere of crisis it produced in Africa. In them we are given a glimpse into the mind of a man who feels that his world can no longer be taken for granted. The certainties of its past are revealed to it as illusory, while the bearings of the future remain unclear. Among the confused emotions of these letters and sermons some of the great themes of the *City of God* were born. It is in this work, and especially in its later books, that we must try to discern the shape of Augustine's thought once it had really come to grips with the historical destiny of Rome as a problem.

44

CHAPTER 3

CIVITAS TERRENA: THE SECULARISATION OF ROMAN HISTORY

THE exploitation of dramatic contrasts has always been one of the favoured devices of rhetoric. Augustine shared a liking for it with his literary contemporaries. There was something about the cast of his mind, however, which made dramatic contrasts a more than normally apt means of expressing his ideas. The schemes in which he thought tended to organise themselves around two poles. The notion of the 'two cities' is only one of many paired conceptions at the foundations of his thought. The division of mankind into two categories is a theme which enters into Augustine's earliest reflection on the course of human history. In one of the earliest of his expositions of the six stages of history, Augustine divides the human race into two *genera*: 'the crowd of the impious who bear the image of the earthly man', and 'the succession of men dedicated to the one God'.[1] The *duo genera hominum* had a long and continuous history in his writings over the next quarter of a century.[2]

In the course of the following decade the idea took more definite shape in his mind: the two 'kinds' of men were defined in terms of two communities they were said to belong to, and their opposition was stated in terms of the opposition of two 'cities', one of the impious, the other of the saints.[3] By about 411, when he was writing the eleventh book of his great Commentary on Genesis, Augustine had formed the intention of devoting a work specifically to the 'two cities'.[4] He began the work which contains this treatise, the *City of God*, some two years later; but strictly speaking, it is its second part, Books XI–XXII, that corresponds to his design. The work contemplated in 411 was begun about 417 and completed

[1] *De vera rel.* 27.50.
[2] On the development of the idea of the two cities in Augustine's writings the most useful study is Lauras and Rondet, 'Le thème des deux cités', also Lauras, 'Deux cités'.
[3] *De cat. rud.* 19.31.   [4] *De Gen. ad litt.* XI, 15.20.

in 426 or 427. The two classes of men, with their divergent ultimate loyalties and their opposed values, were a part of Augustine's earliest scheme of historical interpretation. Quite soon the two categories are seen transposed into a social key and represented in the image of two societies or cities, in their turn typified by the biblical images of Babylon and Jerusalem.

In their origin these ideas of Augustine's are quite independent of his reflection on Roman history. Their outlines were fairly clear and definite long before Augustine had come to entertain the project of devoting a work to them. Even then, in 411, the interest of the theme did not appear to lie in the opportunity it would offer to interpret and to comment upon the significance of Rome in world history. There is nothing in the way Augustine sketched his plan, or in the context, that could suggest to a mind not prejudiced by historical hindsight that Augustine's plan had at this stage any specific historical reference, to Rome or to any other state. There are hints, to be sure, that if pressed, Augustine would have been prepared to identify civil society with the *civitas terrena*.[1] The hints, however, are on the periphery, not at the centre of Augustine's horizon. They reveal what he had been taking for granted, not something he had come to work out. In the years following 411, above all in the early books of the *City of God* (I–X, *c.* 413–16), Rome becomes the concrete historical representative of Babylon, the embodiment of the earthly city. The new emphasis is revealing: Rome itself has now moved to the centre of the stage. The categories in which Augustine will now interpret Rome had long been established in his mind; their applicability to the Roman state had always, though in a shadowy manner, been taken for granted; but Rome was not what Augustine had been interested in. It had, quite simply, not become a problem for him. For this we have to wait for the controversies precipitated by the

---

[1] *Ep.* 91.4, of 408. In *Ep.* 95.5, of the same year, the identification of a *populus terrenus atque Romanus* with Babylon, contrasted with the celestial Jerusalem, is quite clear. As early as about 390 Augustine spoke of the *terrena civitas* as the sphere of the unregenerate man's action, apparently equating it with the Roman state—*De vera rel.* 26.48.

fall of the City in 410, and for the challenge to Augustine from the *salons* of Carthage, swarming with educated Roman refugees such as the pagan Volusianus.

The *De civitate Dei* was intended, from its inception, to be an answer to pagan Romans who were blaming the disaster on the substitution of the Christian religion for the old cult.[1] It was to be a work about the destiny of Rome, and this theme was to be treated —as the choice of the title, *De civitate Dei*, shows—in terms of Augustine's ideas on the two cities. The plan to write a treatise on the two cities and the 'zeal for the house of God'[2] which spurred Augustine on to provide an answer to pagan critics of Christianity had coalesced into a single grandiose design. The outcome was the long and rambling book which is, nevertheless, perhaps Augustine's most carefully planned work.[3] Augustine himself appears to have thought of the first ten books as primarily polemical in nature, of the rest as constructive exposition. With both parts we are here concerned only to the extent that they contain Augustine's mature re-assessment of the Roman Empire and of its significance in the history of salvation.

We saw in the last chapter that until the early years of the fifth century Augustine accepted at their face value the ideas about the Christian Roman Empire generally current among contemporary Christian writers. This world of thought, feeling and imagination owed much to a long tradition of thinking about the Roman Empire.[4] This tradition reaches back at least to Philo; in its Christian form, it was voiced in the later second century by Melito

---

[1] Apart from the many passages in the work itself, cf. *Ep.* 169.1; 184A. 5; *Retr.* II, 43, and the correspondence between Marcellinus and Augustine in *Epp.* 136 and 138.

[2] *Retr.* II, 43.1.

[3] On its plan cf. *Retr.* II, 43, and the Letter to Firmus, ed. Lambot, 'Lettre inédite'; Jones, 'The manuscript tradition'; and Guy, *L'unité et structure logique.*

[4] This has been illuminated by a good deal of scholarly work stimulated, above all, by Erik Peterson's characteristically perceptive essay, *Der Monotheismus als politisches Problem.* Among the later literature, cf. Straub, 'Christliche Geschichtsapologetik', Mommsen, 'St Augustine and the Christian idea of progress', Cranz, 'Kingdom and polity', Opelt, 'Augustustheologie und Augustustypologie', and the survey by Markus, 'The Roman empire'. I wish to thank the editor of the *Downside review* for allowing me to make use in this chapter of some of the material of this article. The contrast between the two traditions was already briefly mentioned by Scholz, *Glaube und Unglaube,* 181.

of Sardis[1] who thought that the unification of the *orbis Romanus* under the emperors was geared under God's providence to the propagation of the Gospel. A century before the conversion of the first Roman emperor to Christianity, Origen gave a classic formulation to this theme in his work against the pagan Celsus. Invoking the Psalm verse 'righteousness arose in his days and abundance of peace' (Ps. 72:7), Origen writes:

God was preparing the nations for his teaching, that they might be under one Roman emperor, so that the unfriendly attitude of the nations to one another, caused by the existence of a large number of kingdoms, might not make it more difficult for Jesus' apostles to do what he commanded them when he said 'Go and teach all nations'. It is quite clear that Jesus was born during the reign of Augustus, the one who reduced to uniformity, so to speak, the many kingdoms on earth so that he had a single empire.

(C. Cels. II, 30, trans. H. Chadwick)

The final establishment of a single polity was something to which Origen looked forward as a possibility for the divine saving work which heals all fragmentation.[2] It was only a short step for his disciple, Eusebius of Caesarea, to see the Constantinian monarchy as part of God's plan for consummating this unification.

Until the time of Constantine, this way of thinking about the Empire was far from universally accepted in Christian circles. It had to compete with attitudes like those of the writer of the Book of Revelation. Here the Empire had been depicted as the Beast to whom the Dragon had entrusted his world-wide dominion (c. 13), or as the harlot arrayed in purple and in scarlet, seated upon the seven hills (c. 17), 'drunk with the blood of the saints and the martyrs of Jesus' (13:6). Among later Christian writers, it is Origen's contemporary, Hippolytus, who expressed such ideas in their most uncompromising form. In Hippolytus's apocalyptic imagination the Roman Empire was identified with the last of the four beasts of the seventh chapter of the prophecy of Daniel.[3]

---

[1] *Apud* Euseb., *HE*, IV, 26.7–8.   [2] *C. Cels.* VIII, 72.

[3] On the image of the four kingdoms, cf. Trieber, 'Die Idee der vier Weltreiche', and Swain, 'The theory of the four monarchies'.

This last 'kingdom' differed from all the others: 'exceedingly terrible, with its teeth of iron and claws of bronze; and which devoured and broke in pieces and stamped the residue with its feet' (Dan. 7:19). It gathered its power by conquest, from every nation on earth. For Hippolytus the Roman Empire was a satanic imitation of the kingdom of Christ: it made the same claims to unity, to universality and to endless duration. The irony is marked by Christ's appearance to summon all nations to his kingdom under Augustus, the founder of the Empire.[1]

Hippolytus mellowed, with age and the passing of the Severan persecution; 'the bearded philosopher seated in dignity on the marble throne found on the Aventine in 1551 was no longer an enemy of the State'.[2] Christians in general were equally quick to change their minds with the passing of the persecutions, and especially, after the recognition granted to Christianity by Constantine. Constantine's biographer and ecclesiastical publicist, Eusebius, turned the theology he had learnt from Origen to good use in his eulogies of the Emperor. Verses from the psalms or the prophets, for instance Ps. 72:7-8, or Isa. 2:4, verses which had traditionally been interpreted in the Church in a messianic sense, are now boldly referred to the person of Constantine.[3] Eusebius introduces his eulogy of Constantine in the last book of the *Ecclesiastical history* as the messianic 'new song unto the Lord':[4] 'Come and behold ye the works of the Lord: what wonders he hath wrought upon earth: making wars to cease even to the ends of the earth.'[5] The final recension of this last book of his great work is written quite uninhibitedly to celebrate the first Christian emperor as the culmination of God's marvellous saving work. Constantine brings to a fulfilment what God himself had prepared

---

[1] *In Daniel.* IV, 8–9.

[2] I quote this judgement from Frend, *Martyrdom and persecution*, 377. This book contains a fine evocation of the contrast between the two traditions, especially in chapters 11–13. Dr Frend is, to my mind, a little too ready to align the two attitudes to the Empire with an East-West division. On the background of ideological opposition to the Empire cf. Fuchs, *Der geistige Widerstand.*

[3] E.g. *Laus Const.* XVI, 7–8; *Praep. ev.* I, 4.

[4] *HE* X, 1.3, quoting Ps. 96:1–2.

[5] *HE* X, 1.6, quoting Ps. 46:9–10.

in Christ and Augustus: he brings about the unification of the world in a single harmonious order, one Empire devoted to the worship of the one true God. Eusebius, naturally, stops short of pressing the implications of this messianic conception to its limits: Constantine is not actually the Saviour, nor is his Empire actually the Kingdom of Christ. Hellenistic conceptions of kingship have here come to his aid and have enabled him to represent the emperor as the image of the Logos, his empire as the image of Christ's kingdom. The Empire and the Church are 'twin roots of blessing';[1] they represent God's sovereign authority and the saving teaching of Christ respectively. Ultimately, in this vision of history, the two are facets of a single reality, only partially and provisionally distinct, and destined to merge in a single Christian 'polity'.[2]

Few Christian writers went as far as Eusebius in applying messianic categories to the rule of the Roman emperors. Nevertheless, the interpretation of the *pax Augusta* in theological terms was widely endorsed in the fourth century, and the Empire was very frequently given an important place in the divine plan of salvation. In the hands of Christian writers, both in the East and the West, it had almost universally become a part of the sacred history.[3] Ambrose of Milan may serve as a striking example of a churchman on whose mind, very differently orientated as it was, these ideas had a deep hold. His comment on Ps. 46:9, for instance, follows closely the classical pattern set by Origen:

Before the spread of the Roman Empire not only did kings of the various cities fight against one another, but even the Romans themselves were afflicted with frequent civil wars...Hence, tired of civil wars, the Romans gave the *imperium* to Julius Augustus, and thus the intestine conflicts were settled. This in its turn served to make it possible to send the apostles through the whole world, as Jesus had enjoined when he said 'Go ye and teach all nations'...Thus all men,

---

[1] *Laus Const.* XVI, 4. This chapter contains the fullest concise sketch of the Eusebian scheme.

[2] On Eusebius's views, cf. Cranz, 'Kingdom and polity'; on the Hellenistic elements in his conception, Baynes, 'Eusebius and the Christian Empire'.

[3] Cf. Peterson, *Der Monotheismus*, 82–8, notes 138–41, citing John Chrysostom, Diodore, Theodoret, Cyril of Alexandria etc.

living under one single earthly sovereign, learnt to confess the sovereignty (*imperium*) of the one God almighty...

(*Expl. s. ps.* 45.21)[1]

The work of Orosius, written after Augustine had completed the first ten books of his *City of God*, is eloquent testimony to the powerful hold that this Rome-theology continued to exercise on Christian minds even after the disasters of the early fifth century. Inevitably, this image of Roman destiny helped to shape attitudes such as those we have seen[2] in the work of Prudentius, writing in the Indian summer of the post-Theodosian era. Prudentius's assessment of the Christian emperors, of Theodosius I above all, springs directly from his conception of the place occupied by the Empire in the scheme of divine providence. This conception permeated much of his verse. It is expressed, with macabre humour, in the prayer Prudentius puts in the mouth of Saint Laurence on his gridiron (unlike the famous joke which precedes it in the poem, this speech, Prudentius assures us, is meant in deadly earnest):

Now all mankind is united under the rule of Remus,
customs once diverse now agree in speech and thought.
This was destined in order that the authority (*ius*) of the
Christian name might bind with one tie all that is anywhere on earth.
Grant, O Christ, to your Romans, that the City become Christian...

(*Perist.* II, 425–34)

The answer to St Laurence's prayer is the Christian Empire of the fourth century. Significantly, Prudentius's defence of the Christian establishment against Symmachus involves a lengthy restatement of the theme.[3] Prudentius's intoxication with the vision of a Christian Empire, realised in his own times, is inseparably linked with his acceptance of a *Reichstheologie* in the tradition of Origen and Eusebius.

Augustine was also, as we have seen, for a while, bewitched by

---

[1] Cf. on the same lines, Jerome, *Comm. in Isa.* I, ii.4 (*CC* 73.30); *Comm. in Mich.* I (*PL* 25.1187–8). It is noteworthy that Ambrose's comments on Luke 2: 1 point in a very different direction—cf. *Expos. in Luc.* II, 37.

[2] Cf. above, Ch. 2, pp. 27–9.

[3] *C. Symm.* II, 583–640; the end quoted above, p. 28.

this Theodosian mirage. Never, however, had he given his assent
to the underlying theology of history. I have found no trace in his
writings of expressions like those which seem to roll naturally
from the pens even of men like Ambrose or Jerome in some of
their isolated comments on prophetic texts or Psalm verses.[1] The
contrast between these and Augustine's comments, for instance on
Ps. 46:9, could hardly be sharper. Augustine happened to be
preaching on this Psalm in Lent, 412. Far from referring its
prophecy—'making wars cease even to the ends of the earth'—to
the *pax Augusta*, he remarks: 'this we have not yet seen fulfilled'.
Hoc nondum vidimus esse completum; and he goes on to dwell, with
curious deliberation, on the conflicts among nations, conflicts
between Christians and pagans, between orthodox and heretics.[2]
Commenting on another Psalm text which had formed part of the
standard repertory of the Eusebian Rome-theology, Ps. 72:7–8, he
expounds these prophecies in purely eschatological terms without
reference to the Empire: when they are fulfilled, when righteousness and peace abound and the Messiah's dominion shall reach to
the ends of the earth, then the end shall be at hand.[3] In the *City of
God* he could scarcely fail to allude to the *pax Romana* in the course
of his polemical *résumés* of Roman history. In the chapter devoted
to the birth of the Saviour he passes over the *pax Romana* in a
single subordinate clause,[4] and carefully refrains from embroidering
its theological significance. Where Jerome, Ambrose and the
tradition in which they stood had commented on the significance
of the Roman Empire for the universal mission of the Apostles,
Augustine refers, in preference, to the dispersion of the Jews:
in being scattered over the face of the earth carrying their Old
Testament with them they spread abroad the world the prophetic
testimonies to Christ. There is no other trace in Augustine's treatment of the Roman Empire of its constituting in his eyes a *praeparatio evangelica*. When he deals with the reign of Augustus, he prefers

---

[1] Cf. above, p. 51, n. 1.   [2] *Enarr. in Ps.* 45.13.
[3] *Enarr. in Ps.* 71.10–11; for Augustine's comments on the verses following these, cf.
above, p. 34, n. 1.
[4] *orbe pacato*—*De civ. Dei*, XVIII, 46.

to dwell on its civil conflicts[1] and on the difficulty with which Roman world-dominion was established. And Roman world-domination, when achieved, is not a preparation for the preaching of Christ's kingdom, but the achievement of 'the new Babylon'.[2]

The *City of God* was very much more than Augustine's answer to the pagan opposition; more even than the realisation of a long-cherished plan to write a treatise on the 'two cities'. The writing of it forced Augustine to take the measure of his own intellectual and spiritual past; of his past not only as a Roman man of letters, but as a Christian scholar and churchman. It is a sustained inner dialogue of a man whose intellectual world has been shaken. In the course of it Augustine came to question, in some cases for the first time, ideas he had taken for granted, or ideas generally current among his contemporaries. He had already abandoned the notions about the 'Christian times' of the Theodosian Empire which he had, in his forties, shared with others of his generation. Now, as an old man, he came to see clearly that what he wished to repudiate was not merely a passing mood of elation. It was nothing less than the almost universal tradition of Christian thinking about the Roman Empire during the fourth century. A number of studies over the last thirty years[3] have taught us to see at least part of the central concern of Augustine's argument in this work as lying in his rejection of the Eusebian Rome-theology.

In the *City of God*, and especially in its second part, the implications of Augustine's theology of sacred history are fully grasped and applied to the history of the Roman Empire. Any attempt to interpret Roman history in prophetic categories is now repudiated. The working out of God's purposes—so the argument runs—does not stand or fall with the fate of Rome or, indeed, with the fate of any particular earthly society. The apocalyptic prophecies are not to be read as referring to any particular historical catastrophe, but to the final winding up of all history;[4] and the time of that no man

[1] *De civ. Dei*, III, 30.   [2] *De civ. Dei*, XVIII, 22.
[3] Cf. above, p. 47, n. 4. On Augustine's standpoint in this regard, see, in addition, Cranz, '*De Civitate Dei*, XV, 2' and Kamlah, *Christentum und Geschichtlichkeit*, especially 175 f.   [4] *De civ. Dei*, XX, 11.

can know, for has not Christ warned his disciples that it was not for them to know the times and seasons of the Father's secrets (Acts 1:6–7)? So it is no use trying to compute the years that are left. All the same, men will go on making their various guesses; but Augustine absolves himself from following them into the intricacies of their reckonings: 'it is unnecessary, for they all rely on human conjecture; there is nothing in them that can claim the support of firm scriptural authority'.[1] The only clue to sacred history is the Bible. Where this is silent, human guesswork about divine purposes in history lacks foundation. The christianisation of the Roman Empire is as accidental to the history of salvation as it is reversible; there is nothing definitive about the *christiana tempora*, we can have no assurance that an age of persecutions will not return. Augustine rejects all arguments aiming either to affirm or to deny that persecutions have ceased as 'rash presumption'. In doing so he must have been well aware of repudiating a view which had been put forward by his own disciple, Orosius, only a few years earlier.[2] Orosius's view, also, it seems, a current one,[3] is an eloquent symptom of the theology which saw in the Christian Empire a definitive achievement which had once and for all brought to an end persecutions—except for the final persecution by Antichrist— and substituted Christianity for idolatry. For Augustine now all such arguments, whether affirmative or negative, have lost their force; they are founded not on prophetic insight, 'but upon human conjecture, which may be right or may be wrong'.[4] The past, when it lies beyond the range of the canonical scriptures, lies outside the scope of sacred history. It is the field for historical investigation;[5] the future is the field for conjecture. Neither is the concern of prophetic insight; both are firmly removed from the dimension of sacred history.

In Augustine's hands the Roman Empire has lost its religious significance. Rome has been removed from the *Heilsgeschichte*, the

---

[1] *De civ. Dei*, XVIII, 53.1.   [2] *Hist.* VII, 27.
[3] Cf. Sulpicius Severus, *Chron.* II, 33.
[4] *De civ. Dei*, XVIII, 52.1.
[5] On *historica diligentia*, cf. Appendix A, pp. 191–2.

Empire is no longer seen as God's chosen instrument for the salvation of men. It is no longer indispensable for the unfolding of his providential plan in history. Nor is it, on the other hand, a Satanic obstacle to its realisation. Augustine now repudiates the application of any prophetic scheme to history since Christ. The Empire is not to be seen in terms either of the messianic image of the Eusebian tradition or of the apocalyptic image as the Antichrist of the Hippolytan tradition. The Empire has become no more than a historical, empirical society with a chequered career, whose vicissitudes are not to be directly correlated with the favour of the gods, pagan or Christian, given in return for services rendered. It is theologically neutral. Here lies the originality of Augustine's mature attitude to the Roman Empire. Christian thinkers of the fourth and early fifth centuries could avoid interesting themselves in questions about the Empire, about human societies, states and their histories. If, however, they did take an interest in such questions, two directions were open to them. They could follow in the footsteps of Origen and Eusebius and give the Empire a sacral significance in terms of the history of salvation. Alternatively they could follow the ancient apocalyptic tradition of hostility to the Empire, assimilating it to the *saeculum* of apocalyptic literature. The Church, in this image, was surrounded by an alien and hostile world in the midst of which it constituted the elect. In a profound sense this image expressed a notion of the Church as essentially and inwardly always persecuted. Those who thought in such terms could take their stand within an ancient tradition of Christian thought, especially strong in Africa. Spiritually, such men lived in the world of Cyprian, Tertullian and of the early martyrs. Beneath the purple and scarlet robes of the apocalyptic whore they could still recognise Rome. In the course of the fourth century the Nicene opposition to the religious policies of Constantius had been nourished by this tradition of thought; in Africa, above all, Donatist theologians kept the tradition alive throughout the fourth century and later.[1] By Augustine's time they were its sole

---

[1] Cf. Frend, 'The Roman Empire'. On Donatism, cf. below, Ch. 5.

representatives. *Odio saeculi gaudemus*, one of them succinctly said,[1] portraying the characteristic posture of its adherents.

The long drawn-out controversy with Donatism which occupied Augustine over many years and called a large number of works from his pen has tended to obscure the extent of the common ground between him and his opponents at this point.[2] Of the two traditions represented in Christian thinking, the Eusebian and the apocalyptic, as we might refer to them for the sake of convenience, Augustine followed neither. For the theologically neutral conception towards which his thought was moving, and which emerges with full clarity in the last books (especially XVIII and XIX) of the *City of God*, I know of no precedent, unless it be in the work of the Donatist theologian Tyconius. From him Augustine learnt much; unfortunately not enough of his work survives for us to be sure about Augustine's debt to him in this particular matter.[3] The ambivalence of Augustine's attitude to Rome is a logical consequence of his repudiation of both of the current Christian interpretations of Roman history. He could accept neither the hostility and opposition to Rome inculcated by the apocalyptic view, nor the near-identification of Christianity and the Roman Empire involved in the Eusebian view. This is the source of the ambivalence which has often misled Augustine's readers and caused scholars to give one-sided evaluations of his position.

The complexity of his attitude is discernible even in the polemically coloured pages of the early books of the *City of God*. His diatribes against Roman idolatry and corruption of manners, against the addiction to the dissipations of the theatre, are too constant a feature of these books to require special mention. What is striking about them is Augustine's determination to use

---

[1] Gaudentius, *apud* Augustine, *C. Gaudent.* I, 26.29.

[2] Notably, in the work of Dr Frend, both in his paper 'The Roman Empire', and in his valuable book, *The Donatist Church*. On the other hand some of the scholars, such as Kamlah, who have treated Augustine primarily from the point of view of his rejection of the Eusebian Rome-theology, seem to me to have exaggerated its extent. This ambivalence of Augustine's attitude has eluded the painstaking study of Maier, *Augustin und das antike Rom*, distorted by the determination to recognise no trace of 'Roman patriotism' in Augustine's work. For an important contribution to redressing the balance, cf. Straub, 'Augustins Sorge'. [3] On Tyconius, see below, Ch. 5, pp. 115–16.

them in denunciation of a contemporary moral decline. Despite the notice devoted to the Christian emperors[1] Augustine does not acknowledge any turning-point in Roman history. Nothing definitive has taken place with the christianisation of the Empire, there is no essential break in Roman history; throughout, Rome is the representative of the *civitas terrena*. Augustine speaks of Rome as an outsider, in the kind of language which would be appropriate to a Christian apologist writing of pagan Rome in the second century. The great figures of Rome's past, her literary achievements —achievements which had, let us recall, nourished Augustine's intellectual life—are continually being referred to as 'yours', and contrasted with the Christian saints and martyrs, or the scriptures, as 'ours'. And yet, we need only dip into Augustine's correspondence, say with the Roman military commander Boniface, or with the African official Marcellinus, to remind ourselves that Augustine was not only a late Roman man of letters but also a bishop in a Roman province whose interests were closely linked to those of the imperial administration. And if we turn back from his correspondence to the *City of God*, we shall discern in its polemic, anti-Roman as it is in intent, the presence of a reverse side to Augustine's real feelings. His tone is often unmistakably and authentically Roman, and full of legitimate pride in the stock *exempla* of Roman virtue; for instance, when he recalls the *indoles Romana laudabilis* to the ancient majesty of the Roman name, invoking the Reguli, the Scaevolae, the Scipios and the Fabricii as the fit objects of admiration and the models for the conduct of contemporary Romans.[2] Few Roman writers can rival Augustine's praise of the self-denial and discipline that went into the making of Roman greatness:

These [distinguished Romans] therefore that neglected their private estates for the commonwealth and public treasury, opposing covetousness, having a full care of their country's freedom and living according to their laws, without touch of lust or guilt, these seemed to go the

---

[1] *De civ. Dei*, v, 24–6, rightly called 'some of the most shoddy passages of the *City of God*' by Brown, 'St Augustine', 8. On Christian emperors, cf. below, Ch. 6.
[2] *De civ. Dei*, II, 29.

right way to get themselves honour, and did so. Honoured they are almost all the world over; all nations very near received their laws; honoured were they in all men's mouths, and now in most men's writings through the world. Thus have they no reason to complain of God's justice; they have their reward. (De civ. Dei, v, 15, tr. J. Healey)

It is not only Augustine's admiration for these representatives of the Roman past and their civic virtue that is given expression here. Expert rhetorician as he was, Augustine manages to combine with this the reminder, contained in the closing allusion to the Gospel (Matt. 6:2), of the limited, earthbound and temporary character of the reward. With this reminder the Roman achievement is neatly 'placed'. Augustine can afford to praise and to admire from the distance which the allusion to the Pharisee puts between himself and the ancient Romans. In the final perspective the Roman achievement, for all its nobility, is unavailing. Taken by itself, it is neutral. It is neither to be repudiated as Satanic, nor to be endorsed as holy, except in virtue of the ultimate allegiances mobilised in this kind of endeavour. 'If nature has given you any praiseworthy excellence'—Augustine apostrophises a personified Rome—'it is purged and perfected only through true piety; impiety consumes and destroys it.'[1] Rome is here suspended, so to speak, between the two 'cities', that of the righteous and that of the unjust. The possibilities of Rome being assimilated to either the one or the other are both left open. This radical indeterminateness of human achievement, and especially of human achievement in society, is profoundly characteristic of Augustine's final estimate of the Roman state. It is implied by many of his utterances concerning Christians bearing secular office: *terrena res publica habet cives nostros administrantes res eius.*[2] Members of the City of God may be found among the ranks of those serving the state, indeed as kings, princes and magistrates.[3]

[1] De civ. Dei, II, 29.1.
[2] Enarr. in Ps. 61.8. The whole paragraph is a particularly revealing one for the complexities of Augustine's terminology. The whole commentary on this Psalm has an outstanding interest in the history of Augustine's ideas about the two cities; cf. Lauras and Rondet, 'Le thème des deux cités', 128–36, and Lauras, 'Deux cités', 143–8.
[3] Among the many occurrences of this theme, cf. Enarr. in Ps. 51.6; Ep. 96.1 and Ch. 6 below on Christian emperors.

Conversely, adherents of the earthly city are to be found in plenty within the Church, even sometimes wielding high ecclesiastical office. Even while denying that belonging to one or other of the two 'cities' can be identified with belonging to the Church or the state respectively, Augustine speaks as if we ought to be able to assume this identification. There is, so to speak, an antecedent presumption that the heavenly city can be equated with the Church and the earthly with the state; but the presumption is shown to have no validity.

The equation of the state with the *civitas terrena* is hinted at in Augustine's earliest reflection on this theme. Rome, in particular, is, with increasing clarity, designated as the *civitas terrena* or as 'another Babylon'. Augustine's identification of the Roman state with the earthly city is as clear in his writings as is his refusal to abide by this identification. His logic is the logic of late antique rhetoric rather than modern formal logic. 'Babylon' is both the city of the impious, and the secular sphere in which good pious Christians may discharge important functions. Without the least sense of inconsistency, Augustine will assert that Rome, or the *res publica*, is the earthly city, or assume this equation, and then go on to speak in ways which imply the contrary: as he does, for instance, when he insists that upright citizens of the *res publica* may belong to the city of God, just as the Church may number within its communion adherents of the earthly city.[1] This overlap of the two cities in actual institutions is incompatible with their mutually exclusive character, which Augustine always emphasises when defining them formally.[2] The two cities are formally defined in terms either of the ultimate loyalties of their members, or of their members' standing in the sight of God. Augustine's most

---

[1] Cf. above, p. 58, nn. 2, 3. In *De civ. Dei*, II, 29 Rome (= *civitas terrena*) is invited to enter the *civitas Dei*, which some of her children, the Christian martyrs, are said to have already entered.

[2] Or when he comes as near to giving a formal definition as he ever does. This problem arises from the systematic ambiguity inherent in Augustine's usage of *civitas*. It has been more fully discussed in connection with the corresponding problem of *civitas Dei* *ecclesia*, on which see Ch. 5, below. On *civitas terrena*, see also Hermelink, 'Dei civitas terrena'.

characteristic formulations of the either/or relation between the two cities are found in his designation of the two cities as that of the saints and that of the unjust respectively;[1] or as comprising those devoted to God and the impious,[2] or the elect and reprobate, those destined to be saved and damned respectively.[3] All these ways of contrasting the two cities imply their mutually exclusive character; and they are manifestly intended to be equivalent ways of stating their fundamental opposition. They are enumerated alongside each other at length, and brought to a common denominator, in the passage in which Augustine first announced his intention to write a treatise expounding the theology of the two cities:

These two loves ['the perverse love which isolates the mind swollen with pride from the blessed society of others', and its contrary, 'charity which seeketh not its own'—contrasted in the preceding paragraph] of which the one is holy, the other impure; the one sociable, the other self-centred;[4] the one concerned for the common good for the sake of the heavenly society, the other subordinating the common good to self-interest for the sake of a proud lust for power...

the two loves—Augustine's catalogue of their contrasts continues— 'have brought about the distinction among mankind of the two cities...the one of the just, the other of the unjust'.[5] The radical opposition between two kinds of love at the foundations of the two cities has deep roots in Augustine's reflection on the springs of human action. It remained central to his exposition of the theme of the two cities in the work devoted to this enterprise: 'two loves have built the two cities: self-love in contempt of God the earthly city, love of God in contempt of self the heavenly...'[6]

No identification of either of the two cities with any institution or with any empirically definable body of people can be reconciled with this radical dichotomy. Membership of the two cities is mutually exclusive, and there can be no possible overlap; but membership of either is compatible both with belonging to the

---

[1] *De cat. rud.* 19.31—here identified with the dichotomy between the humble and the proud, cf. *ibid.* 33. [2] *De vera rel.* 27.50. [3] *De civ. Dei*, xv, 1.1.
[4] *privatus*—on this see Augustine's remarks in the preceding paragraph of his Commentary. [5] *De Gen. ad litt.* xi, 15.20. [6] *De civ. Dei*, xiv, 28.

Roman—or some other—state and with belonging to the Church. This entails a logical loosening of the equation of Rome with the earthly city. Rome can only be called the earthly city in a secondary or derivative sense, in so far as the Empire is a society organised around loyalties with no positive relation to God. To accomplish this identification Augustine dwells on the idolatry of pagan Rome, on the lust for power and the quest for human glory and renown, as well as on the corruption of Romans, even of Christian Romans, of his own day, who swarm to the dissipation of the theatres while the rest of the world mourns the fate of Rome. In ways such as these Rome, both pagan and Christian, is assimilated to the new Babylon. With bold and sweeping rhetoric, Rome is allowed to emerge as the earthly city of the present, despite Augustine's rejection of the possibility of treating any society in so monolithic a manner. But Augustine was also acutely conscious of the limits of rhetoric. Repeatedly he insisted on the ultimately questionable nature of the equation established by its means. 'What is Rome but the Romans?'[1] 'A city consists of its citizens, not its walls.'[2] The dichotomy of the two cities, based on men's ultimate allegiances to the values they set before themselves, was bound to cut across empirical social groupings. Augustine was keenly aware of this and never ceased to stress the fact. He nevertheless continued to use both ways of speaking as it suited his purpose: the one in terms of historical social entities, the other in terms of individual, personal orientations.[3]

Even though its bounds do not coincide with any society discernible in historical terms or definable in empirical categories, the *civitas terrena*, like its heavenly counterpart, is a society. Augustine often speaks of it as a *societas*,[4] and his definition of a *civitas* lays

---

[1] *Sermo*, 81.9.

[2] *De Urbis exc.* 6; cf. *Civitas = concors hominum multitudo—Ep.* 155.3.9; and *multitudo constat ex singulis—De civ. Dei*, I, 15.1; cf. Ch. 6 below, pp. 149–50.

[3] This is often ignored by scholars who lay all the stress on the individualistic direction in Augustine's thought, e.g. Scholz and Kamlah. The most telling critiques of this approach, though both worked out in relation to the *civitas Dei*, are Ratzinger, 'Herkunft und Sinn' and the final chapter in Wachtel, *Beiträge*.

[4] E.g. *De civ. Dei*, XVI, 17; XII, 1.

special stress on the need for some bond to unite a multitude of individuals: 'a city is nothing but a multitude of men linked by a social bond'.[1] The earthly city has its own, unifying, social bond, located somewhere among the perverse, self-centred and temporal purposes aimed at by its members. Their common allegiance to such fleeting values, even though it be, in the end, divisive, suffices in Augustine's eyes to constitute them a genuine society. But it is a society which, again like its heavenly counterpart, does not appear visibly as a society until the last judgement at the end of time. Here and now the two cities melt into one another; their boundaries are invisible and cut across all visible social groupings. 'In this world the two cities are inextricably interwoven and mingled with each other, until they shall be separated in the last judgement.'[2] They are in this sense eschatological entities. The 'dapple' of earthly existence, in Gerard Manley Hopkins's image, comes to an end with the descent of night; then

> Let life, waned,
> ah let life wind
> Off her once skeined stained veined variety upon, all on two
> spools; part, pen, pack
> Now her all in two flocks, two folds—black, white; right,
> wrong...

When 'our night whelms, whelms and will end us', then the two cities will at last be disentangled from their interwoven existence in the *saeculum*.

Augustine saw the whole course of history, past, present and future, as a dramatic conflict of the two cities, that is to say, in terms of a tension of forces which will only appear in their naked reality beyond temporal history. From this point of view the sphere in which human kingdoms, empires and all states have their being is radically ambiguous,[3] and all social institutions and human group-

---

[1] *De civ. Dei*, xv, 8.2; *civitas...nihil est aliud quam hominum multitudo aliquo societatis vinculo colligata*; cf.*Ep.*138.2.10: *multitudo hominum in quoddam vinculum redacta concordiae.*
[2] *De civ. Dei*, i, 35: *perplexae quippe sunt duae civitates in hoc saeculo invicemque permixtae...* Cf. *Enarr. in Ps.* 61.8.
[3] H.-I. Marrou has expressed this eschatologically ambiguous nature of history, with

ings are radically infected with this ambiguity. The distinction between the two cities lies in the dimension of men's wills, in their inner response to their world and their experience: 'Both cities use the same temporal goods, both suffer the same calamities; but they do so not with the same faith, nor with the same hope, nor the same love.'[1] There can be no outward separation, no historically distinguishable careers discernible before the end. Augustine's excision of Roman history from sacred history has left not only Rome, but all historical achievement, problematic. The only exceptions to the universally problematic nature of all history are those societies, persons or incidents where a divine revelation has identified for us the *locus* of the two cities in human history and traced their destinies in time. To the historical careers of the two cities only the Scriptures supply the clues. Beyond this human conjecture runs into the sand, being impotent in the face of the mystery hidden in God.[2] Thus in the *City of God* Augustine breaks off his narrative of the career of the heavenly city at its limit: with the coming of Christ. The history of the Church is no longer—as it had been some twenty-five years before[3]—a part of the sacred history. Here, in the last books of the *City of God*, is Augustine's furthest retreat from the theology of the *tempora christiana*, and the fullest clarity about the implications of his theology of sacred history.

Augustine had set himself two tasks in the *City of God*: to take the measure of Rome, and everything Rome stood for, from a Christian standpoint; and to delineate his theology of the two cities, long ago conceived as symbolising the primordial forces at work in human affairs, but only gradually brought to bear on the problem of 'Rome'. The two tasks coalesced and ramified; but

characteristic distinction, in *L'ambivalence du temps*, and in his second thoughts about it in 'La théologie', as well as in his paper *Civitas Dei*. J. C. Guy has rightly underlined the negative character of M. Marrou's answer with a forceful reminder that the *tertium quid*, Augustine's *saeculum*, is not to be hypostatised. It is, quite simply, the two cities in their intertwined state in history. Cf. *L'unité et structure logique*, 121–2.

[1] *De civ. Dei*, XVIII, 54.2; cf. XIX, 17; I, 8.2 etc.
[2] *De civ. Dei*, XIV, 11.1.
[3] In *De cat. rud*. 3.5; on this cf. above, p. 32.

they did not involve the necessity of thinking out a 'political theory'. In his image of the heavenly city Augustine had sketched the outline of the ideal form of human society, consisting in the concord and peace of righteous men living in union among themselves under God and in God's presence. What need was there to expound the precise status of the many imperfect forms of human association which, in all their variety, inevitably failed to measure up to this ideal? In this sense a 'political theory' comparable, for instance, with Aristotle's discussion of actual states, their working and even their pathology, is absent from Augustine's work. There is, nevertheless, a good deal to be discovered about his views on actual states from his observations on the relations between the two cities. The rhetorical equation of Rome with the earthly city served Augustine well in debate, not only with Roman paganism, but with Eusebian optimism; but if we wish to reach the kernel of his dispassionate estimate of political life we shall do better to scrutinise the area of indeterminacy between the two cities. This, in the last resort, is the theological *locus* in which he places politically organised society.

This can be most clearly seen in the way in which he treats the classical Ciceronian definition of the *res publica*.[1] This much-discussed definition equated *res publica* with *res populi*, and then defined a *populus* as a 'multitude joined together by one consent of law and their common good'.[2] Augustine's critique fastens on the word *ius* embedded in the definition. Following hints he found in Cicero's *De re publica*, from which he quoted the definition, Augustine makes justice (*iustitia*) an essential constituent of the notion of *iuris consensus*, so that 'where there is no true justice, there can be no *ius* either'.[3] It followed that in the absence of true justice in a community one could not speak of a *res publica*.[4] The critique of a state without true justice was anticipated by Cicero; but it is

---

[1] This phrase, too, has a wide range of applications in Augustine's vocabulary. It can mean either of the two cities, the Church, the Roman state etc.

[2] *Coetus iuris consensu et utilitatis communione sociatus—De civ. Dei*, II, 21.2; XIX, 21.1; cf. Testard, *Saint Augustin et Cicéron*, t. 2, 39–43, 64–6.

[3] *De civ. Dei*, XIX, 21.1.   [4] *Ibid.* and *De civ. Dei*, II, 21.2–3.

Augustine's translation of it into Christian terms that converts the Ciceronian *ius* into 'righteousness' in the full, biblical sense of the word. Years before, in a different polemical context, Augustine could make the necessary distinction: 'although a man may, without absurdity, be said to live most justly (*iustissime*) for the purposes of human society, yet he cannot be without sin, so long as "the flesh doth lust against the spirit"' (Gal. 5:17).[1] Now the distinction between sinlessness and a more limited 'justice' *pro consortio societatis humanae* is shelved, and the conclusion follows that the requirements of real justice are met only in the City of God: 'where there is not that justice according to which God alone rules by grace over a society which obeys him...in whose members the body is subject to the soul, the passions to reason, in observance of the right order; in such a manner that the whole multitude lives, as does the just man, by faith, which works through love...'—where all these conditions are not fully satisfied, there, Augustine argues, the Ciceronian definition will not allow us to speak of a *res publica*.[2] On this definition, with its *ius* understood in Augustine's sense, there can be only one *res publica*, and all human kingdoms are in greater or lesser degree 'dens of robbers', according to the extent of their failure to achieve true justice.[3]

Augustine was perfectly well aware that this rhetorical mode of expression was not suited to the realities with which political discourse is concerned. This is the reason why he gave an alternative definition of *res publica*, in entirely neutral, positivistic terms. On this definition a people (and *res publica* = *res populi*) is 'a multitude of reasonable beings, united in agreement over the things they love'.[4] This definition makes no mention of justice or of any other value. According to it, the political organisation of the Athenians, or of any of the Greek cities, the Egyptians or 'the first Babylon of the Assyrians', indeed of any nation at all, can be designated by the phrase *res publica*; let us, for convenience, adopt 'state' as a suitable

---

[1] C. ep. Parm. II, 7.14: *quamvis iam pro consortio societatis humanae non absurde dici possit iustissime vivere...*   [2] De civ. Dei, XIX, 23.5.
[3] De civ. Dei, IV, 4.   [4] De civ. Dei, XIX, 24.

rendering, though not one entirely free of problems. The values which members of a society are united in being committed to are immaterial to the question whether they constitute a state or not. This has to do only with the political expression of a society, a society with some coherent purpose shared by its members, whatever that purpose or set of purposes may be. The quality of the purposes pursued by a society will, of course, be relevant to any judgement on the quality of a given society. Some will be bad, some will be better; only one, the heavenly city, will be good without qualification. But in so far as there is some bond of common loyalty to unite people, they will, on this definition, constitute a society, which, given political form, will rank as a state.[1]

Augustine had defined the two cities in terms of the ultimate motivation of their members, their 'loves', as he put it. 'Love' is also the conception most fundamental to his understanding of the manner in which the two cities are related within any empirically circumscribed grouping, such as a state. Augustine's definition of the state as the political expression of a society 'united in agreement over the things it loves' cannot be understood in isolation from the whole richness of his theory of love.[2] 'Love', in Augustine's vocabulary, represents much more than simple moral—let alone emotive—dispositions. To know what a man's disposition is in regard to a particular object, we need to know not only whether he 'loves' it or not but also, or rather, in what way he 'loves' it. For the love of something for its own sake, without reserve and as the finally satisfying quelling of one's longing, is very different from the 'love' of something desired as a means to something else; the overwhelming, unconditional self-commitment to something, or to some person, differs greatly from the 'love' of something valued modestly on the scale of goods which one appreciates in some way or other. Human excellence is realised in achieving a

---

[1] *Ibid.* Augustine was acutely aware of groups as capable of developing a 'mind' of their own. Cf. *De doctr. chr.* I, 29.30; *Conf.* VI, 8.13.

[2] The finest general study is Burnaby, *Amor Dei.* Also Holte, *Béatitude et sagesse*, 193–300. For a shorter exposition, cf. Markus, 'Marius Victorinus and Augustine', 380–94.

balanced perspective over the whole range of 'loves'. Already long ago, Augustine had spoken of the righteous man as a man who is *rerum integer aestimator*:

the man who has ordered love (*ordinatam dilectionem*), which prevents him from loving what is not to be loved, or not loving what is to be loved, from preferring what ought to be loved less, from loving equally what ought to be loved either less or more, or from loving less or more what ought to be loved equally.

(*De doctr. chr.* I, 27.28)

The identical vision of virtue as the 'order of love' runs through the *City of God*:

Bodily loveliness, though made by God, is nevertheless temporal, carnal, and a lowly good; it is wrongly loved if it is valued above God, the eternal, inward and lasting good. Just as the covetous man subordinates justice to his love of money—through no fault in the money, but in himself—so it is with all things. In themselves they are all good; they can all be loved well or badly. They are loved well when the right order is kept in loving, badly when it is upset.

(*De civ. Dei*, xv, 22)

More particularly, Augustine often distinguishes two attitudes whose misdirection is the perversion of right order which we call vice: 'enjoyment' (*frui*), the attitude we entertain towards things we value for themselves, and 'use' (*uti*), the attitude we entertain towards things we value for the sake of something else.[1] With the aid of these notions, derived from Stoic ethics, Augustine constructs a morality for the Christian on his earthly pilgrimage towards the heavenly *patria*.[2] Nothing but God can ultimately serve as a resting-place in which all human longings are satisfied; to seek to 'enjoy' anything else is to be retarded in one's journey or diverted from its true destination.

The members of the two cities are distinguished according to the objects in which they seek their final satisfaction, that is to say those they wish to 'enjoy' for their own sake, above all else, to the pursuit

[1] Cf. *De div. qu. LXXXIII*, 30.
[2] On this theme cf. Markus, 'Alienatio'.

of which their other concerns are subordinated. The citizens of the heavenly city recognise no object worthy of such ultimate allegiance but God; the citizens of the earthly city prefer some lower good.[1] Augustine's dichotomy between the two cities in these terms—loving God or loving something else—is over-simplified if taken to mean that the citizens of the heavenly city do not 'love' the objects 'loved' by the citizens of the earthly city. They do; the temporal goods on which the latter set supreme value are good in themselves, and fit objects of 'love'. It is the way in which such objects are loved that is in question: whether they are 'used', and thus valued conditionally, in reference to something else of more ultimate value, or loved to be 'enjoyed', that is unconditionally, for their own sake. 'All share in "using" these (temporal) things, but each has his own purpose in using them, and the purposes differ widely.'[2] The heavenly city, then, is constituted by those who set supreme value only on God, and subordinate all other loves to this one love; the earthly city sets up some other objective as its ultimate goal. Augustine likes to define these objectives, especially in Book XIX of the *City of God* in which the overlap between the two cities is under discussion, in terms of 'peace'. 'Peace' is the final state of gratification of all longing, the state of having come to rest in possession of the desired object; it is the *telos*, almost in the sense of Aristotelian cosmology, of all activity in the universe, not only human and rational but also inanimate.[3] Being the end for which all strive, it is, like the striving for it, capable of realisation on many different levels. Thus the restricted sphere to which the earthly city confines its concerns is that of 'temporal peace': the sphere of material needs and their satisfaction, of security, of orderly social inter-course.[4] All these are as necessary to the heavenly city while it is

---

[1] Cf. *inter multa, De civ. Dei*, XV, 7.

[2] *communis est usus; sed finis utendi cuique suus proprius, multumque diversus—De civ. Dei*, XIX, 17.

[3] *De civ. Dei*, XIX, 12–14. On this immensely rich notion, cf. Fuchs, *Augustin und der antike Friedensgedanke*.

[4] *pax terrena—res ad mortalem hominum naturam pertinentes…humanarum voluntatum compositio…De civ. Dei*, XIX, 17.

on its earthly pilgrimage as they are to the earthly city, and they must be rightly valued by its members, too. For them, this range of objects and activities will constitute the realm of things to be valued in reference to the object of their single ultimate concern: 'All use of temporal things is referred by the members of the earthly city to the enjoyment of earthly peace; by the members of the heavenly city to the enjoyment of eternal peace.'[1]

The existence of a wide range of activity which forms the proper object of concern to all men, whatever the values to which they are ultimately committed, accounts for the overlap of the two cities in this realm. The earthly peace is of common concern to all, whether citizens of the heavenly or of the earthly cities;[2] it is valued and 'loved' by both. Augustine's 'positivistic' definition of the *res publica*[3] appears to have been very carefully devised to make room for this overlap. The people constituting a *res publica* are agreed in valuing certain things; they need not be agreed in valuing them on identical scales of value, still less do they need to be agreed on the objects upon which they set supreme value. The *res publica* will inevitably embrace among its members people with a variety of different ultimate allegiances. But these allegiances fall outside the sphere of the *res publica*. So far as these are concerned, within its restricted sphere the state is inherently 'pluralistic', being the sphere in which the concerns of individuals with divergent ultimate loyalties coincide. The worlds of their personal valuations may be differently structured, their personal orientations in respect of what is ultimately desirable may conflict; but this does not preclude agreement on valuing in some manner which need not—indeed must not—be specified, all that Augustine includes within the scope of 'temporal peace'.

Augustine's treatment of the sphere in which the state's function lies has the effect of endowing the realm of politics with a considerable degree of autonomy. In the Eusebian image of the Empire, political discourse was, we might say, part of theology;

---

[1] *De civ. Dei*, XIX, 14.   [2] *De civ. Dei*, XIX, 17.
[3] *De civ. Dei*, XIX, 24; on it cf. above, pp. 65–6.

with the desacralisation of Roman history at Augustine's hands the Empire, at any rate, was removed from this dimension. But his theology of the two cities led him to a more general understanding of the place of human society and of its political life in relation to the ultimate concerns—the faith, the hope and the love—of the Christian believer. The discussions of Book XIX of the *City of God* in effect pushed such fundamental commitments as a man's religious beliefs and the values he lives by outside the field of political discourse. The only links between the realm of politics and the realm of faith and morals were now those which existed inwardly, in the way in which individuals' valuations are structured. At this personal level, political life, as all other aspects of human living, must of necessity have some place in the overall pattern of the values which guide a man's actions, or some place in the pattern of motivations expressed in his activities. But these relations to a wider context of values and motives lie in a dimension which Augustine took care to exclude from the sphere of politics. This is confined to the outward, the social, the area which is defined, formally, by the possibility within it of coincident decisions springing from fundamentally differing structures of motivation. As a consequence of this personalisation of the links between politics and belief Augustine sometimes took a very detached view of political institutions and of the forms of social living: 'In regard to this mortal life, short and transitory, what does it matter under whose rule a dying man lives, so long as those who rule do not compel him to commit impiety or injustice?'[1] The detachment here amounts almost to indifference to secular institutions; but the context is polemical, and the words were written more than ten years before the final maturity of Augustine's thinking in the last books of the *De civitate Dei*. The same theme appears there in a very different guise:

The heavenly city, while on its earthly pilgrimage, calls forth its citizens from every nation, and assembles a multilingual band of pilgrims; not caring about any diversity in the customs, laws and

[1] *De civ. Dei*, v, 17.1.

institutions whereby they severally make provision for the achievement and the maintenance of earthly peace. All these provisions are intended, in their various ways, among the different nations, to secure the aim of earthly peace. The heavenly city does not repeal or abolish any of them, provided that they do not impede the religion whereby the one supreme and true God is taught to be worshipped.

So the heavenly city, too, uses the earthly peace in the course of its earthly pilgrimage. It cherishes and desires, as far as it may without compromising its faith and devotion, the orderly coherence of men's wills concerning the things which pertain to the mortal nature of man; and this earthly peace it refers to the attainment of heavenly peace... (*De civ. Dei*, XIX, 17)

In the course of ten or twelve years the tone has changed markedly. The sphere of politics is relative and restricted;[1] within its restricted area, it is autonomous; but in its very autonomy it is a matter of deep concern to the citizen of the heavenly city. The new emphasis is part of Augustine's most mature reflection on the secular components of human life and flows from his understanding of the *saeculum*, not as a no-man's land between the two cities, but as their temporal life in their interwoven, perplexed and only eschatologically separable reality.

[1] Cf. *De civ. Dei*, XIX, 19. This theme is more fully discussed at the end of Ch. 4, below, pp. 98–104.

CHAPTER 4

ORDINATA EST RES PUBLICA: THE FOUNDATIONS OF POLITICAL AUTHORITY

AUGUSTINE'S ideas about the Roman Empire were the outcome of two debates. One was the long-sustained debate among Christians since the beginning about how to look upon the Empire in relation to the divine plan of salvation. The other was Augustine's debate with himself, the slow realisation of what was implied by his theology, the growth of reservations about contemporary enthusiasms for the victory of Christianity under the Theodosian establishment, all culminating in his final rejection of the attitudes which nourished this enthusiasm. The final spur to the re-thinking involved was given by the perplexity, both within and beyond the Christian community, provoked by the Sack of Rome in 410. Thus at every stage of their development, Augustine's ideas in this sphere unfold against a varied background of contemporary reflection.

It is otherwise when we consider his views on what might be called the fundamental questions of political theory: questions about human society and its institutions in general, and especially in relation to the ultimate purposes of human life; questions about political authority and obedience, about law and social order. The very concept of a 'state' is one in which we credit Augustine with an interest by extrapolating from the direction of his remarks about Rome; but such an extrapolation, though permissible as a logical inference, must be recognised to be a historical anachronism if read back into Augustine. On such topics a little ingenuity and considerable industry can provide a fair harvest of remarks scattered through the works of Christian Fathers and of secular *literati*. But even casual acquaintance with these scraps is enough to dispel any notion that what we have to do with here is anything that could properly be called 'political theory'. Apart from the little theory contained in some of the best thinking of classical legal writers, the whole corpus of utterances concerned with political matters would reveal itself to be a collection of current platitudes and of incidental asides. Of sustained reflection on the social dimensions of human existence there is no trace between Cicero and Augustine.[1] Thus there was no living context for Augustine's thought beyond the platitudes and passing remarks which, in this sphere, constituted the intellectual capital of his contemporaries. When we come to enquire into Augustine's own 'political theory' we are faced with a similar difficulty. There are certainly elements of reflection on political theory to be found in his writings, but his own explicit remarks in this area constitute no clear body of 'political thought'. They are largely commonplaces or asides, rarely at the centre of his interests. If anything like a 'political theory' is to be extracted from Augustine's work, it will appear more in the form of implications drawn from what he has to say on other, though related matters. Thus in the last chapter we have seen some general implications concerning the scope of the state emerge from what Augustine had to say about the two 'cities' and their mutual relations; and for him, it need scarcely be repeated, these thoughts arose from reflection on Roman history viewed in the framework of the history of redemption. In this chapter we shall enquire into the political implications of his views on human nature, on the realisation of ultimate human purposes and human perfection in general.

Augustine's problem in this sphere lay in the apparent conflict between the dominant ideas of the classical and those of the Judaeo-Christian traditions. For the *polis*-centred tradition of Greek thought the political framework of human life was the chief means of achieving human perfection. Life in a city-state was an education for virtue, a fully human life, the good life. Politics was a creative task. It consisted in bringing into being the kind of

[1] Cf. Barker, ed. *From Alexander to Constantine* and Dvornik, *Early Christian and Byzantine political philosophy*, especially Chs. X–XI.

ordering of society which was most conducive to the realisation of ultimate human purposes. In this sense Plato, Aristotle, the Sophists and the rest all upheld fundamentally the same conception of political activity. Where they differed was in their understanding of the order which they wished to see established in social life. For the Sophists it was essentially one devised by men for their own purposes; for Plato the right social order was one founded upon the real nature of things and to be discerned in the ultimate structure of the world by those properly qualified and equipped for the task. Aristotle's more subtle position combined elements of both views. But whatever they thought about the origins or the metaphysical status of the right social order the theme of the *polis* as the means of directing men towards the achieving of the good life runs through the whole Greek tradition of political thought.

In Judaeo-Christian tradition the key-note of political thinking was different. The people of God, whether of the old or the new Covenants, could not think of themselves as citizens involved in creating the right order in society, nor of their leaders as entrusted with bringing such an order into being. Only God's saving act could establish the one right social order. In relation to that kingdom they were subjects, not agents; in relation to all other, human, kingdoms, they were aliens rather than citizens. In relation to neither God's nor men's kingdoms could they therefore think of themselves as active participants in a creative political task. They could not readily think of themselves as having a part in decision-making assemblies or in governing élites. They were more concerned to define the state's right in participating in their own privileged form of life as a worshipping and believing community than in participating in the creation of a social order through the state's machinery. Their whole tradition was dominated by the need to adjust themselves to a society radically alienated from the one ultimately acceptable form of social existence. In such a society they could never feel themselves fully at home. With the rich resources of the Old Testament imagery of exile the rabbis had formulated the attitude towards Babylon appropriate to the chosen people. Even as Hellenised a Jew as Philo never entirely broke through this horizon.[1] To despised, suspected and sometimes persecuted Christian minorities the attitude came with almost natural inevitability. Late Roman bureaucratic government was very congenial to this non-participating political orientation: for many a conservative lawyer or administrator *disciplina* was more important for the running of the Empire than *concordia*.

Augustine initially stood closer to the classical conception of political life than to the Judaeo-Christian. He thought, as we shall see, that politics was a matter first of discerning the lineaments of the right ordering of society in the nature of the world, and then embodying this discovered order in social arrangements. The development of his thought was steadily away from this classical starting point, towards a biblical notion of a transcendent kingdom where alone men would find their true home, and of human societies which could never aspire to provide the means for human fulfilment, societies in which the citizen of the heavenly kingdom could never be more than a *peregrinus*. But although Augustine came to repudiate the 'creative' conception of politics characteristic of the classical tradition, this was only the first major development of his own political reflection. In the end he was not content with this rejection. In the final phase of his thought there is an obstinate sense of a need to give more weight to the political order than it could bear in the perspective of a stark, biblical repudiation of 'creative' politics. A way had to be found for reconciling the Christian's sense of having no abiding city here with some real political participation in and commitment to a city which was far from an abiding one. This reconciliation appears in the writings of Augustine's last years.

How close Augustine stood initially to the classical tradition of thought in this sphere appears from a slip he made in an early writing. In the course of an argument he found himself appealing to St Paul: 'as the Apostle says, All order is of God', [2]*Omnis ordo a*

[1] Cf. Goodenough, *The politics of Philo Judaeus*, especially 83–4.
[2] *De vera rel.* 41.77.

Deo est, as Augustine wrote, citing from memory. The text he had in mind was, of course, from Paul's famous justification of political authority: 'there is no power but of God' (Rom. 13:1). Many years later, when correcting himself,[1] Augustine would argue that although he had misquoted the text, there was nevertheless good authority for his view in the sequel: for the text goes on to say *quae autem sunt, a Deo ordinatae sunt*—'all that is', as Augustine understood it, 'is ordered by God'. The original slip reveals his mind on this point more dramatically than any positive statement, through the association of ideas which made him write *ordo* instead of *potestas*. The first thing that came into his mind when thinking of political authority (which is what *potestas* here refers to) was the idea of order.

Augustine's memory had betrayed him, and betrayed him in a revealing manner. One key-note of his earliest reflection is the idea of order, and in so far as political authority enters the range of his thought at all at this stage, this is the idea in terms of which Augustine understood it. With neo-Platonism he shared the notion of an order which pervades the whole universe, at all its levels, from the transcendent One at its summit to the lowest. Bound up with this image of a cosmic order there is an image of human destiny: the human soul as fallen into its present state and destined to ascend stepwise to its goal. The cosmic hierarchy provides a ladder for the soul's ascent to its state of perfection. The image, though a philosophic commonplace, and destined to become a commonplace of Christian mysticism and theology as well, had found its supreme expression in the *Enneads* of Plotinus, for instance in his description of the soul's journey to the contemplation of absolute beauty.[2] It had made a profound impression on Augustine's mind, an impression that was never completely effaced from his work.[3] Plotinus's own interests never led him to devote any special discussion to the social bearings of his cosmic vision. But ideas of a similar kind had furnished the material for a good deal of writing

[1] *Retr.* I, 13.8. [2] *Enn.* I, 6.7–9.

[3] On this theme, among the many excellent accounts I refer only to Holte, *Béatitude et sagesse*, and to Madec, 'Sur la vision augustinienne'.

on the nature of society and kingship in late Antiquity, both among pagans and Christians. Eusebius, for instance, had not only utilised the prophetic interpretation of the scriptures to endow Constantine with a divine mission in history;[1] he also mobilised Hellenistic ideas of kingship to create an image of the Christian ruler as the reflection and counterpart in the visible world of God's invisible *logos*.[2] The emperor became an intermediary between the terrestrial empire and the heavenly kingdom, the representative and agent of the latter placed at the head of the former. In his own person, the ruler was the point at which human affairs were drawn into the cosmic order. Similar ideas underlay conceptions of kingship such as those of Themistius and Synesius. They became especially influential in Constantinople. Eusebius only gave Christian form to widely current ideas, such as received systematic expression, for instance, in a neo-Pythagorean treatise on kingship preserved by Stobaeus:

That the nature of all living beings is attuned in harmony with the universe and all that is in it seems to me to be proved by many sorts of evidence. Being in sympathy with the universe, and having a connexion with it which is at once inevitable and ideal, the nature of living beings follows the sweep of the whole, and is carried round in it to participation in the general system of good order...

In the parts of the universe, which are many and different in their nature, some one living being has rule over the others in virtue of its innate capacity and its greater share of divinity. In the terrestrial part, where we are ourselves concerned, man is the best endowed by nature, but among men the king is most divine...

The primary and most necessary community for the human race is that in which the king set over us is one partner, and the other is He who orders all things in the whole universe...

(*apud* Stobaeus, IV, 7.64, translated by E. Barker, *op. cit.* 357, 369).

Augustine, though he does mention the social order in relation to his neo-Platonic philosophy of cosmic order, rarely does so in more than passing remarks. These remarks, although they do little more

---

[1] Cf. above, Ch. 3, pp. 49–50.
[2] *Laus Const.* 4–5, and Baynes, 'Eusebius'; cf. also Ambrosiaster, *Q. Vet. &. Nov. Test.* 35 and 91.8.

than follow the social bearings of a neo-Platonic vision of the world, have their interest. The social order, at this stage of Augustine's thought, is understood entirely in terms of its place within the cosmic order. Thus there are hints that for him society is a reflection of a higher, intelligible order of reality.[1] More often, and more clearly, Augustine asserts that social arrangements have their due place in an overriding order which embraces them. 'What is more horrible than the public executioner? Yet he has a necessary place in the legal system, and he is part of the order of a well-governed society.'[2]

Order, for Augustine, is 'that which, if we follow it in our lives, will lead us to God'.[3] Being part of the all-embracing order in the world, human society is one of the stages of man's advance towards God. Hence the importance of ensuring that the social order really does conform to the divinely established order of the universe. Like Plato long ago, Augustine seemed to think, at this stage of his career, that this would be secured by making sure of the perfection of the ruler.[4] He must be a wise man, and education is to procure wisdom. Through this the wise man will achieve an understanding of order at its very heart and source. This understanding places him above the reach of the temptations besetting other men, and he will be able both to understand them and to remain firm in the face of the apparent disorder they bring into human affairs.[5] Thus under the guidance of the wise ruler emancipated from the appeal of what is temporary and partial, the social order assists men in advancing towards their goal. This advance is accomplished by reason, within a universe conceived as substantially accessible to human comprehension and capable of being dealt with by the resources of human reason.[6] Both the vision of a cosmic order and the idea of human society as a means of man's *teleiosis* within this order are commonplaces of classical thought. At this point the

---

[1] E.g. *C. Acad.* III, 17.37; 18.40.
[2] *De ord.* II, 4.12. [3] *Ibid.* I, 9.27.
[4] *Ibid.* II, 8.25. [5] *Ibid.* II, 5.14.
[6] On the whole of this theme, Cranz, 'The development'.

temper of Augustine's mind reveals itself as deeply in harmony with such a cast of mind.

Even in his early writings, however, there is a certain tension between the classical and the biblical elements in Augustine's thinking, disguised only by the occasional coincidence of the vocabularies in which they are expressed. Philosophers and scriptures both spoke of the opposition between the 'carnal' and the 'spiritual' man, of the 'outer' and the 'inner', or the 'earthly' and the 'heavenly'. These pairs of opposites could be taken as roughly synonymous, and they could be understood in terms either of philosophical categories of Platonic origin, or of the biblical categories of redemption. But the categories did not by any means coincide.[1] The imagery derived from the philosophic context is part of a cosmological scheme. The 'spiritual' is on a higher level than the 'carnal' in the cosmic order. Their relation can be pictured in spatial terms, as 'above' and 'below'. The biblical opposition, on the other hand, depends on Christ's redemptive work: the 'spiritual' is what is transformed, the 'carnal' is unregenerate. The opposition is not between something cosmologically 'higher' and something 'lower'. It is one best expressed in temporal rather than spatial terms, as 'new' and 'old'. Thus, though capable of being rendered in the same terms, the two sets of contrasts are in reality essentially disparate. But Augustine did pass from the cosmological dualities of neo-Platonism to the temporal dualities of biblical redemption history. Two things assisted him in this: one was that both sorts of context pointed towards the same moral conclusions, the *ascesis* and detachment of the soul from bodily concerns. The other was his liking for 'figurative interpretations' of the Old Testament. 'There are certain sacred spiritual realities', he once argued, 'which it was proper for the carnal people [the Jews of the Old Testament] to show forth in image so as to prefigure the new people in the bondage of the old...Thus it is most fitting that what is brought about in a rightly educated

[1] Armstrong, 'Salvation', and in *Christian faith*, 55–8, has a penetrating discussion on the general problem.

individual by the order of nature and learning, should also be accomplished in an analogous manner in the whole human race by divine providence.'[1] Here the *disciplina* of the liberal arts and philosophy has become a parable of the *disciplina* of divine providence. By this means Augustine passes from the emancipation of the educated and wise man, who can rise above the vicissitudes to which the less rational remain in bondage, to the historical 'education' whereby God delivers his people from the bondage of the law into the freedom of the spirit. This readiness to equate ideas drawn from quite disparate contexts enabled Augustine to bridge the gulf between Platonic and biblical ideas of the 'inner' and 'outer' man. He could represent the sixfold scheme of world history[2] as equivalent to a Platonic ascent through the various stages of growth to full human maturity.[3] Generally, this type of thinking disguised from him—for a time—the gulf between the redemption history interpreted as a divine educative process and the ascent from the lower to the higher, the material to the spiritual, the sensible to the intelligible, as conceived in the Greek philosophical tradition. This, however, was a precarious synthesis of two essentially disparate bodies of thought. 'He has tried to express his own Christian experience in a language which is basically alien to it', as a modern scholar remarks in the course of a penetrating study of this phase of Augustine's thought.[4] It was only very much later in his career that Augustine saw the real gulf between the Platonic and the scriptural talk about 'two worlds', when he rejected[5] his own youthful identification[6] of Christ's kingdom (which is 'not of this world'—John 18:36) and the intelligible world of Plato's forms. But by the time Augustine became conscious of this, the tensions present in his early synthesis had long since changed the shape of his reflection on human society.

The first major step in this development was the result of his immersion in the Bible, following his ordination to the priesthood,

---

[1] *De div. qu. LXXXIII,* 49.   [2] Cf. above, Ch. I, pp. 17–19.
[3] E.g. *De vera rel.* 26.48–9; *De div. qu. LXXXIII,* 58.2–3; 64.2.
[4] Cranz, 'The development', 277.
[5] *Retr.* I, 3.2.   [6] *De ord.* I, 11.32. Cf. Markus, 'Alienatio'.

and especially of his reading of Paul in the mid-390s. This is the source of Augustine's increasingly stark vision of human history in terms of a simple dichotomy of those predestined to be saved and the reprobate. This dichotomy soon eclipsed the idea of a progress through the successive stages of God's unfolding plan 'educating' mankind. In the more fundamental relation to God's foreordaining will and grace, all ages are identically placed. The Church is recruited from all historical epochs, before Christ or since. All ages receive their meaning through Christ. The 'two kinds of men', or 'two nations'[1] are now more clearly defined in terms of sin and salvation: they are less readily identifiable with an 'inner' and an 'outer' man understood in cosmological terms. Human destiny is now more immediately tied up with the inscrutability of divine judgement. In the last resort mankind is divided into two by God's mercy working in inscrutable ways. Commenting on the Pauline verse (Rom. 9:18) Augustine writes '(God) will have mercy on whom he will and have no mercy on whom he will not: we must believe most firmly and without hesitation that this is the act of some hidden justice, inaccessible to human investigation. . . '.[2] By the late 390s Augustine's reading of the scriptures and of Paul in particular had brought him a long way from the classical belief in *teleiosis* by human effort to ascend through the successive levels of an ordered universe essentially accessible to human rationality.

He could still write about political authority in terms of securing the right order. Indeed, in a somewhat simple-minded way he could comment on Paul's command to obey the powers that be, in the thirteenth chapter of his letter to the Romans, by explaining it in terms of the duality of soul and body: since we consist of both and require the things we need for bodily sustenance in this life, we must be subject to the government. For it is its business to procure these. It is not its business to concern itself with the soul. In this respect we must acknowledge no human superior, for this

---

[1] Cf. above, Ch. 3, pp. 45, 60.
[2] *De div. qu. ad Simpl.* I, 2.16.

does not belong to Caesar's sphere.[1] The conclusion of Augustine's argument will lend itself to be re-interpreted in the context of his later approach to the tasks of government;[2] but the argument here still derives from the scheme of an ordered hierarchy of levels. Paul could still be fitted into the world of the philosophers at this point.

There are still important relics of neo-Platonic cosmology in the *Confessions*, written around 400 and the years immediately preceding, as indeed in later works. The restlessness of the human heart in its striving for God, its ultimate resting-place, with which the *Confessions* begins,[3] and the evocation of the final rest in the eternal Sabbath with which it ends could both be formulated in the language of neo-Platonic philosophy. But the soul's itinerary towards its final resting-place in God has now undergone a fundamental change. All trace of reliance on human powers in the accomplishing of this ascent is gone; even the idea of a gradual ascent through successive steps has lost its significance in the decisive stress now laid on God's initiative in grace. Augustine's final insistence is clinched in the prayer with which the work closes: 'Of You must we ask, in You must we seek, at You must we knock. Only thus shall we receive, thus shall we find, thus will it be opened to us.'[4]

With this transformation of the great perspectives of Augustine's views on human destiny, the social order came to assume a different place in his thought. With the disappearance of the 'ladder of ascent', society could no longer take its place among the rungs of the ladder.

The new perspective of Augustine's reflection on society is determined by two poles: the human drive for wholeness, fulfilment, rest, peace—the yearning expressed at the beginning of the *Confessions*; and, by way of counterpoise, the deep and painful awareness of the human condition, with the vast distance between

---

[1] *Exp. prop. Ep. Rom.* 72; cf. *Ep. ad Gal.* 28.
[2] Cf. above, Ch. 3, pp. 68–70.
[3] I, I.I.   [4] XIII, 38.53.

its realities and the goal of human striving: 'groaning with inexpressible groaning in my pilgrimage, remembering Jerusalem with my heart stretching upwards in yearning for it: Jerusalem, my fatherland...'[1] Augustine never ceased to have the acute sense of being a wanderer, *in via* towards a distant country in which his longing for a fullness denied him here would be satisfied in final repose. The object of this yearning is 'peace'; peace, defined in a formula full of classical echoes, as 'the tranquility of order'.[2] Man's life on earth is defined by its tension towards this peace. Here he lives as a *peregrinus*—a foreigner—in a land where it behoves him to travel light, with ardent love for a distant country. Hope is the characteristic virtue of the wayfarer: by this he is anchored to his real home. With painful recognition Augustine now denied that the order which leads through all things to God is to be found in human affairs: *hoc nondum est*.[3] The possibility of securing it through the government of wise men, or of men perfectly dedicated to God, is dismissed as an illusory option. The condition of man consequent on Adam's fall does not allow for the achievement of the harmony and order in which alone man can find rest. Tension, strife and disorder are endemic in this realm. There can be no resolution, except eschatologically. Human society is irremediably rooted in this tension-ridden and disordered *saeculum*.

It was this radically 'tragic' character of existence for which ancient philosophy, in Augustine's view, could find no room. His break with the classical idea of 'creative politics'[4] appears at its clearest in his rejection of the 288 actual and possible philosophical statements concerning the ultimate good of man.[5] Like the ancients, Augustine believed that the life of the wise man is a social life;[6] what must be rejected, he thought, is the claim that felicity can be found in it, that the *polis* can be the means of securing perfection. More fundamentally, what is being repudiated is the idea of a final end within the range of human achievement. 'For it is written,

---

[1] *Conf.* XII, 16.23.   [2] *De civ. Dei*, XIX, 13.1.
[3] *De Trin.* III, 4.9.
[4] I borrow the phrase from the late C. N. Cochrane's lectures to be published posthumously.   [5] *De civ. Dei*, XIX, 1–4.   [6] *Ibid.* 5; cf. below, pp. 99–100.

"the just man lives by faith": neither do we yet see our good, wherefore we must seek it believing, nor is upright living something we can achieve of ourselves.'[1] In Augustine's mature view the radical vice of Greek philosophy as of Roman political ideology was the belief in the possibility—he did not know of Plato's bitter disillusion with it in the *Laws*—of perfection through the *polis* or the *civitas*. 'God resists the proud but to the humble he giveth grace':[2] the scriptural sentence quoted at the opening of the *City of God* was to Augustine's mind the most fundamental comment on classical pretensions to human self-determination, as expressed in Vergil's line, quoted in dramatic juxtaposition, on the historic mission of Rome:

> parcere subiectis et debellare superbos   (*Aen.* vi, 853)

Here is Augustine's final answer to the illusion of a *teleiosis* through rational and human means; and it is the more poignant for being a repudiation of a heritage which, as we have seen, had some power over his mind in his youth.

From the late 390s Augustine's political thinking was dominated by this repudiation. Never again did he consider the institutions of society and government as agencies concerned with helping men to achieve the right order in the world. Their task was now to minimise disorder. This is the meaning of Augustine's insistence that political authority is not natural to man, but a result of his sinful condition.[3] Here, again, he was reaching back to an old Christian tradition. According to this tradition, the purpose of the state and of its coercive machinery was to deal with the disorganisation and conflict resulting from the Fall: to prevent men from devouring each other like fish, as Irenaeus put it in a graphic image, itself culled from rabbinic tradition.[4] As with other early Christian commonplaces, the publicity of the Christian emperors since Constantine had done much to obliterate this notion from the general currency of Christian thought on politics in the fourth

---

[1] *Ibid.* xix, 4.1.   [2] Prov. 3:34, quoted in *De civ. Dei, Praef.*
[3] Cf. Appendix B for a detailed analysis of Augustine's statements.
[4] *AH*, v, 24.2.

century, and other ideas, classical, Hellenistic and neo-Platonic, had come into fashion. Augustine himself, as we have seen, had not been immune to their attraction. Nor was he the first, however, to mount an assault, in his mature writings, on the philosophical image of the ruler as set over his subjects in the overarching cosmic order embracing them. Dissenters from the imperial orthodoxy in the fourth century could call the emperor Antichrist; and in more dramatic fashion Ambrose's determination to treat the Christian emperor as a *filius ecclesiae* had dealt a decisive blow to the Hellenistic image of the ruler. In the West, at least, the 'pious humility' which Augustine praised in Theodosius,[1] the penitent sinner subject to ecclesiastical discipline, had rapidly become part of the popular imagery of Christian kingship.[2] It could now be seen as an eloquent symptom of the human condition in which not even rulers were immune to the endemic liability to sin. If all here was subject to distortion and instability, then the ruler's claim to obedience could no longer be based on his standing as the representative of a higher order into which his subjects are to be drawn through his agency. 'Like a running stream, so is the heart of a king in the hand of God: He turns it wherever he will' (Prov. 21:1):[3] how could he serve as the linchpin of an order in human affairs which embodies a stable, universal and objective order? The imperative to obey constituted authority which the New Testament imposed on the Christian had therefore to be reinterpreted. There was no longer any place in Augustine's conception for a ruler as God's agent in helping men achieve their ultimate destiny.

The need to obey rulers could, in fact, be stated without any reference to the purpose of the state. It could be derived from a more general view of man in a world largely beyond his control. In preaching obedience to lawful authority, what Augustine is

---

[1] *De civ. Dei*, v, 26.1.

[2] Cf. Duval, 'L'éloge de Théodose'.

[3] Quoted by Augustine in *De gratia et lib. arb.* 21.42. In his anti-Donatist polemic, however, the first part of the statement could serve to justify religious coercion by rulers. Cf. La Bonnardière, 'Quelques remarques', 77–8.

attacking, before all else, is the 'delusion of self-determination'.[1]
The duty to obey the 'powers that be' is of a piece with man's duty
to bow to God's will in general:

A man is humble before his rulers because he is humble before God. His
political obedience is a symptom of his willingness to accept all processes
and forces beyond his immediate control and understanding. Thus he
can even accept the exercise of power by wicked men. In this, Augustine's
view of obedience is strictly analogous to his view of illness, another
phenomenon plainly beyond man's control and constantly frustrating his
intentions. What does he do, he once wrote to a friend, when he feels
depressed, and cannot preach well? *Flectamur facile ne frangamur*—'let us
bend easily lest we be broken'...The Christian obeys the state because
he is the sort of man who would not set himself up against the hidden
ways of God, either in politics or in personal distress.

(Brown, *loc. cit.* pp. 5, 9)

Such are the grounds on which lawfully constituted authority
must be obeyed—though, of course, obeyed within limits. Man
must obey the state, but not because it can claim to promote the
good life, or to educate him in the ways of the order in the universe.
Although, however, the state cannot claim to secure order in this
positive sense, it did, for Augustine, constitute an order of another
kind. The analogy with a man's readiness to accept illness or
distress is illuminating: like political authority, these are among
the consequences of man's fallen condition. Like illness and distress,
political authority, in claiming a man's obedience, cannot claim
to 'perfect' him in any immediately obvious sense. God's hand
is, to be sure, present in all his dealings with men, in the disease
and sorrow with which he tries them and the rulers to whom
he subjects them; and in this sense they all form part of the hidden
'order' of God's will. But this is a very different thing from the
cosmic and political order as conceived in the classical, Hellenistic
or neo-Platonic views which had played so great a part in Augustine's early thinking.

Augustine himself took some care to distinguish the two kinds

[1] Cf. Brown, 'Saint Augustine', 4. On this point I owe much to this deeply perceptive
study.

of order in the course of his prolonged meditation on the ways of God's providence in human affairs. In his Commentary on the creation story, Augustine came to think of the creation of rational beings as introducing a forking of ways in the universe. Up to this point the processes established in the world could all be described as 'natural'. God was at work in a great garden, 'giving growth even to the trees and the grass'. But at this point the divine gardener grafted reason into the universe 'as on to a great tree of things', and thereby inserted an element of novelty which could no longer be subsumed among 'natural' processes. The activities of rational beings, though still present to God's providence, were present to it in another way. Providence henceforth operates through two channels: through the order of nature, and through the acts of wills and the events in which these issue. Augustine calls the providence behind the first *providentia naturalis*, that behind the second *providentia voluntaria*.[1] Dependent on the two streams of providence, there are two kinds of order to be found in the world: the order of nature and the order expressed in human choices and enacted in human action and its results. This duality of order in the world underlay all Augustine's later reflection on society.

Augustine's philosophy of law played an important part in helping him to formulate these thoughts. Its development ran very closely parallel to the development of his views on society and its institutions—indeed, it forms part of that development. His concept of law, his classification of its various kinds and their mutual relations have been amply studied,[2] and this ground cannot be covered again here. It will be relevant, however, to draw attention to Augustine's change of mind on the status of human law and on what it could be expected to contribute to man's itinerary towards his perfection. There are passages in his earlier writings in which human law is conceived as no more and no less than a kind of reflection of the eternal law. Taking its cue from Stoic thought,

---

[1] *De Gen. ad litt.* VIII, 9.17; cf. below, Appendix B, pp. 203-4.
[2] Cf. Schilling, *SSLAug* ch. 18 for the fullest account. Also Schubert, *Augustins Lex-aeterna-Lehre*.

especially from Cicero's exposition of some of its tenets, Augustine's notion of law revolves around the idea of a rational principle at work in the cosmos, which can be described either as a divine (or 'eternal') law, or as a principle immanent in nature,[1] and accessible to men through reason—a *lex non scripta sed nata*, as Cicero called it.[2] Like so many of the Christian Fathers, Augustine accepted the substance of this teaching, and often expressed it in a form determined by his theory of human knowledge as dependent on divine illumination. Thus the precepts of the eternal law are 'written in the heart of man', or engraved upon it as an 'impression' of the eternal law.[3] This, in a somewhat fluctuating terminology, remained Augustine's unchanging teaching on this subject.

It is in respect of human or civil law and its relation to the eternal law that Augustine's views appear to undergo change. In his earliest discussions of it—at this stage called *lex temporalis*—Augustine held the view that in order for this law to be valid, it must be 'derived' from the eternal law.[4] Though variable from place to place and time to time, human laws belong essentially to the apparatus whereby men are directed towards the achievement of their proper perfection. They must therefore be the public embodiment of the eternal law, or a part of it, in so far as that is accessible to human knowledge. No legislation that fails to measure up to the requirements of the eternal law can be just, or indeed deserve the name of law, for 'it is just that all things should be perfectly ordered'.[5] Justice is almost synonymous with the right ordering of human affairs; and the right ordering of human affairs is part of man's itinerary to God: 'order is that which, if we follow it in our lives, leads to God; and unless we do follow it, we shall not come to God'.[6] Justice and human law considered as its embodiment and instrument are in Augustine's early writings part of the ladder of man's ascent to God.

---

[1] On the various ways in which these were related, cf. Grant, *Miracle and natural law*, 21–8, where Grant notes that the distinction between divine and natural law tended to be more stressed in neo-Platonic than in Stoic thought, which tended, rather, to identify the two.   [2] *Pro Milone*, IV, 10.

[3] Cf. Markus, 'Marius Victorinus', 366–9 and 388–9.   [4] *De lib. arb.* I, 6.15; 5.11.

[5] *omnia esse ordinatissima—ibid.* 6.15.   [6] *De ord.* I, 9.27.

Within two or three years of his first explicit discussion of law Augustine's absolute rejection of any enactment not in accord with the eternal law is softened. Already in his *De vera religione* (*c.* 390) Augustine's argument is not that legislation must, in order to be legitimate, reflect the eternal law, but that 'the temporal legislator, *if he is a good and wise man*, will bear in mind that eternal law...so that he may lay down for his own time what is to be enforced and what is to be prohibited according to its unchanging rules'.[1] The eternal law has become a worthy model and the legislator is recommended to keep it before his eyes. But conformity with it is no longer a *sine qua non* of validity. Henceforth there is no mention in Augustine's writings of the eternal law prescribing, positively, the shape of human law.[2] So far as the public law of societies is concerned, the eternal law has become a negative criterion: what is in conflict with it cannot be just. A man may not be required by the public authority to act against its precepts, and if so required, is entitled—even in duty bound—to withhold his obedience.[3] Even in his earlier writings Augustine sometimes suggests that human law is concerned with externals and is powerless or neutral with regard to the internal dispositions of men, whether they act in conformity with the law or break it.[4] In his later remarks on the purpose and scope of human legislation the emphasis shifts towards stressing this external character of the law. It cannot make men good, but it can secure public order, security, the rights of property. Stated more generally, its purpose is to help in avoiding conflict and to maintain the 'earthly peace'. Its role in directly

---

[1] 31.58.

[2] Cf. Deane, *The political and social ideas of Saint Augustine*, 90: 'As far as I have been able to discover, in none of the works written during the remaining forty years [after the *De vera rel.*] of his life does Augustine ever state that positive law must conform to God's eternal law or to the law of nature to be valid.' See also Ratzinger, *Volk*, 310–14 on the dichotomy of divine and human *ius* in Augustine's thought.

[3] E.g. *Sermo* 62, 8.13; *Enarr. in Ps.* 145.15; *Ep.* 185, 2.8.

[4] E.g. *De lib. arb.* I, 15.32: the eternal law is concerned with what a man loves; the temporal law cannot punish wrongful loving, only the wrong done to others. On Augustine's use of this argument in defence of the punitive measures adopted by the government against schismatics, cf. *inter multa*, *Ep.* 153.6.16; *C. litt. Pet.* II, 83.184, and Ch. 6, below.

promoting the progress of the individual towards the ultimate destination of his earthly pilgrimage has been quietly dropped.

For Augustine's theory of the relation between the political order and the eternal law a formula which appears in his writings by about 400 is of crucial importance. He had by now abandoned his earlier belief in the possibility of human salvation and perfectibility through human society.[1] Now, in his *Contra Faustum*, written around 398, a new formula makes its appearance: 'the eternal law is divine reason, or the will of God, which orders the preservation of the natural order and prohibits its transgression'.[2] This seems to have commended itself to Augustine as a formal, technical definition, repeatedly used or assumed. Its importance for our present purpose lies in the fact that it speaks of the natural order and of the eternal law as two separate things.[3] Previously the two things had been almost identified, or related as original and its image or reflection, as the manifestation or 'impression' of the eternal in the created order. Now they are more clearly distinguished: the eternal law (or God's will) *orders (iubet)* the conservation of the order of nature. It is not said to be embodied, or even reflected, in the order of nature, but stands behind it as its ultimate source and sanction. The importance of this separation is that it allows Augustine to restrict the scope of the 'natural order' while safeguarding the all-embracing sweep of the eternal law (God's will). It is now possible for Augustine to say—though this is not yet being said here—that there are human realities which are not subject to the 'order of nature'; but if so, they, too, will be subject to the 'eternal law' of God's will, just as is the natural order. The assertion that there are indeed two distinct realms, a natural order

---

[1] Cf. above, pp. 75f. and Cranz, 'The development', a discerning study to which I owe much at this point.

[2] *ordinem naturalem conservari iubens, perturbari vetans—C. Faust.* XXII, 27. The same formula recurs *ibid.* 28, 30, 43, 61, 73, 78 and looks like a recently devised formula, adopted by Augustine with some enthusiasm. I have found no precedent for it, though the doublet *iubens–vetans* (or *prohibens*) is, of course, common in Cicero; cf. e.g. *Rep.* III, 22.33, *Leg.* I, 6.18.

[3] Cf. Cranz, 'The development', 301: 'the new phrasing is more easily harmonised with a sharp contrast between God and the creature, between the creator and the natural order'.

determined by its own law and an order shaped by wills, both subject to the 'eternal law', followed not many years later, when Augustine was meditating on the ways of divine providence in the created universe.

The new formula used in the *Contra Faustum* for defining the scope of the 'eternal law' is tailor-made to suit Augustine's theory of a providence channelled in the two streams of 'nature' and of 'wills'. When he wrote the eighth book of his long Genesis Commentary and devoted it to this very problem, he had, as we have seen,[1] become conscious of a distinction between two spheres, both of which are subject to God's will. One of them he described as consisting of the operations of nature, determined by the hidden principles inscribed in things by their creator, according to which they function; the other is the sphere of human action, choice and contrivance. The earlier assimilation of all order, human, social, political, to a single cosmic order which manifested the eternal law is now decisively rejected. Such order as there is in human affairs, in the societies of men, their arrangements and their historical careers, is no longer part of a cosmic or natural order. But, like the natural order, this, too, falls under the sovereign providence of the one Lord.

The Lord of nature is also the Lord of men acting freely, and hence of history, the totality of such actions. This scheme henceforth determined the way in which Augustine portrayed divine operation in the world. It underlies the more informal account of the workings of God's providence in the *City of God*. The chapter devoted to the curious workings of providence in Roman history argues from the premise that not only the whole of nature, but also all the works of man are subject to divine providence, to the conclusion that the kingdoms of men, their rise and fall, are not to be thought exempt from 'the laws of his providence'.[2] Here, as in the crucial chapter (XIX, 15) concerning subjection among men, providence is pictured as operating not only in a natural sphere clearly

---

[1] Cf. above, p. 87.

[2] v, 11. This is anticipated, in a general way, though without the precision which use of the notions of *providentia naturalis* and *voluntaria* could give it, in *De vera rel.* 28.51.

distinguished from a social or historical one, but also in the sphere of society and history. The 'law of divine providence' is also the law which Augustine says ordained the subjection of men to men: 'penal servitude is ordained by that law which orders the conservation of the order of nature and prohibits its transgression'.[1] Far from asserting that penal servitude is an ordinance of nature, the clear sense of the statement, taken in the light of the theory of providence which forms its background, is that penal servitude is no less ordained by that 'law' (the eternal law, i.e. God's providence) which has also ordained the observance of the order of nature and prohibited its transgression. It does not say that penal servitude is part of this natural order, or even that it is to be assimilated to it. It asserts only that God's sovereignty is all-embracing, extending over human affairs no less than over nature. In his later writings Augustine made strenuous efforts to make it clear that human society cannot be treated in terms appropriate to the natural order.

Corresponding to the dual order of providence, Augustine distinguished two sorts of subordination of inferior to superior. One is the 'natural' subordination of 'lesser' to 'greater', of all created things to their creator, 'of corporeal things to spiritual, irrational to rational, earthly to heavenly, female to male, the less worthy to the nobler, the more restricted to the more comprehensive'.[2] The order of human affairs, however, and their government, derives from the other stream of God's governance. The relations of dependence, subordination and superiority which obtain here are not 'natural', though they are subject, as are the 'natural' relationships, to divine providence. His theory of a dual providence led Augustine to deny that social or institutional forms of subjection among men were 'natural' in the way, for instance, that subjection within the family to its head, or subjection of the passions to rational guidance could be called 'natural'. In this latter type of case the regulating element in the relationship—the father, man's

---

[1] *poenalis servitus ea lege ordinatur quae naturalem ordinem conservari iubet, perturbari vetat.* Cf. Appendix B, p. 204 on this.

[2] *De Gen. ad litt.* VIII, 23.44.

reason—could be recognised as in some sense 'naturally' superior to the regulated—the child, the passions. This 'natural' superiority was the foundation for the control exercised by the superior over the inferior, and where this kind of foundation existed, the subjection of the inferior to the superior could be called 'natural'. But no such foundation of 'natural' superiority can be found in the case of ruler and ruled, or master and slave. Here, if there is any 'superiority', it is simply the *de facto* relation in which one of the partners in the relationship finds himself to the other. His being in a position to control his inferiors is not here founded upon an antecedent 'superiority', but is in fact the only thing in which his superiority consists. And this *de facto* superiority Augustine refused to recognise as 'natural'. The bare superiority of being established in a controlling position is the only kind of superiority Augustine could concede to the master over his slaves or to the ruler over his subjects; in no other sense were his 'inferiors' inferior. For this reason Augustine rejected the classical models according to which political authority was represented as analogous to the authority wielded by God over the world, of the mind over the body or a parent over his children.[1] The authority of rulers over their subjects could not be related to an intrinsic superiority over their subjects, and the duty of subjects to obey their rulers does not derive from any natural inferiority or subordination, in virtue of which they need the guidance of their superiors for the achievement of their own perfection. In some ideal, but fictional, society rulers might be the wisest and best men, through whose guidance and rule the less excellent are enabled to achieve perfection. But this is a model Augustine rejected. The whole realm of politically organised society with its institutions of government can only be spoken about in a language appropriate to a world in which the harmonious order of such natural relationships is irretrievably distorted.

The fundamental index of this radical dislocation of our world, in Augustine's eyes, came to be seen in the passion to dominate, to subjugate, others to one's will: the *libido dominandi* of which

[1] Cf. Appendix B, pp. 206–7.

Augustine so often speaks. This is the perverse and selfish love which produces the 'earthly city'.[1] It has no place in the hearts of the just who live by faith. In the rule of such a just man over his subordinates there is no trace of the passion to dominate or the pride of rule.[2] If such a one is called to exercise office in the state, he will conduct himself on the model of the *paterfamilias*. This is the model which Augustine often recommends to his highly placed friends: 'fulfil as a Christian magistrate the office of a kind father', he wrote to Marcellinus.[3] But though the image of the *paterfamilias* could serve as a model for conduct in public office, Augustine refuses to allow that it can serve as model for explaining political institutions. For these involve relationships essentially different in kind from those based on 'natural' subordination within the family. Indeed, Augustine had once asserted that no ruler ever in fact does rule in accordance with this model: for God alone rules 'without pride'.[4] It is possible that in his youth Augustine would have been prepared to base political authority on intrinsic superiority: wherever we look around us in the world, he once wrote, we see order, law, constancy, harmony and beauty; and among their evidences he enumerated the 'authority of command owed to the better'.[5] But though the picture of a cosmic order with 'superior' levels rightfully regulating the 'inferior' remained a permanent feature of Augustine's thought,[6] he ceased to apply this scheme to political authority. The hierarchy of nature and the hierarchy of society had been prised apart. The two kinds of order do not coincide in society, as he insisted in his Commentary on the creation story. Political subordination cannot be assimilated to natural subordination.

In Augustine's mature thought there is no trace of a theory of the state as concerned with man's self-fulfilment, perfection, the good life, felicity, or with 'educating' man towards such purposes. Its

[1] Cf. above, Ch. 3, pp. 60–9.
[2] *De civ. Dei*, XIX, 14, 16 and Appendix B, pp. 197–9.
[3] *Ep.* 133.2; cf. *Ep.* 134, to Apringius etc.   [4] *Conf.* X, 36.58.
[5] *De ord.* I, 8.26. It is by no means certain that Augustine here had political authority in mind.
[6] Cf. e.g. *C. Faust.* XXII, 27; *In Joh. Ev. Tr.* 8.2.

function is more restricted: it is to cancel out at least some of the effects of sin. Political authority exists to resolve at least some of the tensions inevitable in human society. Inequality among men is not only a symptom and a consequence of the loss of primal integrity. It is itself mobilised under God's providence in this sinful world to keep sin in check. Political authority serves to remedy the conflict, disorder and tensions of society. In a world of radical insecurity—'this hell on earth'[1]—the state exists *propter securitatem et sufficientiam vitae*. All the institutions of political and judicial authority, with their coercive machinery, serve this purpose: 'while they are feared, the wicked are held in check, and the good are enabled to live less disturbed among the wicked';[2] *ut tuta sit inter improbos innocentia*[3]—to secure the space for the free exercise of virtue in a society racked by the insecurity which is woven into the very texture of human existence.

Augustine never doubted that social life itself was 'natural' to man in a way in which politically organised life was not.[4] Man was created from a single stock that he might live in concord with his fellows; even the life of the wise and of the saints in heaven is a social one. 'There is nothing as social by nature and as anti-social (*discordiosum*) by corruption as the human race';[5] there is less conflict among the fiercest of beasts than among the societies of men.[6] The ultimate goal of man's yearning is 'eternal peace'; but this is to be had by the citizens of the heavenly city only at the end of their earthly pilgrimage, in the spontaneous harmony of love which characterises that society. The great need here, in Augustine's sombre vision of the nasty brutishness of man in his fallen condition,[7] was for bulwarks to secure society against disintegration. In its coercive machinery the state turns human ferocity itself to the limited but valuable task of securing some precarious order, some minimal cohesion, in a situation inherently tending to chaos.

---

[1] *De civ. Dei*, XXII, 22.4.   [2] *Ep.* 153.6.16.
[3] *Ibid.* Cf. *De Gen. ad litt.* IX, 5.9: *ne contrariae voluntates pacem cohabitantium perturbarent...*
[4] Cf. Appendix B, pp. 209–10.
[5] *De civ. Dei*, XII, 28.1.   [6] *Ibid.* 23.
[7] On some of the analogies between Augustine and Hobbes on this subject, cf. Wilks, 'St Augustine and the general will'.

Violence was always liable to erupt in Augustine's North Africa, and the check to it by the authorities was clearly visible as a positive good. Characteristically, it is the thirteenth chapter of the Letter to the Romans that will come to Augustine's mind when he is preaching to a congregation which has just been guilty of lynching a local officer. No doubt, Augustine says, he deserved his fate; but what has that to do with you? What is one to call the killing of a man unheard, unjudged, without the authority to punish? 'The state has its judges, it has its authorities: *ordinata est res publica.*'[1] 'Control of the wicked within the bonds of a certain earthly peace'[2] remained Augustine's fundamental thought about the purpose of government, at least from the time he had worked out the implications of his views on divine providence.

The check to violence was the public authority's most immediately obvious contribution to resolving some of the tensions in society. But there are expressions, especially in Augustine's earlier writings, which suggest that the public authority of the state would also make some contribution in securing a space for the development of the amenities and the arts of civilisation. In his youth he had lavished eloquent praise on all the varied fields of intellectual, artistic and constructive achievement.[3] He thought of them as bound up with the life of politically organised society. Although he was much more reserved about the 'useless arts' only ten years later, he still valued social institutions for the sake of more than the bare possibility of life and its continuance. They also help to make life civilised, they facilitate social intercourse and they define the quality of a common life within a shared culture.[4] Augustine knew too well that a society resting on no cohesive bond other than the coercive power of its public authorities was doomed to disintegration. On these grounds all the institutions which fostered human intercourse and a shared culture were matters of concern to a Christian.[5] Even in the *City of God*, a work whose polemical

---

[1] *Sermo* 302.13.
[2] *De Gen. ad litt.* IX, 9.14.
[3] *De quant. an.* 33.72.
[4] *De doctr. chr.* II, 25.39–40.
[5] *Ibid.* and II, 39.58.

orientation is not the most conducive to giving this concern much prominence, Augustine's statements about the purpose of the state suggest that it included more than providing the framework for minimal security. The 'temporal peace' which is of concern to both 'cities' appears to embrace not only the whole sphere of material needs and their satisfaction, of security, of orderly social intercourse, but also the 'fostering of a certain coherence of men's wills'.[1] Augustine tends, in his work, to minimise this 'coherence of human wills', for his aim was to present the deep divergence of wills at the roots of the two 'cities', and his argument is precisely that in the state these radically opposed orientations of will must coexist. Thus, although he thought of 'the coherence of human wills' as limited in scope, he nevertheless gave it real value within his limits. In matters falling short of the ultimate purposes society must concern itself with shaping the pattern of its common values.

His first insistence, of course, remained the denial that society was in any way the agency of man's pursuit of his ultimate good. His downgrading of society by confining it to the sphere of the temporal needs of men in their fallen condition is the counterpart of his secularisation of history, considered in the previous chapters. In those, and especially in our mapping of his ideas on Rome, it has been possible to achieve greater chronological precision than has been possible in tracing the development of his ideas on human society in general. The reason for this is twofold. First, it is plain that the basic themes of political philosophy, such as the concepts of the state, or of political obligation, were never the central objects of Augustine's interests, whereas the destiny of Rome did become a crucial issue for him in the years following 410. Secondly, the change in Augustine's approach to society which we have followed in this chapter is largely compressed into the first ten or twelve years of his literary career. During this relatively short time he had abandoned the notions of society inspired by Greek philosophical conceptions. The parting of the ways had come much earlier;

[1] *ut sit eis de rebus ad mortalem vitam pertinentibus humanarum quaedam compositio voluntatum—De civ. Dei*, XIX, 17. Cf. Ch. 3, pp. 68–70.

thereafter Augustine's ideas underwent little fundamental change compared with the slower development of his views on the Roman Empire.

The 'downgrading' of society which we have described in this chapter can be looked upon as the preparation for Augustine's final estimate of human achievement in the Roman state. The realisation that society in general cannot be considered as part of the mechanism provided for man's self-perfecting opened the way for a fresh approach to man's social condition. Instead of the 'cosmological' terms in which he had seen society as part of a universal order, he had now come to see it in historical terms, as part of the 'order' of God's historical providence. The question about the role of social arrangements in assisting men to achieve their ultimate good was superseded by another: what is the relation of the historical career of a society—the Roman—to the divine plan for the salvation of men? Augustine, in the end, answered that question[1] in terms of his theology of the 'two cities': the Empire—as all actual societies of men—hovers between the 'earthly' and the 'heavenly' cities, or, more precisely, it exists in the region where the two cities overlap. Its achievement is radically infected with the ambiguity of all human achievement. In a sense this answer had been anticipated in Augustine's rejection of the classical 'politics of perfection'. Only his later thought about the two 'cities' could give the rejection sharpness; but in the view that the state is essentially bound up with man's fallen condition, we already have the germs of this insistence on the ambivalence of social institutions in relation to the ultimates of human destiny. With these ultimates—either the satisfaction of all man's yearning in the eternal 'peace', or his final estrangement from his *patria*—social arrangements are emphatically not concerned. They have their place between these ultimates; they meet more limited needs, with no immediate relation to perfection or salvation.

Moreover, even the limited need for security, for the material framework of everyday living and for the amenities of civilised

---

[1] Cf. Ch. 3, above, pp. 64–70.

intercourse is met, in Augustine's final view, at terrible cost. There is perhaps nothing in all Augustine's writing that expresses quite so shattering a sense of the radical dislocation of order even within the *ordinata res publica* as the chapter he devoted in the *City of God* to 'the errors of human judgements, when the truth is hidden'.[1] In Book XIX Augustine sets out to give the Christian answer to the philosophers' quest for felicity. Having disposed of all human techniques and strategies for the achievement of felicity, and of all the classical expositions of what it consists in, he returns[2] to the classical insistence on the social character of the life directed to human fulfilment. Cicero, Varro and the philosophers say that the life of the wise man is a social life: *Nos multo amplius adprobamus*—we insist even more strongly, Augustine replies;[3] but what is social life? Something very different from what they envisaged, as Augustine goes on to show in his sombre catalogue of the inescapable tensions involved in social living, the endemic insecurity, the painful exigencies of trying to be moral man in immoral society. There is a deeply disturbing realism in Augustine's parable[4] of the conscientious judge who, 'even in the most peaceful of states', finds himself frustrated in his quest for justice by the very conditions of human life. The inescapable dilemmas, the uncertainties surrounding human justice even at its best, are Augustine's epitome of social living.

Life in society is, as the ancients insisted, a necessity. Without society, Augustine agrees, no human maturity is possible; indeed there can be no image of human perfection that is not essentially social in character. In this sense man was certainly social by nature, for Augustine. But the parable of the conscientious judge compelled *malgré lui* to dispense injustice shows how little he was inclined to understand man's social nature in the sense of Plato or Aristotle. If social life is natural, it is nevertheless, in the actual conditions of a politically organised community of sinful men, a burden, like a disease. 'Will a wise man sit as judge in this darkness

---

[1] *Brev.* XIX, 6. [2] *De civ. Dei*, XIX, 5.
[3] *Ibid.* [4] *De civ. Dei*, XIX, 6.

of social life (*in his tenebris vitae socialis*), or will he not dare?'
Augustine asks in concluding his parable, and his answer is clear:
'Of course he will sit. For the solidarity of human society, which
he deems wicked to abandon, lays upon him this duty and draws
him to its performance.'[1] This answer reveals the mature complexity of Augustine's attitude to social institutions. They have a
real claim upon men, they impose duties which Augustine repeatedly describes in terms which evoke their binding character:
they 'compel' or 'constrain' men to carry out their social duties,
they lay men under a 'necessity'. Such claims may not be resisted
without guilt; but—Augustine returns to the point—let us not
deceive ourselves: there is no felicity to be realised among the
'necessities' of this social existence. The conscientious judge who is
Augustine's epitome of the man most fully engaged in the 'necessities' of society, while fully responsive to the claims it exerts on
him, is also the first to 'recognise the misery of these necessities,
and to shrink from his own implication in them; with true piety
he would cry out to God with the Psalmist: "Deliver me from
my necessities."'[2]

This sums up the old Augustine's assessment of the claims made
for politically organised society (the *civitas*, as he calls it here) by
the classical tradition. When he had just begun the composition of
the *City of God*, thirteen or fourteen years previously, Augustine
had already perceived that the idea of a Christian society was a
mirage, and concluded that Christ's servants, whether kings or
their subjects, could only hope to 'stick it out' with patience, and
must be content with working here to secure for themselves a
place in the sun in 'that heavenly society where God's will is the
law'.[3] Now, Augustine was much too sensitive to the claims of
the earthly state on the members of the heavenly city to let it go
at that. Concern for this temporal order, in its very temporality,
had become for him part of a Christian's duty to God. This is the
discovery which lies between the early and the final books of the

[1] *De civ. Dei*, XIX, 6.   [2] *Ibid.*
[3] *Ibid.* II, 19.

City of God. Book XIX is in substance his exploration of the consequences of this discovery.

We have already seen[1] that for the old Augustine, engaged on the final books of the *City of God*, the affairs of the *saeculum* assumed significance just because he now saw the *saeculum* as the historical, empirical, perplexed and interwoven life of the two eschatological cities. At the most fundamental level, that of their ultimate allegiance, men were starkly divided between the two cities. But the *saeculum*, and the societies, groups and institutions whose careers constitute it, embraced both poles of the dichotomy. With John Stuart Mill, Augustine held that mankind 'are more easily brought to agree in their intermediate principles, *vera illa et media axiomata*, as Bacon says, than in their first principles'.[2] These intermediate principles sufficed to stake out a large tract of territory common to the two cities in their temporal being. To speak of the *saeculum* as the region of overlap between the heavenly and the earthly cities, while true, is misleading if understood in terms of the logical notion of an overlap between two mutually not exclusive classes. For in their eschatological reality the two cities are, of course, mutually exclusive, while in their temporal reality they are indistinct: here the primary *datum* for Augustine is the integrity of the *saeculum*, or, more precisely, of the social structures and historical forms in which it is embodied. The account of the *saeculum* in terms of the temporal co-existence of the two cities applies to the *saeculum* an eschatological perspective. In any perspective shorter than this, the primary reality is the ambiguous world of historical experience. The very terms of Augustine's critique of the sacralisation of the Roman Empire implied a protest against the readiness to see within any society the ultimate eschatological conflict prematurely revealed in visible, identifiable form. All we can know is that the two cities are always present in any historical society; but we can never—except in the light of a biblical revelation in the unique strand of 'sacred history'—

---

[1] Cf. above, Ch. 3, pp. 62–70. The analysis of *De civ. Dei*, XIX in Ch. 3 stands behind the following pages.　　　　　[2] 'Bentham', 91.

identify the *locus* of either. Hence concern for the secular realities
of any society, with all their ultimate ambivalence, was itself
forced upon its members by the quality of their ultimate concerns:
their faith and their love. The citizen of the heavenly city was no
more a stranger to the *saeculum* than was the citizen of the earthly
city, for here and now the two cities between them are, quite
simply, what the *saeculum* is. It is neither a third thing somewhere
between them, nor is it, except eschatologically, resolvable into
its two constituents. For the citizen of the heavenly city, concern
for the *saeculum* is the temporal dimension of his concern for the
eternal city.

This is the ground for Augustine's mature consciousness of the
real and deep claims which bound a Christian to a temporal society
devoted to the service of objectives which lay well on this side of
the final goals of life. In the work of his old age there is a strong
sense of 'membership', a concept which Raymond Williams has
described as

an individual's positive identification with the society in which he lives.
The member of a society feels himself to belong to it, in an essential way:
its values are his values, its purposes his purposes, to such an extent that
he is proud to describe himself in its terms. He is of course conscious of
himself as *a* member—an individual within the society to which he
belongs—but it is of the essence of membership that the individual, so
far from feeling that the society is opposed to him, looks upon it as the
natural means by which his own purposes will be forwarded.

The long revolution (Pelican ed. 1965, 102)

Within the sphere of purposes which fall short of the most ultimate
of human purposes, Augustine would have accepted this. In Book
XIX of the *City of God* he set about the task of defining a secular
sphere in which it was possible for a Christian to think of himself
as a member of a temporally limited society. The needs and concerns which men shared, even when their ultimate allegiances
diverged, established a human community sufficient to mobilise
men's loyalties and to focus their sense of belonging.

Augustine's conception of the *saeculum* made it possible for politics to resume some of the significance of which his attack on the Platonic tradition (in which politics had *ultimate* significance) had deprived it. The complexity and poise of his final estimate of politics stem from his conviction that the quest for perfection and happiness through politics is doomed. The archetypal society, where alone true human fulfilment can be found, is the society of the angels and the saints in heaven: not a *polis*. Aristotelian theologians in the middle ages would be claiming the weight of Augustine's authority in support of their belief that the political order formed part of the natural order established by God in the universe;[1] rationalists and romantics in the eighteenth century would draw from his diagnosis of man's loss of his original innocence the conclusion that a redeemed society was within the reach of human contrivance, if only men would follow nature, disclosed either through reason or through moral sentiment.[2] Augustine would have disowned both: the one as a conservative, the other as a revolutionary deformation of his thought. In both he would have seen a betrayal of the basic insight which had come to him as he learnt to dissociate himself from the classical heritage of a 'politics of perfection': the insight that man had lost his autonomy before God. To recover the right, divinely intended, 'natural' or 'traditional' order among men, men must look beyond human institutions. *Garriebam tamquam peritus*, Augustine wrote[3] in his middle age, recalling his youthful illusion of human self-determination—'I chattered like an expert.' As a young man he had spoken[4] of the transformation of the inexpert (*imperitus*) into an expert (*peritus*) through education; now, seen in his confrontation with Christ, the expertise is doomed: the *peritus* is transformed, in a word-play which contains a deliberate allusion to his youthful ideas, into the *periturus*; the expert is doomed to perish, for One alone is the Way.[5]

In the last resort man's destiny is not within his control. Not

---

[1] Cf. Appendix C.
[2] Cf. Vereker, *Eighteenth century optimism*, especially Chs. 8–10.
[3] *Conf.* VII, 20.26.   [4] *De ord.* II, 9.26.   [5] *Conf.* VII, 20.26.

even in society can men work out their salvation. And this being so, as the functions, institutions and the quality of a society cannot be assessed in terms of the ultimates of human destiny, then the relevant language of politics must move in a more limited sphere, the sphere of the needs which social life exists to satisfy. Augustine's repudiation of the classical 'politics of perfection' prepared the ground for a political theory which he never in fact elaborated beyond the bare indications that its realm is that in which the two 'cities' overlap. But he saw the direction and indicated it clearly. The realities of the *saeculum* must be spoken of in historical or political, not in theological, terms.

CHAPTER 5

AFER SCRIBENS AFRIS: THE CHURCH IN AUGUSTINE AND THE AFRICAN TRADITION

FOR Augustine the institutions and the life of politically organised society were irretrievably infected with man's sin. Human society could not heal the dislocation nor bridge the gulf between the ineradicable tensions of this life and the peace of the heavenly city. The depth of this gulf became ever more apparent to Augustine in the course of the Pelagian controversy. Though created good, all men are born in sin; to what we inherit, we add what we do. In sum, the world is evil—but for its redemption by Christ. His coming has created another world, where division is healed, multiplicity restored to unity and corruption to integrity. Humanity has 'trickled apart': let us rally, return to oneness, collect what has been scattered, restore what has been broken. The reconciled world *is* the Church: *mundus reconciliatus Ecclesia*, as Augustine said in one of his finest sermons on this favourite theme of his.[1] This commonplace of Western theology discloses the richness of its meaning only in the context of Augustine's dialogue with a long history of reflection on the Church in its relation to the 'world', especially in Africa.[2]

Augustine belonged to two very different worlds. In Rome and, especially, in the Milan of Ambrose, he encountered a cosmopolitan Church, wielding wide influence over emperors and officials, occupying a place of leadership in society, confident of its power to absorb, mould and transform it.[3] This image of the Church cast a

[1] *Sermo* 96.6–8.
[2] Inevitably, this is far too large a subject for anything like a full discussion within the limits of one chapter. I have been content to give my own version of the story without seeking to justify even the more controversial of my views, and without attempting to refer to the whole of the evidence on which it is based. A basic list of the secondary literature on the subject of this chapter is given in the Bibliographical note (p. 234).
[3] Cf. the fine evocation by Brown, *Augustine of Hippo*, 225.

spell over his mind which had some power even after he had come to build his conception of the Church on different foundations. On his return to Africa, however, Augustine encountered an ecclesiology which had become dominated by a very different tradition. The Church was thought of as an alternative to worldly society and as a refuge from it. Since the days of Tertullian and Cyprian, African Christians had come to think of the Church as standing uncompromisingly over against an alien and hostile world. In the third century, persecution gave this image a reality whose power can still move the reader of some of the more restrained *Acta* of the martyrs. The characteristic features of the African ecclesiological tradition were born during the age of the persecutions; but they showed a tenacity which ensured their survival long after.

For Tertullian, writing around 200, the Church was the community of the elect, defined by its separation from the pagan world of idolatry and falsehood, and from the multitude of the heretics, its offspring. His deep conviction that the Church as the Bride of Christ had to be 'without spot or wrinkle' was to drive him outside the communion of the Catholic Church. In the writings of his Montanist period the true Christian community stands over against not only the world of unbelievers and heretics, but also against the 'psychics', the Catholic Church, which at this very moment was admitting—as men like Tertullian and Hippolytus saw the matter—the 'world' with all its impurity and profaneness into the Holy of Holies.[1] For Tertullian and men of his cast of mind 'world' and 'Church' were mutually exclusive. If the 'Church' allowed itself to be penetrated by 'world', then the threshold of the sanctuary had to be moved back to a point beyond the reach of contamination, to a realm where the purity of the Spirit would hold sway.

The idea of a Church of the 'elect' was scarcely novel. In Tertullian's theology it was the outcome of a stark dichotomy

---

[1] Cf. the perceptive though impressionistic chapter of Kamlah, *Christentum*, 116–29 on the 'Callixtan revolution'.

between 'truth', 'purity' and 'holiness' ranged against 'error' and 'idolatry' which epitomised the 'world'. His powerful rhetoric lent itself well to stating such stark oppositions: 'What has Athens to do with Jerusalem? The Academy with the Church? Heresy with Christianity?'[1] In so far as the Church failed to identify itself in such an antithetical relation *vis-à-vis* the world and was prepared to acknowledge some common ground with it, it could not be the true Church. Here was the first appearance of that characteristic need of African ecclesiology for a 'counter-Church' which would be a kind of diabolical parody of the true Church. This was a simple solution of the problem raised by the lack of relation between holiness and the established ecclesiastical structure—the *ecclesia numerus episcoporum*, as Tertullian called it—and its appeal was both strong and widespread. Especially in the aftermath of the persecutions, so long as Christians felt outraged by the presence within their community of those who had compromised in the time of testing or betrayed their true Christian calling, a Church which failed to repudiate and exclude such 'traitors'[2] from its communion could itself be repudiated and excluded from the 'true Church'. The situation was common wherever persecution had been widespread. There were controversies similar to the controversy over Donatist repudiation of *traditores* in Rome, Egypt and Palestine; but even in Egypt, where the Melitians formed a sect, they never played the part that the Donatists played in Africa. What gave Donatism its standing in Africa was that it could claim to be, quite simply, *the* African Church.

For it was the African Church itself, in the time of Cyprian, in the fifties of the third century, that had cast its official theology within moulds which belonged to Tertullian's spiritual universe. Essentially Cyprian's ecclesiology differed from Tertullian's only in that it identified the Church of the bishops with the Church of the pure. The exclusive categories in which Tertullian had thought of the 'spiritual' Church, true, holy and removed from

---

[1] *Praescr.* 7; cf. *Apol.* 46.
[2] *Traditores:* those guilty of handing over copies of the scriptures to the authorities during times of persecution.

the contaminating world, were now applied to the Church of the bishops.

Cyprian, though no great speculative theologian, was the intellectual heir of Tertullian. In an age of uncertainty his influence became decisive for the African Church. His personal disposition was far from extremist. Temperamentally, he may have been much further from the rigorist fanatics in the African Church than he stood from those who wished to treat people who had 'lapsed' during the persecution of 250 with leniency. His circumspection, his refusal to act without carefully weighing the principles of action,[1] and his distrust of all *Schwärmerei* must incline us to take his final stand on the 'purity' of the Church all the more seriously. This was no intransigent rigorism. There are sure to be tares among the wheat, and they must be tolerated, he wrote to some confessors, liable to their occupational disease of wishing to separate themselves from the tares.[2] But so far as the sacramental structure of the Church is concerned, and those who administer it, 'whosoever hath a sin or blemish, let him not approach to offer sacrifices to the Lord', Cyprian will insist, in the words of the Old Testament laws of ritual purity.[3] Sin and impurity disqualify the minister and invalidate his ministry; from such clergy a community must separate itself.[4] Sacraments administered by such clergy have no power to save. In this, their ministers are like heretics. Baptism administered by heretics or schismatics fails to sanctify; in the Church alone do the *sancti* sanctify.[5] The purity required for the sacramental ministry fixes a gulf between the Church and the world as deep as any that divided Tertullian's Jerusalem from Athens: 'What can lies have in common with truth, darkness with light, death with life, the Antichrist with Christ?'—from such dichotomies, so reminiscent of Tertullian's, Cyprian draws his conclusion: 'so we must hold to the unity of the Catholic Church and yield nothing to the enemies of faith and truth'.[6] In a revealing

---

[1] Cf. Monceaux's fine character sketch, *Histoire*, vol. 2, 341 f.
[2] *Ep.* 54.3.
[3] *Ep.* 65.2, quoting Lev. 21:17; cf. the other OT quotations here.
[4] *Ep.* 67.3.   [5] *Ep.* 70.2.   [6] *Ep.* 71.2.

comparison he once spoke of the Church as the lines held under God's generalship against the enemy on a battlefield. The task of Christ's soldier is to hold them, not yielding an inch.[1]

Cyprian's views on baptism, and with them the image of a closed, pure and holy Church, were endorsed by the African bishops who met in council in 256. The bishop of Rome might denounce them, but the African Church did not consider it necessary to defer to his views if they compromised the truth. Cyprian's doctrine remained its official doctrine, and rebaptism its normal practice. Cyprian's death soon after the council, in the persecution of Valerian, was followed by the great age in the christianisation of North Africa. Especially in the rural Hinterland and in the comparatively un-Romanised regions such as the Numidian High Plains, 'the victory of the Christian Church in North Africa was won probably in the latter half of the third century A.D.'.[2] This great Church of perhaps not far from 300 episcopal sees by the end of the third century—possibly double what it had been when Cyprian died—took shape and formed its mind at a time when the legacy of Cyprian held undisputed sway over African Christianity. The Church which emerged in Africa from the great persecution at the beginning of the fourth century bore the stamp of Cyprianic Christianity.

It was, alas, also a Church torn with dissension. The See of Carthage, its chief See, was now the object of dispute between two rivals and the parties gathered around them. It was the appeal of one of these to Constantine, the new emperor, for recognition as the true Catholic Church in Africa that gave Rome its chance to get its own back on the African Church. In 256 Pope Stephen had failed to get Cyprian and the African bishops to agree to repudiate rebaptism; now rebaptism became the badge of heresy. Overnight, their lack of agreement with the Roman and other Western Churches turned the African heirs of Cyprian, confident of being recognised by unprejudiced Gallic eyes as his true successors, into

[1] *Ep.* 73.10—the famous letter to Jubaianus, treasured by the Donatists in their collection of Cyprian's works.
[2] Frend, *The Donatist Church*, Chs. 6 and 7. The quotation is from p. 94.

heretics outlawed by a Christian emperor.[1] The schism born of rival claims to the See of Carthage, assisted by the conflict of provincial jealousies between Numidia and Carthage, was thus transformed into a schism with European implications. The 'Catholic' party came to be identified by its agreement with transmarine customs, and by its readiness to communicate with overseas Churches less particular than the African about tolerating *traditores* in their ranks. This compliance brought in its train the enjoyment of official support and of imperial favour. But it meant disowning what had hitherto been African Christianity. For nothing can disguise the fact which the 'Donatists' (as the party of Majorinus will now be known) never tired of stressing, the fact which even Augustine was compelled to recognise, that theologically the Donatists were the true heirs of Cyprianic Christianity. They owed their new status as schismatics from a 'Catholic' Church simply to a decision made abroad, in defiance of the old traditions of autonomy in the African Church, a decision upheld by the emperor. From an African point of view the newly designated 'Catholic' Church had betrayed African Christianity, with its sense of independence in relation to 'overseas Churches', its commitment to ritual purity and rebaptism, its fiercely exclusive stand towards the 'world' and opposition to its powers as alien or hostile. 'Catholicism' was an import to Africa. The Council of Arles of 314 and the first Christian emperor can claim the full credit for its establishment in Africa.

Inevitably, the newly imported Catholic Church failed to make much headway, especially among the sections of the population more remote from Roman influence. African Christianity, now officially labelled 'Donatism', remained the religion of the

---

[1] As late as 314, at the time of the Council of Arles, Africans were known to have their own usage in this matter, and it was now prohibited. It is impossible to discover when the party of Caecilian gave up the custom of rebaptism. Optatus and Augustine assume that Catholics and Donatists had been divided on this matter from the start. The Roman synod of October 313 called by Constantine to settle the conflicting claims to the See of Carthage censured only Donatus in this respect. Perhaps Caecilian had been far-sighted enough to adopt Roman customs in good time. His readiness to comply must, in any case, have been known. It is unlikely that the attitudes of the two parties towards *traditores* were initially very different.

economically underprivileged, the African 'masses' of the country-side, especially away from the Romanised urban centres or the great Roman estates. In Numidia in the 390s the Donatists were still the established Church. When Augustine arrived in Hippo, the Catholics were an insecure minority there. To the very end, the right of the imported Church to the title of 'Catholic' was passionately contested by its rival, conscious of being the true heir of what had been African Christianity before Constantine. Charges of *traditio* had been flung around on both sides at the time of the original schism between Caecilian and Majorinus at Carthage. The Catholics, despite their claim, upheld by an official enquiry, to vindicate Caecilian's consecration as untainted by *traditio*, had been identified by the Donatists as the Church of the *traditores*. It may well be, if the dossier of official documents compiled by Optatus and Augustine can be relied on, that the Donatists were the more vulnerable, as a matter of historical fact, to the charge they levelled against Caecilian's party. But the historical facts, though the subject of endless bickering, conceal the real issue in the conflict. This concerned not the origins of the two Churches, but what they actually were. With greater or lesser clarity both parties recognised what was at stake. The Donatists persisted in calling the Catholic Church the Church of the *traditores* with a cavalier indifference to the evidence adduced by the Catholics; after all, what could the possible purity of Caecilian's consecrators matter in face of his Church's manifest readiness to communicate with bishops consecrated by *traditores*, and its refusal to rebaptise? The Catholics, on their side, were quite clear that questions about the origins of the schism constituted an irrelevance. Their strategy at the great conference with the Donatists in 411, from the moment in the muddled proceedings at which Augustine took the lead on his side, was aimed at separating the two issues. Do the Donatists wish to accuse our predecessors of crimes? If so, we shall defend them with the aid of documents drawn from the public archives:[1]

[1] *Gesta coll. Carth.* III, 187; cf. *ibid.* 155, 197, and Augustine, *C. Cresc.* IV, 45.53.

we shall take up their cause as that of our brothers. If they be proved guilty to us, we shall anathematise them to-day—but we shall not on that account relinquish the Church...

If it be the Church we are to enquire into—its identity, its nature, its qualities—then we must have recourse to divine testimony.

Let them [the Donatists] choose: if they will cease accusing men of crimes, we shall cease appealing to documents, and divine authority alone shall speak: let the divine scriptures, to which we both bow, be brought into court.

What was at stake was the right way of conceiving the Church and of representing it in relation to the world.

The Donatists clung to the old image of a pure, unspotted Church, standing over against a godless world in a stance of permanent hostility. They thought of themselves—with some justification—as the Church which 'suffers but does not inflict persecution'.[1] The 'world' was always waging war on their Church. All their favourite images underlined the Church's separation from the world around it: it was the 'garden enclosed, a sealed fountain' (Cant. 4:12)—an image that had been particularly dear to Cyprian;[2] the Ark, that old image of the Church, was caulked with pitch both inside and out (Gen. 6:14) in order to prevent, as they preached, leaks either from or into it.[3] Their theology, like Cyprian's, and like Tertullian's before him, was dominated by the stark dichotomy of 'inside' (*intus*) and 'outside' (*foris*):[4] all light, purity and godliness within, darkness, sin and godlessness without. 'Darkness will not mix with light, gall with honey; life will not mix with death nor innocence with guilt...':[5] the simple contrasts and the antithetic rhetoric take us back into Tertullian's and Cyprian's universe. How could sacraments administered outside the Church possibly sanctify? How could sinners possibly bestow what they did not themselves possess?

[1] *Gesta Coll. Carth.* III, 258.
[2] Cf. *Ep.* 69.2; 74.11; Parmenian, *apud* Optatus, *De schism.* I, 10, II, 13; Cresconius, *apud* Augustine, *C. Cresc.* I, 34.40, IV, 63.77 etc.
[3] *Ep. ad Cath.* 5.9.
[4] Cf. for some references to typical passages Congar, *Traités*, 53.
[5] Petilian, *apud* Augustine, *C. litt. Pet.* II, 39.92.

The whole Donatist theology of the sacramental ministry is no more than the application of the old doctrine of the Church as the sole and exclusive abode of holiness. The Donatist conception of 'catholicity' was closely linked to this: 'catholic', as one of their bishops said at the conference of 411, 'means the fullness of the sacraments, unspotted wholeness'.[1] They rejected the 'Catholic' Church's claim to this reality, and its interpretation of the word.

'Catholicity', for the Catholics, consisted in agreement with the Churches of the world and communion with them. For Augustine, born in the Catholic stronghold of Thagaste, and baptised in Ambrose's Milan, Christianity could only be envisaged in its cosmopolitan character. In Italy he had encountered an expanding Church, assured of its mission, confident of conquering a world which had been promised to it by the prophecies of the Old Testament. From the first the true Church for Augustine was the *ecclesia toto orbe diffusa*,[2] and this it always remained for him. If the Italian Church considered itself to be the heir of the future, the Donatists in Africa certainly saw themselves as the sole heirs of the African past. Their narrow, exclusive and self-contained world was too small for Augustine, on his return from Milan and Rome. 'The clouds of heaven proclaim the house of God being built over the whole earth; and the frogs croak from their pond: "We only are Christians."'[3] The horizons of Augustine's whole experience as a Christian, as a writer and thinker, were too wide to allow him to identify himself with Cyprian's true heirs. His Church could be nothing other than the one Church spread over the earth. To the Donatists' plea at the confrontation of 411 that since the whole business concerned Africans alone no account be taken in the proceedings of views held abroad, he replied simply by recalling that for 'African Catholic Christians' this was just the kernel of the whole matter. What gave them their sense of self-identity in

---

[1] *Gesta Coll. Carth.* III, 102.

[2] The phrase appears as early as *De Gen. lib. impf.* I, 4, here in a formula with interesting Donatist affinities: [*Ecclesia*] *quae Catholica dicitur, ex eo quia universaliter perfecta est, et in nullo claudicat, et per totum orbem diffusa est.*   [3] *Enarr. in Ps.* 95.11.

Africa was precisely their communion with the *universus orbis Christianus*.[1] This unwavering conviction is what drove Augustine to devote so much of his energies for more than twenty years to upholding the claims to 'Catholicity' of the Church which was in communion with the Christian world. Of course, this meant upholding the claims of a Church which, in Africa, owed its existence to a 'transmarine' judgement and to official recognition by the Christian emperors. It meant, in Africa, upholding the terms of the ecclesiastical settlement of the Constantinian revolution, and upholding them in an age when the emperors were often less reserved about exploiting their alliance with the Church than Constantine had been. If Augustine did not flinch from these implications, it is nevertheless not the case that 'he appears as the theorist of the Constantinian revolution'.[2]

We have already seen[3] the gulf that divided Augustine's thinking about the Christian Roman Empire from that of the real prophets of the Constantinian (or Theodosian) settlement, such as Eusebius, Prudentius, or even Ambrose. Now, when we come to examine Augustine's doctrine of the Church, we shall be driven to recognise that despite his defending the results, in Africa, of this settlement, his conception of the Church in its relation to secular society and the public authority had more in common with the views of his Donatist opponents than with the theorists of the Constantinian revolution; that he was not prepared to throw to the winds the African theological tradition on which the Donatists took their stand; and that much of the old African sense of autonomy survived in Augustine's Catholicism. If he upheld the claims of a Constantinian importation, it was not with the aid of a theology well suited to the purpose. He shared too much of the intellectual capital behind his opponents. Augustine was always conscious of being an African in Africa; he would remind a fellow African of the

---

[1] *Gesta Coll. Carth.* III, 99–100.
[2] I quote the phrase from Brown, 'Religious dissent', 99. The interpretation it describes is a common feature of modern historians', e.g. Frend's and Brisson's, accounts. The most determined attempt to expound Augustine on these lines is Diesner, *Studien*.
[3] Ch. 3, above.

fact soon after his return to this much more provincial world from Italy,[1] and some twenty years later he would still, a little self-consciously, remind the cosmopolitan Count Marcellinus of his 'Africanity'.[2] Always receptive and responsive to his intellectual environment, it did not take Augustine long to absorb much of the African theological capital on which Catholic no less than Donatist theology drew. We have recently learnt to appreciate the force of these native traditions in Augustine's theology.[3] His ecclesiology was a 'Catholic' one; but it was at the same time peculiarly 'African' in inspiration.

Augustine not only appropriated some of the basic insights of the Cyprianic theology of the African Church; he also learnt to re-interpret them with the aid of concepts supplied to him by the work of the greatest of Donatist theologians, Tyconius.[4] Tyconius, whose attractive personality and elusive thought this is not the place to consider,[5] had been excommunicated by the Donatists for rejecting their conception of 'Catholicity' in favour of the Catholics' conception of it as 'universality';[6] he had rejected the Donatist idea of a 'pure' Church and recognised that in the Church the few saints rubbed shoulders with a majority of the un-righteous;[7] and rebaptism, as a consequence, went by the board. To Augustine's lasting incomprehension, he nevertheless did not become a Catholic. Of the reasons suggested for this[8] only one is of direct interest to this study: that to Tyconius the whole historical development since 313 represented 'a diabolical innovation, a

---

[1] *Ep.* 17.2, the source of the heading of this chapter.

[2] *Ep.* 138.4.19.

[3] Cf. especially Ratzinger, *Volk*; and, in another context, Bonner, 'Les origines africaines', has shown the surprising extent to which Augustine's theology seems to have been drawn from African sources of which he was the mouthpiece rather than the creator.

[4] A trivial but revealing example of Augustine's adoption of Tyconius's exegesis of a passage in place of Cyprian's, which he had previously followed: *Retr.* II, 18.

[5] On him cf. Monceaux, *Histoire*, vol. 5, 165–219; Hahn, *Tyconius-Studien*; Pincherle, 'L'ecclesiologia' and *idem*, 'Da Ticonio a Sant'Agostino'. For the reconstruction of the Commentary on the Apocalypse from Bede's Commentary, cf. Bonner, *Saint Bede*, esp. the Appendix. More briefly, cf. also *idem*, *Saint Augustine of Hippo*, 245 f.

[6] Augustine's reports to this effect are confirmed by *The Turin fragments*, §323, p. 139.

[7] *The Turin fragments*, §52, pp. 61–2.

[8] Cf. Hahn, *Tyconius-Studien*, 100; Monceaux, *Histoire*, vol. 5, 177; and J. Ratzinger, 'Beobachtungen'.

falling away from Christ, a becoming worldly of the Church'.[1] The Constantinian settlement, and the Church dependent upon it in Africa, were the work of Antichrist. Daniel's prophecy 'is being enacted in Africa'.[2] The most weighty reason for Tyconius's continuing rejection of the Catholic communion was perhaps the abhorrence with which he viewed its readiness to call in the state to persecute fellow Christians, and, more fundamentally, his underlying sense that it had betrayed the Church of the martyrs by its very being, identified with the Empire and kept in being by this alliance. We have already seen how much Augustine had in common with this evaluation of the Constantinian revolution.[3] It may be that the lonely voice of the dissident Donatist had struck a chord in his mind. Whatever the truth of the matter on this point, there was a fundamental insight behind Augustine's theology of the two cities which he had undoubtedly learnt from Tyconius.[4]

This was the realisation that the stark antithesis between iniquity and righteousness had a theological validity, but that it could not be expressed—contrary to the insistence of African theology from Cyprian to the Donatists—in sociological categories. Tyconius expressed this insight in various, sometimes not wholly felicitous ways. The Body of Christ had 'two parts', or the one Body, the Church, could be seen simultaneously as holy and as wicked.[5] This was the insight for which Augustine above all praised

[1] Ratzinger, *Volk*, 309, n. 1, referring to Hahn.

[2] *Reg.* vi (Burkitt, 67).

[3] Cf. above, Ch. 3, especially pp. 51-7. On Augustine's attitude to religious coercion, cf. Ch. 6, below.

[4] Ratzinger, 'Beobachtungen', criticises the commonly held view that the 'two cities' originate in Tyconius's work. On this it is necessary to remark that in this article Ratzinger confines himself to the *Liber regularum*—thereby excluding vital evidence. Ladner, *The idea of reform*, 262-3 and n. 101, argued convincingly that the 'two cities' were part of Tyconius's *Commentary on Revelation*; his arguments are much strengthened by the occurrence of *duo populi* in *The Turin fragments*, §172, pp. 96-7, and by the reconstruction of the text from Bede's commentary by Bonner, *Saint Bede*, 27, who quotes a passage from it (*PL* 93.185A) which contains the 'two cities'. Despite Ratzinger's argument in this paper, he does assert the conclusion in his book, *Volk*, 321, that Tyconius and Augustine showed the impossibility of the earlier African attempt to identify the *göttliche Rechtgestalt* directly and without qualification with the *sichtbare Rechtgestalt* of the Church. This is the conclusion I state below in terms of 'eschatological' and 'historical' (or 'sociological') categories.

[5] *Reg.* ii (Burkitt, 8 f.).

Tyconius: that whatever the sense in which the Church is 'holy', this must admit the possibility—the need—for tolerating sinners within it until the end;[1] that the Church's holiness is not invalidated by the presence of sinners in her.[2] In practice, the Catholic Church had, of course, long acted on this principle; and even the Donatists —quite apart from being compromised by their defection from 'purity' in their policy over the Maximianist schism[3]—were also ready to admit the presence of sinners in their Church. What they stressed was the purity of their ministry, and above all its freedom from the taint of *traditio*. But Tyconius was the first to have elaborated a theology of the Church's holiness as eschatological. The two 'sides', 'parts', 'peoples' or 'cities' were bound to co-exist within the one Body until their separation at the final judgement.[4]

This was the foundation on which Augustine built his theology of the 'two cities'. We have already considered his *civitas terrena* in its relation to politically organised society, and to the Roman state in particular.[5] More briefly, we must now examine his views on the *civitas Dei* in relation to the Church. What was said above[6] about the logic which allowed Augustine both to assert and to deny the identification of the *civitas terrena* with the (Roman) state, is also true in this case. There is a whole series of terms such as 'Church' (*ecclesia*), 'Kingdom of God' (*regnum Dei*), 'Body of Christ' (*corpus Christi*) and 'City of God' (*civitas Dei*) which Augustine uses at one moment as synonymous, at another as distinct though overlapping in meaning. As in the case of the 'earthly city', we must recognise that the 'heavenly city', too, both is and is not identifiable with a particular society. The society here in question is, of course, the Church; and its identity with the

---

[1] *C. ep. Parm.* III, 3.17; *Ep.* 249. [2] *C. ep. Parm.* I, 1.

[3] Cf. De Veer, 'L'exploitation du schisme Maximianiste', who shows that the Donatists could have defended their conduct on their own principles; cf. Brisson, *Autonomisme*, 229.

[4] It will be clear that I am using the term 'eschatological' in a sense different from, e.g., that of Kamlah's, *Christentum*, 136 f., who asserts that the whole tradition of the ancient Church insisted on the 'eschatological' character of the Church's holiness. Cf. below, pp. 178 f.   [5] Cf. Ch. 3.   [6] Above, pp. 59 f.

City of God, the heavenly Jerusalem, had been taken for granted by Augustine all along. In this the development of Augustine's thought on the 'heavenly city' is not quite parallel to the development of his thought on the 'earthly city'; and consequently, the logic of the two concepts is slightly different. The Roman Empire was drawn into the scheme of the 'two cities' relatively late, when the theme of the 'two cities' or the 'two kinds of men' already had a long history in Augustine's thought. Augustine had divided men into two classes according to their inner dispositions or their final destinies long before he faced the question: where does Rome belong in the scheme? Underlying the language and imagery of the 'new people of God',[1] however, one can discern the clear identification of it in Augustine's mind with the Church from the very start. In a definite though unanalysed manner the identity of the Church and the 'heavenly city' was something with which Augustine began as given. Whereas with Rome the question was: given the dichotomy of the 'two cities', where does Rome fit into the scheme?, with the Church the question was rather: given the identity of the Church and the 'heavenly city', where is the 'earthly city' to be found within the Church?

The question had to take this form, because Augustine knew, from Tyconius, that in any given society on earth both 'cities' must have their members. With Tertullian, Cyprian and the Donatists, Augustine had always thought of the Church as God's holy people; with Cyprian he identified this holy people with the community gathered around their bishop in sacramental communion; with Tyconius he made room in his theology of the Church for sinners within it. It was with the aid of Tyconius that Augustine reinterpreted the tradition within which he took his stand. The Church was primarily the society of the redeemed, the holy, the pious gathered in worship and sacrifice. This was its fundamental reality, unimpaired by the hidden workings within it of an 'underground movement'.[2] The Church could therefore be

---

[1] *De vera rel.* 27.50.
[2] Cf. Wachtel, *Beiträge*, 123 for some excellent remarks on this.

said to be the City of God in a way in which a state could not be identified, *tout court*, with the earthly city. Idolatry or the lust for power might disfigure a state such as the Roman, and thus identify it with the earthly city; but in a sense this identity is accidental. Rome, or some other state, may in fact be idolatrous, but it is not defined as a state by its idolatry or its lust for power; whereas it is just such a permanent and essential link which identifies the Church with the City of God. A state, simply as such, without some disfiguring idolatry, for example, being written into its constitution, is neutrally 'open' to both cities. In its essence as a form of politically organised society of men, a state can be assimilated to one or other city only in virtue of its citizens' allegiances;[1] and these, one must assume, are generally an unpredictable mixture. This is equally true, in Tyconius's as in Augustine's conceptions, of the Church's members on earth. Nevertheless, the Church is not neutrally 'open' to both cities in the way the state is. It is identical with the City of God in a way in which no other human grouping can be with either city. For only here is salvation to be had, only here are the fruits of Christ's saving work available for the redemption of men into the heavenly kingdom.[2] This fact constituted a link between the sacramental community and the heavenly City which entered into the very definition of 'Church'. The Church is the historically visible form of the City of God. Its very substance lies in its continuity with God's eschatological community, into which it is always growing. Looked at causally, the Church is simultaneously the medium in which and through the instrumentality of which this growth takes place, and its final, heavenly outcome. Looked at from the point of view of God's predestining choice—a point of view which increasingly dominated Augustine's thought —the Church showed forth the continuity between an inevitably mixed visible human group and the purified group of the finally

---

[1] Cf. above, pp. 56-9.

[2] On the problem of where the frontiers of salvation lie in relation to the frontiers of the visible Church and to the scope of valid sacraments, cf. the debate between Greenslade, *Schism in the early Church*, xiv f. and 168 f., and Butler, *The idea of the Church*, 87–138. Wiles, *The making of Christian doctrine*, 146–52 has some brief but illuminating remarks.

chosen. How much this radical identity of the Church with its final, purged reality meant to Augustine may be seen in a comment he made on Tyconius's terminology about the Church being Christ's 'bi-partite' body, embracing wicked and holy alike: he would rather avoid this language, he said, and speak instead of Christ's 'true body' and his 'diluted (*permixto*) body', or 'something of this kind'; for 'that which will not be with the Lord in eternity should not really be called his body'.[1] There is almost a more vivid sense than in Tyconius of the strength of the old African and Donatist exclusiveness in this wish of Augustine's to restrict one of his favourite designations for the Church—'the Body of Christ'—to the eschatologically purified community.[2]

Augustine was too much of an African to forget what 'Church' had above all meant to his countrymen for centuries. But he was also a Catholic bishop; and Tyconius had furnished him with the means of reconciling the old African theology with the new Catholic fact. For it was Tyconius who had taught Augustine to transpose concepts which earlier African theology had understood in empirical, sociological or historical terms, into an eschatological key. This did not mean, for either of the two theologians, that the two 'cities' had no existence here and now, in history, but would only come into being at the final judgement. It meant rather that they owed their existence here and now to the presence in history of what would be revealed in its clear, separate identity only at the end. The Church is subject to the permanent tension between what is here and now and the eschatological reality to be disclosed in and through it. This eschatological tension is what underlay the ambivalence of Augustine's concept of the Church. Primarily, the Church *is* what it will be; but thanks to the Tyconian 'eschatologisation' of the concept, it is also, in the interim, what it will not be at the end. Though identical with the City of God, there is room in it, for the time being, for the earthly city, too. Thus for Augustine the Church is always caught up in the tension and duality between *qualis nunc est* and *qualis tunc erit*.[3] Failure to reckon

De doctr. chr. III, 32.45.   [2] Cf. Ratzinger, *Volk*, 148–9.   [3] E.g. *De civ. Dei*, XX, 9.1.

with this complexity in Augustine's conception has led to much dispute about whether the Church could or could not be identified with the City of God.[1] The Donatists who criticised Augustine in 411—and some modern critics who have followed their hints— were quick to put their fingers on what seemed to them the weak point of Augustine's concept of the Church, but what was in fact the crucial novelty of the Tyconian conception he had adopted. They charged him, as the spokesman of the Catholics, with speaking of 'two Churches, one which now has the wicked mixed in its ranks, and another which after the resurrection will not have them'.[2] Their objection would certainly have force within the context of a theology in which the 'Church' of the angels and saints in glory, and the 'Church' of sinners battling here on earth in the weakness of the changing body are sharply separated. We need here only recognise that for Augustine this separation was impossible. How far his theology of the Church's unity, achieved through 'charity' and through 'sacramental communion', was successful in solving this problem, this is not the place to examine.[3] The simple fact remains that in his vocabulary the Church was the City of God, even though it certainly numbered citizens of the earthly city among its members 'while on its earthly pilgrimage among the wicked, living by faith'.[4]

Not for nothing had Tyconius been excommunicated by the

---

[1] Congar, 'Civitas Dei et ecclesia' gives a brief résumé of these controversies. Thanks to Cranz, 'De Civitate Dei, XV, 2' this debate may now be said to be of no more than historical interest.

[2] Brev. Coll. Don. III, 10.19. It may be remarked that Augustine's answer as here summarised by himself could have done little to convince his opponents that their charge was misdirected: 'as if the saints who are to reign with Christ were not the same people as those who now, living justly, put up with the wicked for His name's sake'—ibid. The question was not whether these people were the same or not, but whether the Church which contained only them could be said to be the same Church as one which contained them along with sinners. This question could not be answered in terms of membership, for this was precisely the question at stake. Some other criterion of what constitutes a 'church', such as for instance 'sacramental communion', would need to be employed. According to his own summary of the debate, this was not done on this occasion.

[3] Cf. p. 119 n. 2, above. Augustine's later views on predestination are also part of his attempt to solve this problem raised by his ecclesiology.

[4] De civ. Dei, Praef.

Donatists. The most powerful theological onslaught Augustine could mount on their position in the great confrontation of 411 was no more than an application of the lessons he had learnt from Tyconius. A Donatist spokesman had given an eloquent exposition of the theology of the unspotted Church. He had invoked the parable of the wheat and the tares (Matt. 13:24–30): in the world the good and the wicked must be tolerated to co-exist, he said, until the harvest; but the Church is not like this.[1] Against the simple commonplaces of this old African ecclesiology Augustine deployed the theology of the Church as a *corpus permixtum*, its holiness and purity as eschatological.[2] The Donatists were quick to see the implications, and came back with the telling answer that Augustine had changed the Church into the image of what Jesus had said of the world: for had not the Lord himself, elucidating this parable, explained to his disciples that the field containing the tares and the wheat was the world?[3]

We are in the presence, in this interchange, of the most fundamental cleavage between Donatist and Augustinian theology. What was at stake was the relation between 'Church' and 'world'. For the Donatists, these were mutually exclusive alternatives. In their view, for a Christian, the only thing to do with the world—if it could not be baptised or rebaptised—was to withdraw from it into a society uncontaminated by it. Sacred and secular were two separate spheres, each contained within its own sociological milieu: the Church of the pure face to face with a hostile, persecuting world, with secular society and the Roman government, and with an apostate Church which had come to terms with them. The 'secular' was irretrievably 'profane'. Augustine's theology rejected the dichotomy of sacred and profane displayed in this image. Sacred and profane, for him, interpenetrate in the *saeculum*; the 'secular' is neutral, ambivalent, but no more profane than it is sacred.[4] His image of the Church is that of a 'secular' institution:

---

[1] *Gesta Coll. Carth.* III, 258.   [2] *Ibid.* 261, 265, 273.   [3] *Ibid.* 274, citing Matt. 13:38.
[4] For the sense in which 'sacred' and 'secular' can be distinguished in history, see Ch. 1. On Church history as not forming part of 'sacred history', but as 'secular', see above, Ch. 2, pp. 32 f. and below, Ch. 7, pp. 179 f.

the language in which it is described is that which the Bible applies to the 'world'.[1] 'World' and 'Church' are co-extensive: there is a real distinction to be drawn between them, but it is eschatological rather than sociological or historical. They are separable only in the final judgement, and their distinct—but not separate—being here and now in the *saeculum* consists of the relation they bear to that judgement. So in the last resort the Church *is* the world, the world reconciled in Christ.[2]

The opposition, on which all Donatist theology hinged, between 'within' and 'without', is transposed into the opposition between what 'is now' and what 'shall be'. With the *bouleversement* of the old sociological categories, all the points of conflict between the Church and the world are also transposed into an eschatological key. The line between sinner and saint or the persecutor and his victim can no longer be drawn at the frontiers of the visible Church. These concepts and their oppositions have no validity on the plane of empirically observable, historical reality; they have validity only in eschatological terms. *Persequitur mundus damnatus: persecutionem patitur mundus reconciliatus.*[3] In the end there is no test for discerning the *locus* of the persecutor and the persecuted; no group has a monopoly of either. The discrimination cuts into the very substance of the Church, as it cuts into the world; indeed, it cuts into the inner being of a man himself. The enemy is rarely external. The key categories of 'inside' and 'outside' are deprived of meaning: 'Within, that which is of the Devil is to be repudiated; and outside, that which is of Christ is to be acknowledged.'[4] The conflict with the powers of darkness cannot be confined within

---

[1] Cf. above, p. 122, n. 3. This is a commonplace in Augustine's sermons—cf. e.g. *Sermo* 5.8; 47.5.6 and *ibid.* 10.17–18; 88.19.21; *Enarr. in Ps.* 42.2.

[2] *Sermo* 96.8, quoted at the beginning of this chapter, p. 105. Augustine was well aware that this conception of the Church grew out of his rejection of the Donatist conception. It can be seen emerging from the actual debate at the point where Augustine observes that *mundus* and *ecclesia* can be interchangeable terms in the Gospel, for instance when the Lord himself said that he had come 'not to judge the world but to save it' (John 12:47): for as we all know (he was speaking among Africans) the Lord will save only the Church: so here 'the world' must mean the same as 'the Church'—*Gesta Coll. Carth.* III, 265.

[3] *Sermo* 96.8. Cf. *C. Gaudent.* I, 21.24.   [4] *De bapt.* IV, 9.13.

labelled frontiers. It is epidemic even to the extent of penetrating into the recesses of man's inner world. A man cannot be sure even of himself, Augustine once wrote; how much less of another! 'Therefore do not pronounce judgement before the time, before the Lord comes, who will bring to light the things now hidden in darkness and will disclose the purposes of the heart' (1 Cor. 4:5).[1] Before God, man, as Augustine had experienced, is always a 'question to himself'.[2] Augustine had come to terms with the impossibility of penetrating into the darkness of his own self in the tenth book of his *Confessions*. His acceptance of himself as ultimately problematic gives us a glimpse into the deepest springs of his impatience with Donatism. A man must learn to accept the darkness within himself and pray to be able to live as a question in God's sight: how much more must a Church do likewise!

Augustine's 'answer' to Donatism was on a level different from that of previous theological debate. This change of level is the result, in large part, of the new perspectives opened in Augustine's thought by his reading of Tyconius in the 390s. Historians of this debate have sometimes overlooked this change of level; they have been content, on occasion, to represent Augustine simply as a theorist of the Constantinian (or Theodosian) establishment, *vis-à-vis* an African Church with deep roots in indigenous culture and a mind formed by a long native theological tradition. We have now seen how firmly Augustine stood within this native tradition, reinterpreted with the aid of another African theologian. We have already followed Augustine on his pilgrimage which led him ever further from the publicists of the Constantinian settlement, and from the mirage about the Theodosian establishment current among his contemporaries.[3] The conflict with Donatism often failed to bring the best out of Augustine; but it did not, at any rate, change the course of his intellectual development on this question.[4] His views on the Church pointed to implications in regard to secular society which are very close to the views we saw him

[1] *Ep.* 130.2.4.   [2] *Conf.* x, 33.50.   [3] Chs. 2 and 3.
[4] But on his attitude in practice, see Ch. 6.

adopting on the role of the Roman Empire in relation to God's providence.

His theology of the Church set out to undermine the Donatist claim to be the true Church, and as such, the object of persecution by the secular power and its ecclesiastical creature, the Catholic Church. Augustine's alternative to Donatism depended on the challenge it contained to the simple sociological categories in which the Donatist claim was formulated. The valid application of the categories by which the Church was distinguished from the world was no simple matter of labelling empirically circumscribable human groups. It was fraught with much greater ambiguity. Thus the old talk of a hostile world persecuting the true (i.e. Donatist) Church was not untrue: its very vocabulary was exploded, or made sense only after a systematic translation of all its terms. The true Church was both holy and worldly; in some sense it had also always to suffer persecution from the world. In no way, at any rate, could it be identified with any worldly institution, and conversely, no worldly institutions could ever validly claim to be 'Christian' or 'sacred'. In Augustine's eschatological perspective the distance between the only true Christian society and any historical society, past, present or future, was infinite. His recasting of the vocabulary of ecclesiology implied that in so far as one could speak of any society possessing any quality of sacredness, one could do so only in virtue of its eschatological orientation. The eschatological orientation required was identity with the City of God; and this was the sole prerogative of the Church. There could be no other 'Christian society'. In the final analysis, there are only the two 'cities'; there is no hierarchy of related societies. Augustine sharply rejected the notion that any society might be modelled on the heavenly city, or reflect it as an image reflects its archetype.[1] The application of the ultimate categories in terms of which societies can be distinguished as 'sacred' and 'profane', or as 'Christian' and 'diabolical', produces

[1] Cf. Cranz, 'De Civitate Dei, XV, 2', whose brief article finally clinches a conclusion on this matter.

only the stark duality of the two 'cities' in their eschatological separateness and their temporal inextricability. To speak about human societies on earth or historical states less ultimate, narrower and more provisional categories of discernment are needed. The application of these will never produce a 'Christian state'. For Augustine, at least in his mature thought, such a phrase would have seemed like a category mistake, linking a non-eschatological, historical concept with a quality which can only be given eschatological meaning. Talk about a 'Christian state' would have involved the precipitous anticipation of a judgement no man can make, and one which could, in any case, not bear upon states. The bottom has fallen out of any theology of a sacral society, and with it, of the Constantinian establishment.[1]

Notwithstanding Constantine or even Theodosius, then, the Empire has remained 'secular' in Augustine's estimation. One large side of the ancient tradition of Christianity, a side which had been kept alive in Africa for a century since the conversion of the first Roman emperor to Christianity, has been salvaged by Augustine and incorporated into the foundations of his theology. More, undoubtedly, was lost in respect of the other perennial distinction of the African Church: its spirit of autonomy and independence in relation to the 'overseas Churches', especially in relation to the Roman See. Rome and the 'overseas Churches' had presided over the birth of the Catholic Church in Africa in 314. Inevitably, during its struggle with its rival, this Church came to lean on its progenitors. It may be that the 'eclipse of Carthage behind Rome'[2] owed something to the struggle; but the extent of this eclipse has

---

[1] Cf. above, Ch. 3, and the reference to modern studies, p. 47, n. 4. It is noteworthy that a distinguished student of Augustine's ecclesiology in its 'African' context could conclude his enquiry with the observation that 'in contrast to Optatus's acceptance of the idea of a state-Church [staatskirchlicher Ansatz], Augustine in effect provides a foundation for the position of the Church of the catacombs in his sketch for the relation of Church and state. The Church no longer appears as the active element in the relation, the idea of "christianising" the state or the world just forms no part of Augustine's programme...Of a subordination of the state to the Church in Augustine there can be no question...', Ratzinger, Volk, 316. Of the view that Augustine did advocate a Christian state, the most distinguished surviving representative is M. J. Wilks. See his 'Roman Empire'.

[2] Monceaux, Histoire, IV, 192; cf. Frend, The Donatist Church, 324.

been seriously overestimated. Africa certainly never sold out to Rome. Too much of the old African autonomy survived—not only in Augustine's theology, but also in the conduct of the Church of Augustine, Aurelius, and their friends, and indeed, of their successors.

The story of the African Church's relations with Rome during Augustine's tenure of the See of Hippo is well known. The moments of tension and the occasions of crisis, arising from a variety of matters, including questions concerning the treatment of Donatists, from the Pelagian affair and then the appeal of an obscure African cleric, Apiarius, to Rome, have often been described, and cannot be retold here.[1] Throughout, the African Church's conduct was impeccably correct by its own standards. Its practice, codified into an African canon law during these very years,[2] may look 'anomalous',[3] but only to the extent that one considers the Donatists as the exclusive heirs of Tertullian and Cyprian. If one recognises that Augustine, and the Church of which he had been an acknowledged leader since 393, also have a claim to a share in this heritage, then their conduct and the principles behind it will appear rather as part of an enduring pattern. Here again we find that combination of deference towards the *cathedra Petri*, the desire to ascertain the views of its bishop, to enlist the support of his judgement, with the polite but firm adherence to the decisions of ecumenical councils and their own African councils, whatever the Roman bishop's views might be. The history of the great series of African Councils inaugurated by the Council of Hippo in 393 does not bear out the suggestion that Carthage—or Hippo—had sold out to Rome.

It was Augustine who had spurred the new bishop of Carthage, Aurelius, into action. A letter[4] Augustine wrote to his own bishop soon after his return to Africa, calling for conciliar action to stamp

---

[1] See most of the better Church histories. Among Roman Catholics good accounts of this crucial period are to be found in Duchesne, *The early history of the Church*, 140–80; Batiffol, *Le catholicisme*, 402–10, 438–72. Cf. also Hofmann, *Kirchenbegriff*, 425 f.

[2] Cross, 'History and fiction', is indispensable.

[3] Cf. Brisson, *Autonomisme*, 230–9.   [4] *Ep.* 22.

out the evils afflicting the African Church, was followed, within a
year, by the council which met, significantly, at Hippo in 393.
Augustine, still a mere presbyter, was commissioned to preach
before the bishops. From this moment he would be one of the
leading figures in the African Church for more than a quarter of a
century. There is no evidence for dissociating Augustine from the
African episcopate's will to independence, shown in each of the
situations of tension and crisis in these years. In 426 they rebuked the
Pope sharply for his high-handed action in the case of Apiarius,
and asked him not to bring into the Church conduct conducive
to the 'murk of worldly pride'.[1] Augustine's name is not among the
signatories of this famous letter, but he had undoubtedly supported
the African Church's policy throughout the preceding years.
Apart from what we may infer from the policies of the African
councils during the period of Augustine's influence, there are only
stray hints in his writings to provide clues to his attitude to the
papacy. This was not a matter on which he felt it necessary to
spell out his position. He was content to follow both the traditional
practice and the old ideas of the African Church.

On occasion events prompted Augustine to express his mind on
the status of the Roman See. This happened, for instance, in 416,
at the height of the campaign against Pelagianism, when two
councils had met in Africa to condemn Pelagius and wished to
rouse the Pope to follow their lead (for, they had heard, Pelagianism enjoyed the favour of some circles in Rome). On this occasion,
several letters were sent to Rome, including one from Augustine
writing, together with Aurelius and some of his closest friends
among the bishops, privately to Innocent. There was no question,
now, of any conflicting claims to jurisdiction, and they wrote
with great deference to the Pope, whom they wanted only to spur
to action. The image of the Church that came to their minds was
that of an irrigation system. The bishop of Rome, with his
abundant water supply, will not need the contribution of their little
trickle, as they modestly described their lengthy document. They

---

[1] *fumosus typhus saeculi*; *Cod. eccl. Afr.*, 138, in Bruns, *Canones*, 202.

wished merely to be reassured that their little trickle came from the same source as the Pope's more abundant stream.[1] The image came from Cyprian.[2] For Cyprian, as for Augustine and his co-signatories, the source of the fertilising waters was not, of course, the Roman Church, but the one Lord, the one faith and the one apostolic Church from which both the Roman and the African drew their water supply. It was not, however, in terms of this old African image that the papacy saw itself. In his reply Innocent neatly altered the application of the metaphor: the Africans were commended for referring their case to the Roman See, so that 'just as all the streams which come forth from their common source flow through all the various parts of the world, keeping the purity of their source, so all the other churches may draw from the authority of this source the knowledge of what to teach, whom to absolve...'.[3] With a sleight of hand the Pope transformed both the juridical relationship between the African and the Roman churches, and the theological understanding on which that relationship rested.

The image of the Roman See as itself the 'source of waters', compared with the old African image, was born of a new conception of the papal office, elaborated in Rome only in the course of the later fourth century. Augustine's thought, where we can trace it, remained entirely within the older mould. Thus the favourite proof-text on which the Popes were building their claims, 'You are Peter and upon this rock (*super hanc petram*) I will build my church' (Matt. 16:18), was silent, for Augustine, on the Roman claims to primacy. He had changed his mind, he informs us, about the interpretation of this verse. Originally, he took it as referring to Peter, though to him as 'representing the whole Church';[4] but, as if even this interpretation might seem to place a

---

[1] *Ep.* 177.19. Cf. the penetrating treatment of this in Caspar, *Geschichte des Papsttums*, I, 330–7, with nn. 605–7.

[2] *De eccl. unit.* 5.

[3] *Ep.* 181.1; cf. *Ep.* 182.2. Caspar, *Geschichte*, 333, also points out that the papal answer transformed the African action into an appeal to the Apostolic See, for which the legal forms had only recently been created. Cf. also Hofmann, *Kirchenbegriff*, 439 f.

[4] *totius ecclesiae figuram gerenti...Ep.* 53.2.

man at the foundation of the Church, he came to prefer another. So later, he tells us, 'most often' he interpreted the verse in a sense such as to mean that the Church was founded on Him whom Peter had confessed as the Messiah: 'thus Peter, so named by that rock (*petra*), would represent the person of the Church which is built upon the rock...; he was not called *petra*, but Peter: the *petra* was Christ...'[1] Augustine left it to his readers to opt for whichever exegesis they preferred; but, either way, it made no difference to his ecclesiology. 'In himself, Peter was a man by nature, a Christian by grace, the first of the apostles by a more abundant grace. But when he is told "To thee I will give the keys...", he stands for (*significabat*) the whole Church...whose person he represents by his symbolic universality.'[2] The whole unity of the Church, not one man, is the recipient of the power of the keys; Peter is the symbol of that unity and catholicity.[3] Christ alone is the head of the Church, his body, and he holds the primacy.[4] On the one occasion when Augustine speaks about Rome as the source of true teaching, this has nothing to do with Petrine primacy: Paul's teaching on grace is contained for the most part in his letter to the Romans, 'so that the preaching of this doctrine might be spread over the whole world as from the head of the world'.[5] We are in the Vergilian world of Rome as the *caput orbis*, not the papal world of Rome as the *caput ecclesiae*.

What is more significant about these passing remarks than what they state is what they pass over in silence. For although Augustine never worked out, consciously and deliberately, a conciliar theology[6] to pit against the monarchical theology launched in Rome and fast gaining ground, his remarks show that he belongs firmly within an older ecclesiological tradition, that of Cyprian and of the whole African episcopate down to his own time. This

[1] *Retr.* I, 21.1.
[2] *cuius ecclesiae Petrus apostolus, propter apostolatus sui primatum, gerebat figurata generalitate personam.—In Joh. Ev. Tr.* 124.5.　　　[3] *Sermo,* 295.2.
[4] *Sermo* 157.3, quoting Col. 1:18.
[5] *velut a capite orbis toto orbe diffunderet. Ep.* 194.7.
[6] Approaches to this may, however, be seen in *De bapt.* II, 9.14; IV, 6.8; *C. ep. Parm.* II, 13.30; *Ep.* 43.7.19.

was just the tradition from which the bishops of Rome had been anxious to extricate themselves since the 360s. Both in jurisdiction, and in terms of the ecclesiology required to furnish a basis for the jurisdictional claims, they were seeking to transform the Roman See into the 'head' of the Church in a sense entirely foreign to Cyprian, to the African—and indeed to the Greek—Church, and to Augustine. The papal programme was embodied in a clear and simple plan: it was to be, in Erich Caspar's image, a pyramid with its sides converging on Rome as its apex. With this building of the papal plan, Caspar contrasted the 'solid building' of Augustine's conception: 'built on a more complicated and more problematic groundplan, and further, more difficult to survey on account of the infinitely greater spiritual riches and the greater depth of the ideas in which the structure was embodied'.[1]

The foundations of Augustine's building lay deep in African soil. The building survived until the very end of Christianity in Africa, resting on the strength of the tradition which had nourished Augustine, and which his work, in turn, enriched. In Western Europe the papal programme was making triumphant headway. In Africa, neither a century of Vandal occupation nor another century of Byzantine rule could wipe out the accumulated legacy of its native Christianity. In the middle of the sixth century, the African Church drew on its inspiration once more to sustain the vitality of its protest against Justinian's attempt to meddle with Chalcedonian orthodoxy, condoned by a weak and bullied Pope. The most distinguished spokesman of the African opposition, Facundus, bishop of Hermiane, thundered against the emperor and his 'manufactured Churches', 'upheld by imperial edicts', in accents reminiscent of Tertullian and Donatus. Facundus drew on an ancient Christian tradition in denouncing a Church based on force and secular power as one which could only be an imitation, contrived by human artifice, of the true Church. Augustine had been led to denounce this same charge of its being a *figmentum*,

---

[1] I owe much to Caspar's marvellous comparison between Augustine and Innocent I, *Geschichte*, 337–43. The quotation is from p. 343. Since this was written, important further clarifications have been made by Klinkenberg, 'Unus Petrus'.

levelled against the Catholic Church, as Donatist blasphemy.[1] In Augustine's day the Donatists were the upholders of this ancient conviction; but more deeply, in his whole theological orientation, Augustine shared much with them and with the tradition in which they stood. Facundus knew this, and could invoke—not Donatus, or Petilian—but Augustine, 'that adamantine man', as he once referred to him, in support of his opposition to the emperor's 'manufactured Churches'. For his pains Facundus earned deposition and exile from the government and the reputation of being a Donatist among the clergy more compliant with the imperial will.[2]

At the very end of the sixth century Pope Gregory the Great, finding himself unable to exercise the authority of Rome in Africa —especially in Numidia—would once again interpret the fierce independence of these churches as a revival of Donatism.[3] For a final moment, almost on the eve of the extinction of imperial rule in Africa, the strength of the tradition of 'dissent' in African Christianity was turned against a monothelite emperor and all his works. But before the end of the seventh century Africa was in Arab hands. Rome had now lost the most tenacious challenge, at any rate in the West, to its intentions. Carthage had been the one great Christian centre in the Latin world that could look Rome in the face. By its submergence, Rome gained undisputed status in the West, but the Western Church lost more than Africa. It lost the last survival of an older structure of ecclesiastical authority, and lost, with it, the vital contribution of a cast of mind, a theology, a conception of the Church and of its place in the world, which it had discarded in 313. Augustine certainly belongs to the long tradition—as Facundus knew—which had served faithfully to keep that memory alive and effective.

[1] C. Gaudent. I, 33.42.
[2] The substance of the previous paragraph is discussed more fully in Markus, 'Reflections'.
[3] For a fuller discussion of this, see Markus, 'Donatism'.

CHAPTER 6

COGE INTRARE: THE CHURCH AND POLITICAL POWER

To reconstruct the mind of a writer from his works is an activity in some ways very like formulating a hypothesis, working out its implications, and testing it by continual reference back to the texts. So far this procedure in the first five chapters of this study has yielded a remarkably consistent reconstruction of Augustine's reflection on history, society and the Church. The strands of his thought on these related subjects, always closely interwoven, produced a single, coherent body as it matured. At the risk of representing Augustine as a precursor of modern 'secularist' theology, it is not out of place to describe his mature thought in this sphere as a synthesis of three themes: first, the secularisation of history, in the sense that all history outside the scriptural canon was seen as homogeneous and, in terms of ultimate significance, ambivalent (Chapters 1 and 2); second, the secularisation of the Roman Empire (Chapters 2 and 3) and of the state and social institutions in general, in the sense that they had no immediate relation to ultimate purposes (Chapters 3 and 4); third, the secularisation of the Church in the sense that its social existence was conceived in sharp antithesis to an 'otherworldly' Church such as was envisaged by a theology of the Donatist type (Chapter 5). These three strands together constitute what we may call a theology of the *saeculum*. The *saeculum* for Augustine was the sphere of temporal realities in which the two 'cities' share an interest. In Augustine's language, the *saeculum* is the whole stretch of time in which the two cities are 'inextricably intertwined'; it is the sphere of human living, history, society and its institutions, characterised by the fact that in it the ultimate eschatological oppositions, though present, are not discernible:

...the enchainment of past and future
Woven in the weakness of the changing body,
Protects mankind from heaven and damnation.

(T. S. ELIOT, *Burnt Norton*)

The coherence of this picture is disturbed, and the truth of the hypothesis threatened, by an aspect of Augustine's mind not so far considered: his readiness to endorse religious coercion by the authorities of the state. His statements on the duties of Christian rulers to enforce orthodoxy, above all his notorious defence of religious coercion with the aid of the Gospel text 'Compel them to come in' (Luke 14:23) have earned Augustine the reputation of being the first theorist of the Inquisition. Certainly, he deployed a massive argument for using the repressive machinery of the state in support of Christian orthodoxy against the Donatists' insistence on religious freedom and their denunciation of state interference in matters of religion.

These facts cannot be denied. Do they invalidate the interpretation of his theology of the *saeculum* which has disclosed a very different direction in his thought? It could be that at this point Augustine's mind appears like one of those drawings which can be read in two alternative ways, according to the way one looks at them. If so, it has at least been worth attempting to look at Augustine's theology from a point of view not often adopted, to see what sort of sense it makes considered as a critique of the 'establishment' of the Church in the Roman Empire. If we should now find that one side of his mind just makes no sense if looked at from this point of view, we should have to be content with leaving the matter there, and to concede either that Augustine faced in two irreconcilable directions or that the hypothesis in which we have interpreted him is unfounded. In the case of a man with Augustine's acute self-knowledge and reflectiveness the first option is not open. He was not the man to act on impulse, under pressure, or in defence of self-interest in flagrant denial of his principles and to disguise such action from himself. But it is too soon to abandon our hypothesis. With a highly differentiated personality like Augustine's, with his complex and subtle mind, it would be a counsel of despair to begin with the assumption that his thoughts and attitudes should have a simple, monolithic consistency about them. We must at least explore the possibility that Augustine's attitude to religious coercion is related in some way to the fundamentals of his theology, including among these the fundamentals of his theology of the *saeculum* as we have interpreted them, even if the relation is far from simple. In this chapter, then, I shall enquire whether and how far Augustine's views on religious coercion cohere with the theological reflection whose growth we have traced in the preceding chapters. The details of his views and arguments have been much studied.[1] They are of interest to us here only in so far as they affect the answer to the question: can they be reconciled with the other facets of his thought?

Augustine took the lead in the African Catholics' struggle against Donatism very early in his career. As a priest, he composed a work in the form of an extended jingle to state the case against Donatism in a popular form. He was already a leading figure in the African Church when he composed this, in 393, the year in which the first of the great series of African Councils was inaugurated with the Council held, significantly, in Hippo.[2] Two years later, he succeeded to the See of Hippo, and attended most of the Councils of Carthage held during his long episcopate. He became a close friend of Aurelius, the bishop of Carthage, and remained the centre of an intimate group of disciples several of whom had become bishops in neighbouring Sees. It will be as well to consider Augustine's attitude in relation to what the African episcopate thought about religious coercion.

The Catholic bishops were by no means averse to the use of repressive measures against pagans. Indeed, in 401, they asked for

[1] The most illuminating study, to which I owe much, is Brown, 'Saint Augustine's attitude'; cf. also Joly, 'Saint Augustin et l'intolérance', and Zepf, 'Zur Chronologie'. Among works covering a wider ground there are useful accounts in Frend, *The Donatist Church*, 227 f.; Willis, *Saint Augustine*, 36 f. The facts are exhaustively re-told in Grasmück, *Coercitio*. For the actual working of coercion in practice, Brown, 'Religious coercion' and Tengström, *Donatisten und Katholiken*.

[2] Cf. Ch. 5, above, p. 128.

their intensification. Encouraged, apparently, by the success of the previous two years, which had witnessed a feverish burst of repressive activity by the authorities in Africa, the bishops asked the government for further legislation to extirpate 'the last remnants of idolatry'.[1] Augustine must have been in full agreement with his colleagues at this time. Whether he actually advocated such policies at the two councils of 401 or not, he was certainly already prepared to endorse them on principle in works written about this time,[2] and later on, when justifying the use of coercion against Donatists, he would often write as if there had never been any doubt—in his own mind or anybody else's—about coercing pagans.[3] His agreement with the conciliar policy may even have been enthusiastic. His preaching and writing about the 'Christian times' rose to a great crescendo in the very years around the turn of the century. Around 399–401 he had no reservations about endorsing the Theodosian establishment, with its forcible methods of repressing paganism and heresy and its recourse to legislation to enforce Christian orthodoxy. This phase of the Empire's history seemed to him, in these years, to mark the climax of its role as the vehicle of divine purpose in history. Through the agency of the Roman Empire, God was fulfilling the promises made of old, the world was being brought to serve his name as the prophets had foretold.[4] In his theology of the 'Christian times' Augustine possessed a fully fledged justification for religious coercion. Theodosius and his successors were the instruments of a divine purpose in uprooting the idols and in subjugating their peoples to the worship of Christ. Augustine certainly had no grounds for disagreement with his fellow bishops in 401. He may even have been the chief theorist of their policies.

At this time, however, the Catholic bishops were still seeking peaceful means of converting Donatists,[5] and it was not until three years later that they changed their views in this respect.

[1] *C. Carth. V*, Can. 2; *VI*, Can. 18.   [2] Cf. e.g. *C. ep. Parm.* I, 10.16.
[3] *Inter multa*, cf. *Epp.* 93.3.10; 97.2–3.
[4] Cf. Brown, 'Saint Augustine's attitude', and Ch. 2, above, pp. 30–7.
[5] Cf. *C. Carth. VI*, Can. 1–3.

During these years the struggle between the two Churches grew in violence. Even so, however, the Catholic bishops wanted to conduct the struggle *more ecclesiastico*, by preaching, by discussion and in public debate. At their Council in 403 they still clung to this policy, and though they invoked the support of the Proconsul, it was only to the extent of asking him to have official archives opened to them for their search for documents to support their case in debate, and to have the schismatics summoned 'honourably' to appear in public to discuss the matters at issue under 'the friendly moderation of the law'.[1] But the Donatists, following the lead of their bishop in Carthage, refused the challenge, and would not appear for these public debates. During the following year the tension rose. At their Council in 404 the Catholic bishops decided to ask the government for repressive measures against Donatists. Even before the arrival of their emissaries in Ravenna, the Court had already decided to act. The 'Edict of Unity', together with some supporting legislation, was despatched to Africa in February and March 405.[2] This inaugurated a sustained attempt by the government to repress the schism.

But at this time Augustine's attitude did not amount to anything like full support of the policies advocated by his fellow bishops and adopted by the government. It may even be that the bishops' delay in adopting against the Donatists the coercive policies they had already advocated against pagans—though it can be explained by the situation they were faced with—was due, at least in part, to the restraint on them of Augustine's reluctance. For we have it on his own authority that he did not agree with the policy of coercion decided upon in 404, and that it was not until some time after the Edict of Unity (405) that he had embraced such a policy. Writing in 408 he explained the reasons for this inhibition: what, he had thought, was the use of legislation to convert heretics into 'feigned' (*ficti*) Catholics? He would have preferred at the time, he says, not to coerce the schismatics for fear of producing a mass of 'feigned' conversions, but to continue with preaching and discussion and to

---

[1] *Gesta Coll. Carth.* III, 174.   [2] *Cod. Theod.* XVI, 5.37, 38; 6.4, 5; 11.2.

prevail by the force of reason. But subsequent events have reconciled him to coercive methods. In his own city of Hippo he had seen the success of the Edict of Unity in operation: multitudes who needed only this external impulse to abandon the error they had clung to from force of habit and prejudice were now grateful for having been helped to the truth by the Edict.[1] There is every reason for accepting Augustine's explanation of his reluctance at its face value. The multitude of semi-Christian converts ushered into the Church by the social pressures on pagans constituted a serious pastoral problem, one to which Augustine had been particularly sensitive in the early years of his priestly and episcopal ministry.[2] He was very apt to interpret the low standards of popular Christianity as the result of the hypocrisy of pagans whose conversion to Christianity was little more than outward conformity. He feared a worse corruption of standards as a consequence of a possible landslide of coerced Donatists. But he overcame his fears. Perhaps he had become less fastidious and learnt to accept the peculiarities of popular religion. At any rate within a year or two of the Edict of Unity, having seen its working, his doubts were dispelled. His own congregation had successfully absorbed the converts who had been 'brought over to the Catholic unity by fear of the imperial Edicts'.[3] With growing confidence in his Church's power to assimilate the masses, Augustine's chief inhibition about the policy of coercion now lost its force. Some time between 405 and 408 his consent followed, and thereafter he never wavered. At the end of his life he recalled that long ago—around 398—he had written a work *Contra partem Donati*, in which he had rejected recourse to the secular power to bring schismatics forcibly into communion. 'I rejected it at that time because I had not yet learnt from my experience either how much wickedness they could resort to if left unpunished, or how much they could benefit from the application of discipline.'[4]

---

[1] *Ep.* 93.5.17.
[2] Cf. Van der Meer, *Augustine the bishop*, 46 f.
[3] *Ep.* 93.5.17.   [4] *Retr.* II, 5.

Augustine, then, did change his mind on the advisability of coercing Donatists, and we are in the comparatively rare position of having his own statement not only pin-pointing the change of mind, but also giving a convincing explanation for it. This change of mind gives no grounds for speaking of a 'conversion' of Augustine from previously 'liberal' ideas to the repressive policies of the African espiscopate and the Roman government. We have seen that he was probably in full agreement with coercing pagans in 401, and that his theology down to about 399–401 would have provided the support of principle for the policy. His 'conversion' to coercion against Donatists is no more than a delayed extension to their case of a policy already endorsed against pagans.

Within three or four years of the letter (*Ep.* 93) containing his apologia for sanctioning coercion Augustine had, however, come to reject decisively the views about the Theodosian establishment which he had held around the turn of the century[1] and which were one of the chief theoretical props of religious coercion. By the time of this famous letter (written in 408) the flow of positive statements about 'Christian times' and indeed about the scope of political action in religious matters had dried up. This loss of enthusiasm did not turn into explicit repudiation until a few years later, the early years of the second decade of the century, when he began elaborating a theology cast in a very different mould. But although the chief theoretical foundation of religious coercion built into his theology had thus disappeared, Augustine never repudiated the policies which had been based on it. This is the central paradox of Augustine's attitude to religious coercion when placed in relation to his fundamental theological development. To solve it, if it can be solved, we need to enquire into two things: what were the theoretical foundations, if any, for Augustine's *continued* approval of coercion? and if these principles did not lie in the sphere of his theology of the *saeculum*, but elsewhere, how were they compatible with his thought in that sphere?

[1] Cf. Ch. 2, above, pp. 37–41.

This study is concerned with theological reflection, and therefore confined to abstract, general ideas. But a man's attitude to an issue such as that of religious coercion is something too complex, and something that operates on too many levels, to be treated exclusively in this abstract dimension.[1] Only a part of it will be captured in the net of a 'doctrine' of coercion. In Augustine's Africa, coercion was one of the facts of life, and a provincial bishop was deeply involved in its exercise. Administrative routine, if nothing else, made the distinction between Church and State inapplicable in this context. An African bishop was not faced with the question whether coercion was justifiable or not; in innumerable ways his position in society, even his episcopal functions, involved him in a repressive régime.[2] We are not here concerned with the working of religious coercion in Augustine's Africa, or even with the way in which Augustine participated in its working. But it is as well to keep these administrative, social and human complexities in mind as a permanent backdrop to define the middle distance. We confine our attention to the chosen foreground, the ideas involved.

Augustine's 'theory' of coercion was, from beginning to end, part of a pastoral strategy.[3] As a young priest he explained his mind to his elderly bishop on how to curb sinners: 'abuses are to be cut off "in a spirit of gentleness" [Gal. 6:1], as it is written... These things are not to be removed, it seems to me, by harshness or in a sharp, imperious way (*non ergo aspere...non duriter, non modo imperioso*): but by teaching rather than commanding, by admonition rather than with threats. This is how to proceed with the majority; severity is best kept for dealing with the sins of the few.'[4] Harshness, fear, threats, coercion are not, even at this early stage, rejected on principle. They are modes of the exercise of pastoral office, but modes which must be kept in reserve, not to be

---

[1] Brown, 'Saint Augustine's attitude', has some penetrating remarks on this.

[2] For its workings, see Brown, 'Religious coercion'.

[3] Berkhof, *Kirche und Kaiser*, 105–22, on the strength of a very cursory investigation, asserts, rightly, that this is where the novelty of Augustine's position lies in relation to earlier theories of coercion. Cf. Crespin, *Ministère*, esp. 162–8, 174–5.

[4] *Ep.* 22.5.

used indiscriminately. Episcopal office seems, however, to have weakened Augustine's resolve to keep pastoral 'severity' within such narrow bounds. His confidence in his ability, and that of his congregation, to cope with 'corrected' sinners, pagans and schismatics in large numbers overcame his reluctance to sanction large-scale coercion. The change of his mind after 405 concerned only the scale on which he envisaged that coercive measures could be applied. They remained, for him, primarily an application of pastoral *severitas*.

The importance of pastoral considerations in sanctioning the use of force is evident from Augustine's Letter 93. He had never doubted that violence should be controlled by the public authority and that Donatist terrorists should be punished; and before now he had spoken of the government's competence to 'persecute schismatics'.[1] But these considerations had not, up to now, tilted the scales in favour of his sanctioning coercion. That, evidently, was done by the 'pastoral' arguments deployed in Letter 93. The key-note is struck in the opening paragraph: 'We see many who have renounced their former blindness; how could I begrudge them their salvation, by dissuading my colleagues from exercising their fatherly care, by which this has been brought about?'[2] Throughout this long letter Augustine considers religious coercion from this perspective. It is likened to medicine administered to an unwilling patient for his own good;[3] it is a true work of love, for 'it is better to love with severity than to deceive with indulgence';[4] even God—and no one can love men more than He does—is always scourging those whom He loves. Can we doubt that people should be compelled to righteousness when we read that the master of the house commanded his servants: 'whomever you find, compel them to come in' (Luke 14:23)?[5] Throughout the Bible we read of punishment being administered as a remedy.[6] After some paragraphs in defence of religious coercion by the secular power, Augustine returns to the gratitude shown by ex-Donatists

---

[1] *Ep.* 87.7.   [2] *Ep.* 93.1.1; cf. *ibid.* 5.19.   [3] *Ibid.* 1.3.
[4] *Ibid.* 2.4.   [5] *Ibid.* 2.5.   [6] *Ibid.* 2.6–8.

for having had the imperial edicts to break them from procrastination, to help them overcome the force of habit and prejudice, for having brought them to an unclouded vision of the truth previously obscured by rumour; for making them do, in short, what they would have wanted to do had they known better.[1]

This kind of argumentation is the kernel, not only of this most self-conscious of Augustine's writings on this question, but of his whole attitude to coercion of schismatics from the moment he endorsed it. The case for coercive measures against the Donatists was fundamentally different from the case—which Augustine never actually deployed in full and whose basis he came to reject—for coercing pagans. With pagans it had been a question of forcing them to accept a truth to which they were blind and to accept a historical destiny expressed in the Christian Church and its alliance with the Roman Empire. With the Donatist schismatics it was a matter of *recalling* them to the flock to which they rightfully belonged and from which they had strayed. Coercing schismatics was, in a sense in which coercing pagans could never be, part of the Church's pastoral activity among its own flock. When preaching on the shepherds of Chapter 34 of Ezechiel, Augustine's mind turns quite naturally to bringing the strayed sheep—the Donatists—back to the one sheepfold;[2] even with the help of inflicted pain, if need be, this is part of *diligentia pastoralis*.[3] In the last of his anti-Donatist tracts, written some thirteen years after Letter 93, he would write, still in the same vein, to a Donatist bishop who had barricaded himself in his splendid cathedral against the imperial official sent against him, and was threatening to burn himself and his congregation in it: 'the tribune sent against you is not your persecutor; he is persecuting your persecutor, that is, your error...'[4]

This horrible doctrine, with all its potentialities for being insidiously and cynically generalised, derives from Augustine's notion of *disciplina*. This was the seed from which his theory of

[1] *Ibid.* 5.18. [2] *Sermo 46, De pastoribus;* cf. also *Sermo 47, De ovibus.*
[3] *Ep.* 185.6.23. [4] *C. Gaudent.* I, 18.19.

persecution grew. Its beneficial value, as we know from his own statement,[1] Augustine realised only late. But once he had come to accept it, Augustine, characteristically, found many threads linking the idea of *disciplina* to the basic texture of his theology. Especially from his late fifties on, he considered freedom of choice less and less as something incompatible with constraint and fear. God had made use of constraint and fear in the long education to which he subjected his chosen people. The divine *disciplina* uses external pressure to bring about an internal moral development. In his justification of religious coercion Augustine would often quote from the Book of Proverbs: 'Give occasion to a wise man, and he will become wiser' (9:9).[2] To the notion—deeply enough established in Christian tradition, even to the extent of finding an echo in Constantine's 'Edict of toleration'—that belief is a matter of free decision, not of compulsion, Augustine replied by rejecting the dichotomy. Free choice and compulsion were not incompatible: 'It is not true that nothing is accomplished by external pressure. For not only is the wall of hardened habit breached by human terrors, but the mind's faith and understanding is at the same time strengthened by divine authority and reason.'[3] A sermon Augustine once preached—his only one actually on the text of the parable of the wedding feast—closed with the reminder that the Lord did not just invite the willing; he gave instructions for the unwilling to be compelled to come in: 'Let constraint be found outside: the will is born within.'[4]

This remained Augustine's settled response to the objection that 'the unwilling are not to be brought forcibly to the truth',[5] urged frequently especially by his Donatist opponents. The notion of *disciplina*, with its cognates—*correctio, per molestias eruditio*—remained the kernel of his 'theory' of coercion. Indeed the power of these ideas increased in his mind with the development of his views on grace, on predestination and on man's freedom, from the

[1] *Retr.* II, 5; cf. above, p. 138, n. 4.
[2] E.g. *Ep.* 93.5.17; much later, *C. Gaudent.* I, 33.43. [3] *Ep.* 89.7.
[4] *Foris inveniatur necessitas, nascitur intus voluntas*—*Sermo* 112.8; cf. also *C. litt. Pet.* II, 84.186.
[5] *C. Gaudent.* I, 25.28.

time of his conflict with Pelagianism, around 410. As a young philosopher, recently converted to Christianity, Augustine had defended the freedom of the will against Manichaean determinism. But long before his encounter with the teaching of Pelagius he had been deeply conscious of the difficulty of achieving the good life in one's conduct. The force of habit (*consuetudo*; apt to become *consuetudo carnalis*) held a man's freedom of action in the grip of his own past. For Pelagius, the grip of past habit on the personality could be broken. In his 'theology of discontinuity' baptism and conversion marked the Christian's emancipation from the power of his own past over him.[1] For Augustine, the man reborn in the Spirit was not so free from the power of the past. For him, the force of habit was not something external to the personality and capable of being discarded in conversion, but something that entered deeply into a man's make-up. This 'wall of hardened habit' was the barrier Augustine saw between the schismatic communities and the unity of the one fold.[2]

To summarise: it seems that Augustine's ideas on religious coercion sprang from several different contexts. First, it is clear that he was never entirely opposed to *severitas* as a pastoral method. His later statements, especially from Letter 93 onwards, place most weight on the notion of coercion as an exercise of this *severitas*, as an infliction of *disciplina* for the education and the ultimate benefit of the coerced. In this sense his later ideas are substantially in line with his earliest, and only constitute a development from them in two respects: first, in the scale on which he was later prepared to sanction the use of methods which he had at first envisaged as applicable only to a few; and second, in the wider resonances his ideas on *disciplina* acquired in the course of his reflection on grace, freedom and predestination during his controversy with Pelagianism. There is, however, another source, of quite a different kind,

---

[1] Cf. Brown, 'Pelagius'. It is one of the singular merits of this deeply impressive paper to have thrown this aspect of the difference between the two men into clear relief. On the importance of Augustine's teaching on grace and freedom for his ideas on coercion, see Brown, 'Saint Augustine's attitude'.

[2] *Ep.* 89.7; cf. above, p. 143, n. 3.

which also nourished his readiness to endorse coercion: his theology of the Roman Empire as a divinely willed instrument of the Gospel. This was a phase of his thought which rose to a climax around 399–401, thereafter declined in importance, and was decisively repudiated soon after 410. It must have played some part in his agreement with his fellow bishops in 401 over coercing pagans, but probably none in securing his consent to coercing Donatists around 406–8, and soon after 410 Augustine must have been conscious that this reason for the policy of coercion was gone. But it made no difference in practice: there were other, equally strong reasons which remained, and could serve to justify continued adherence to the policy. Moreover, Augustine was being increasingly drawn into meditating on the deep mysteries of human freedom and on God's ways with the wills of men. He could equate God's action on human will with external impingement: 'God himself is doing this [recalling you to the fold] through us—whether by pleading, by threats, by rebukes, by punishment and by troubles; whether through his own secret admonitions and visitations, or through the power of the temporal law.'[1] His last anti-Donatist work, *Against Gaudentius* (421), compared with the anti-Donatist writings of 400–11, shows clear traces of enrichment from this more recently developed context of Augustine's thought.[2] The role of rebuke, punishment, fear and all salutary constraint did not cease to preoccupy Augustine. One of his last works was devoted to these very problems.[3] Grounds for approving coercion were therefore well embedded in other spheres of Augustine's thought than in a relatively short phase of his reflection on politics and the Roman Empire.

We may then conclude that Augustine's views on coercion need not be taken as part only of his reflection on history and on politics, indeed that this reflection would have supported them only during a relatively short period and would not have done so at any rate during the last twenty years of his life. The theoretical

---

[1] *Ep.* 105.4.13. [2] See for instance *C. Gaudent.* I, 19.20.
[3] *De corr. et gratia* (426–7); cf. also *Ep.* 210.

background of his views on coercion was a changing constellation of ideas belonging to different realms of thought, and the views themselves are part of a complex set of attitudes rather than implications drawn with rigorous logic from any theory.[1] It does, however, remain true that there is an unresolved tension between Augustine's mature theology of the *saeculum* and his views on coercion. His endorsement of official enforcement of Christian orthodoxy, whatever its theoretical foundations, is not well at home in the repudiation of the Theodosian 'Christian times', nor in the setting of his scepticism about a Christian Roman Empire and about legal and institutional means of christianisation.

Augustine was assisted in concealing this tension from himself by a habit of mind which is revealed in his customary manner of dealing with the theme of the 'Christian ruler'. In discussing this theme, Augustine came up against the central problem of the intersection of two spheres of discourse: the Christian ruler or magistrate can be thought of either as a member of the Church, or as part of a system of governmental institutions; either as a servant of God or of the *res publica*. In his earliest pronouncements on this subject Augustine tends to by-pass the problem of relating these two spheres. Thus in a work written soon after his conversion to Christianity he apostrophises the Church as the guardian of all the virtues distinctive of all stations in life. Among the several kinds and conditions of men taught their proper place in the world are rulers and their subjects: 'You (the Church) teach kings to care for their people, you admonish peoples to be subject to their rulers.'[2] Here the Church appears as the guardian of all established order and of all proper human relationships, and in the passage as a whole there is an implicit but effective rhetorical identification of the existing with an ideal order. At this stage, of course, Augustine

---

[1] This is well brought out by Brown, 'Saint Augustine's attitude', 107–8. It is for this reason, too, that one cannot in the end, as a historian, identify Augustine with some of the caricatures to which his teaching easily lends itself. Cf. the concluding paragraphs of Brown's paper: 'But remove the foundation of honesty for one moment from this attitude, and Augustine's phrases become fallacious, horrible and insidious...', *ibid.* 115.

[2] *De mor. eccl.* I, 30.63.

would not have rejected such an identification.[1] Rulers were the agents of founding an order among men grounded upon the universal order established by God in the world. The tasks and interests of Church and State necessarily coincided in the person of the ruler.

This coincidence was further strengthened by the Eusebian type of theology of the Empire, from whose sway Augustine only learnt to free himself after 400. The Empire was the instrument of a divine purpose, the Emperor a quasi-messianic figure with a transcendent mission; Church and State were only provisionally distinct aspects of a single Christian 'polity'. Although Augustine never wholly identified himself with the more extreme forms of such a theology, it did, as we saw (Chapter 2), shape his thinking about the Empire for some years. In the context of such a conception the problem of defining the respective spheres of Church and State was again by-passed, for the two were, at root, identical. It is in the later period of his thought, when he had rejected both the idea of the political order as part of a universal, cosmic order, and the idea of a Christian Roman Empire, that we might expect to find traces of a consciousness of this problem in Augustine's writings. But in fact Augustine continued to speak of Christian rulers and officials owing specific service to God in their public, official capacity. In 405 he wrote: 'Uprooting the idols from the face of the earth—promised so long ago—is not something any private citizen can command. Kings thus have their own status in human society in virtue of which they can serve the Lord in ways not open to those who are not kings.'[2] 'When we ask something of our rulers for the benefit of the Church, we are not placing our hope in them: we are admonishing them to place their hope in God.'[3] The same thoughts are expressed twelve years later, in a letter to the Roman commander Boniface concerning 'the correction of the Donatists'.[4] Kings' specific service of God, as kings, consists in 'commanding what is good, prohibiting what is wicked, not only in matters pertaining to social relations between

---

[1] Cf. Ch. 4, above, pp. 75–80. [2] *C. litt. Pet.* II, 92.210.
[3] *Ibid.* II, 97.224. [4] *Ep.* 185.5.19.

men, but also in those pertaining to divine religion'.[1] Augustine sums it all up in the famous 'mirror for princes': Christian emperors achieve their true felicity if, among other things, 'they make their power serve God's majesty by using it to the utmost to spread his worship'.[2]

There is no trace of any reservation about the scope of imperial or royal authority in such statements, no suggestion that it is in any way restricted to 'temporal' matters. If there was a tension between Augustine's views about the function of the state or of the Roman Empire, as they were developing at this time, and his views on the duties of Christian kings and emperors (including the duty to enforce true religion),[3] Augustine seems not to have been aware of it. Once he remarked, in a letter to the Proconsul of Africa, that the 'business of a province is one thing, that of the Church another';[4] but this was no attempt to define distinct spheres of authority. On the contrary: the purpose of this distinction of spheres was to persuade the Proconsul to deal leniently with Donatists, so that through his mercy, the mercy of his mother, the Church, might be made manifest. 'For when you act, the Church acts, for whose sake and as whose son you act.'[5]

Here is the clue to the reason why Augustine could write as he did about the duties of Christian rulers and about religious coercion by the public authorities long after he had ceased to believe that the state had any religious purpose or function. Neither in his dealings with imperial officials nor in his writings in defence of religious coercion did he ever consider Christian rulers and civil servants as parts of a governmental machinery, of the 'state'. He thought of them as members of the Church. Through them, it is the Church that 'uses power'.[6] Once he even spoke of coercion *by* the Church.[7] The concept of the 'state' is conspicuous by its absence from all Augustine's discussions of this theme. When, on a rare occasion,

---

[1] *C. Cresc.* III, 51.56.   [2] *De civ. Dei*, v, 24. Cf. above, p. 57, n. 1.
[3] The quotations in the previous paragraph cover the years *c.* 405 to 417; the same thoughts still occur in 421, *C. Gaudent.* I, 35.45.
[4] *Ep.* 134.3.   [5] *Ibid.* 4.   [6] *Ep.* 173.10.
[7] *Ep.* 185.6.23. It was no slip of the pen, for the thought is implicit *ibid.* 2.11.

he recalled that there was something wrong—as his own principles must have suggested—with the whole coercive establishment of the Theodosian Empire, he formulated the objection not in terms of the state's proper function, but from the point of view of the Church's well-being: through the service rendered to it by kings the Church is exposed 'to greater and more serious temptation'.[1] The reason why it did not occur to Augustine to restrict the scope of the state's proper sphere of action when he was thinking about religious coercion is simple: it did not occur to him to think in terms of the 'state' at all in this context. It is striking that when Augustine defends the exercise of coercive power by the secular authority in the religious sphere, he always does so in a vocabulary of persons rather than of institutions. Although he did have at his disposal words such as *imperium* or *res publica*, which may suitably be rendered in abstract political terminology, these are not the words he uses for this purpose. He will speak of emperors rather than of empire, of kings and magistrates rather than of state or government. Thus he could continue to speak without inhibition of Christian emperors long after he had abandoned all talk about a Christian empire.[2]

This is no accident of linguistic habit. Augustine's linguistic preferences here are an index of some of the profoundest preoccupations of his mind. The reasons for his choice of vocabulary are embedded in the perpetual liability of his conception of the state to dissolve into a kind of atomistic personalism. 'A city consists of its citizens, not of its walls.'[3] Especially when he wished

---

[1] *De perf. iust.* 15.35. Cf. Ch. 2 above, p. 40, n. 6.

[2] There are signs, however, that even in his speech about Christian emperors Augustine was deliberately reserved. A meticulous recent study, Duval, 'L'éloge de Théodose', has disclosed the extent of the independence of Augustine's judgement from that of the writers on whose work he drew for information. In his eulogy of Theodosius (*De civ. Dei*, v, 26.1) he drew heavily on Rufinus's recently completed translation and continuation of Eusebius's *Ecclesiastical history*. But there is no trace in Augustine's presentation of the emperor of any of the quasi-messianic features which Rufinus, in the Eusebian tradition, had projected onto his hero. On the contrary: Augustine prefers to single out the typically private virtues for special praise in Christian emperors: their humility in the face of the seductions offered by high office, their submission to God and their grateful recognition of his gifts.

[3] *De urb. exc.* 6. For further passages of this kind, cf. Ch. 3 above, p. 61, n. 2.

to comment on the moral quality—the piety or turpitude—of a society, Augustine liked to dismember it in this fashion into its constituent, personal atoms. 'Where a king, a council, officials, people are to be found, there is the *civitas*'; wickedness is not something to be found disembodied in 'cities', it does not exist in institutions but in individuals who are 'the constituent elements and atoms of cities'.[1] This somewhat simple-minded approach to political morality, with its exclusive interest in persons and neglect of structures, does not, of course, represent the whole of Augustine's mind on the matter. He could give much weight to the quality of a society's institutions, traditions, and its collectively upheld ideals.[2] But the protest against objectifying the mixed ultimate personal allegiances current in any social group into a collective entity capable of simple moral assessment was a vital part of his rejection both of pagan Roman and of Christian Eusebian ideology.

It was this protest that was at the roots of his insistence that in any human grouping the two eschatological 'cities' always coexist and overlap.[3] Once he had embarked on the writing of the *City of God*, and on the sustained meditation on God's purposes in history which lie behind it, what interested Augustine increasingly were the eschatological ultimates as they were interwoven in the *saeculum*. Terms such as the 'state' disguised the fact that, from this point of view, the entity designated by them was a composite one, consisting of the two 'cities' in their overlap. But this was precisely what Augustine had to stress in order to empty the 'state' of eschatological significance. To preserve its neutrality between the two 'cities' and to transfer to them the whole burden of being the exclusive bearers of all ultimate significance, what was required

---

[1] *elementa et semina civitatum—Enarr. in Ps.* 9.8. The tendency of the abstract political concepts to dissolve into 'personalistic' terms is, of course, very much in line with the development of late Roman government. The 'patriarchal' situation of the great estate was becoming increasingly characteristic of the social and administrative life of the Empire. The 'state' was becoming increasingly eclipsed as an abstraction only dimly visible behind the peculiarly personal and quasi-feudal authority of the senatorial governors of the Western provinces.

[2] Cf. above, pp. 66 f., 96 f.

[3] Cf. Ch. 3, above, pp. 64–71. What follows summarises the argument there given in full.

was a kind of invisible re-grouping of the state's citizens into the two mutually exclusive bodies of the citizens of the earthly and of the heavenly cities: Rome could not have any ultimate, eternal destiny because it was—as is any other actual body of men— necessarily a mixed body. Only the two 'cities' are in the relevant sense 'unmixed'—but in their historical existence they can never be discerned in their unmixed state. This invisibility of the presence of eschatological categories in historical realities is the foundation of Augustine's theology of the *saeculum*. In order to insist on the ultimate eschatological ambivalence of all empirical human group-ings and institutions Augustine had to by-pass their collective, in-stitutional character, and to break them down (though with the rider that this could never in fact be carried out with assignable named individuals) into terms of individuals with their personal loyalties to different, and very mixed, ultimate values. This is why his habit of reducing political institutions into their component personal atoms is linked with some of his most fundamental con-cerns, at a fundamental level.

We come thus to the paradoxical conclusion that both Augus-tine's 'desacralisation' of the Roman Empire, with the 'secular' theology of society implied in it, and his defence of religious coercion spring from a single root. More precisely, although his views on coercion sprang from another context, it was the funda-mentals of his theology of the *saeculum* which, on the one hand, pointed in a very different direction, and, on the other, by virtue of their formulation, disguised from Augustine this divergence. The main lines of his thinking about history, society and human institutions in general (the *saeculum*) point towards a political order to which we may not unreasonably apply the anachronistic epithet 'pluralist', in that it is neutral in respect of ultimate beliefs and values. On the other hand, it was this very reflection itself, and its terminology, that undermined the solidity of Augustine's political vocabulary, with the effect that concepts such as that of the 'state' tended to dissolve in his hands. The concept of the Church was less susceptible to this 'atomisation'. It was, for obvious reasons, less easy to dissolve into its members, whereas the idea of the 'state' could not so easily survive the tendency to break down into terms of the individuals who compose it. In consequence it ceased to be a concept which engaged the centre of Augustine's interests, or in terms of which he discussed other related questions in which he was interested. Among such questions is the one we have been considering in this chapter, that of religious coercion. Perhaps, had Augustine thought of this issue in terms of the proper function of the 'state', he might have come to take another view of the matter than he did; perhaps he would at least have been more conscious of an unresolved tension than he appears to have been. These are conjectures. At any rate, we may say that the fact that he did not think of this problem in terms of the state, but in terms of individual members of the Church who held secular office, disguised from Augustine the acute tension between his consent to coercion and the implications of his theology of history and society. The 'atomistic personalism' bound up with the latter is what, in large part, made it possible for him to elaborate a 'theory' of coercion of the type he did.

That this was a theory of coercion by the Church, not by the state, is of vital importance for understanding Augustine's mind on the matter, though the difference is, of course, irrelevant in practice. There was, indeed, little foothold for such a distinction in the actual circumstances of Augustine's Africa. In the course of the early middle ages, with the increasing difficulty of applying the concept of the 'state' to anything that could be found in Western Europe, the categories of Augustine's 'atomistic personalism' found more ready application than ever. For centuries it was much easier to think of political realities in terms of rulers, officials, their duties and ideals, than in terms of abstract political concepts such as the 'state', 'government', or 'public authority'. Hence that 'political Augustinianism' so characteristic of the middle ages which, though scarcely in line with the grain of Augustine's own thought, has been aptly defined as 'a tendency to absorb natural law in supernatural justice, the right of the state in that of the

Church'.[1] Not for nothing was the *genre* of Augustine's 'mirror for princes'[2] one of the favourite forms of medieval political writing. For all that, the argument of this book is that if we wish to understand the political bearings of the fundamental theological structures of Augustine's thought, we do better to pursue the implications of the hypothesis in which we have reconstructed the shape of that thought than to remain content with what he actually said about the duties of Christian rulers and subjects.

[1] Arquillière, *L'augustinisme politique*, 4.   [2] *De civ. Dei*, v, 24.

CHAPTER 7

CIVITAS PEREGRINA: SIGNPOSTS

WE have come to the end of our investigation of a complex strand of Augustine's reflection, that concerned with divine purpose in human history, with the function of politically organised society, and with the place of the Christian Church within it. Following Augustine's lead, we have adopted the term *saeculum* to refer to the realm to which this reflection refers. Our investigation has shown that as Augustine's thought in this sphere took shape, it lent itself less and less to interpretation in terms of a 'theology of the Constantinian (or Theodosian) establishment'. It is, of course, plain that as a provincial bishop Augustine was nevertheless very much an 'establishment' figure. The conditions of the organised life of his Church and of bearing episcopal office in it would scarcely have allowed anything else. Even though, in the years following 410-11, Augustine lost his earlier enthusiasm about the alliance between the Roman Empire and the Catholic Church,[1] he could hardly have renounced it in practice. Indeed, he went so far as to invoke this alliance repeatedly, especially where coercing schismatics or heretics was concerned. In terms of his theology of coercion, conceived as an activity of the Church and as an exercise of pastoral care, Augustine could take such an attitude without dishonesty. His practice accorded well with principles which had deep roots in his mind. In the last chapter we have tried to disengage these principles from a tangled context, and to indicate how Augustine could reconcile them with the dominant emphasis of his theology of the *saeculum*. We concluded that he could do so

[1] Brown, *Augustine of Hippo*, 337, has noted this loss of enthusiasm about the alliance between Church and Empire, without, however, bringing it into relation with Augustine's theological development. He relates it more immediately to the judicial murder of Augustine's friend, Count Marcellinus, the very man who had presided over the Catholic–Donatist Conference of Carthage in 411, which marked the zenith of the alliance of Church and State in Africa. I would not wish to deny the importance of this.

quite simply because for him coercion was an act of the Church, not of the state. His hold upon the concept of 'the state' was not firm enough to force him to question whether its absorption by the 'Church' in the exercise of religious coercion was consistent with his theology of society. Augustine certainly had his share in accustoming the minds of Christians throughout the centuries to sanctioning many enormities perpetrated in the name of the principle 'Compel them to come in' to which he had given currency. But this fact should not be allowed to obscure the presence in his theology of a radical challenge to all political thinking on such lines. Augustine was certainly no critic of the 'establishment'; but his theology is a critique of 'establishment' theology.

At this point the historian and the theologian have reached a parting of the ways. The historian, even if he confines his interest to the history of ideas, will wish to understand as fully as he can all the ideas which went into the making of Augustine's mind, and to seize the full complexity of their tangled interplay in its development. The theologian can recognise that, abstracted from the context of Augustine's attitude to the ecclesiastical establishment of his place and time, in all its complicated detail, there are two quite distinct sets of questions to be distinguished here. One concerns the internal, pastoral activity of the Church; the other concerns wider questions about history, society, human destiny, and the Church's relation to them. In this final chapter I keep entirely to this second set of themes. I shall attempt to sketch the directions of the signposts provided by Augustine's reflection on history, on society and on the Church.

It cannot be concealed that there is an element of hazard about such a procedure. To extrapolate the directions discerned in a body of thought across more than fifteen centuries, and to claim to read off its implications for the present is futile. The historian can understand Augustine better without such a preoccupation, and the theologian may be credited with the ability to construct a relevant theology of history, of society and of the Church without such dubious assistance from a remote past. As against this caution, however, no historian would wish to deny that if the past is to be understood, it must be understood in and from the present. Conversely, the theologian is of all men the most apt to look over his shoulder, if not for 'authorities', at least for a tradition in which to locate his own thought. On the assumption, which this is not the place to defend, that this look over the shoulder is an essential part of the Christian theologian's work, I now consider some of the ways in which Augustine's thought can nourish, deepen and set the direction for relevant thought on these subjects in our day. In theology, true continuity is not so much a matter of drawing out implications from, still less of repeating the substance of assertions made by, the Fathers; it is rather to be found in loyalty to their ultimate doctrinal aims.[1] Having observed Augustine's doctrinal aims taking shape with growing clarity of focus in his writings, I now trace the direction, without following the signposts very far, in which the insights Augustine can furnish to twentieth-century theology point.

Naturally such a task cannot be confined to the horizons of Augustine's world, even of his intellectual world. I shall have to go beyond them increasingly in the course of the argument; least so in the first section, which is devoted to the theology of history. In the second, on the theology of society and politics, while remaining fairly close to the horizons of Augustine's thought as they have emerged in the course of the first five chapters, I discount as a distracting complication for my present theological purpose the historical facts of Augustine's own positions studied in Chapter 6. Finally, in the last section, that on the Church, it must be acknowledged that neither has Augustine's immensely rich ecclesiological thought been examined in this book nor have I sought to tap its resources in this epilogue in order to point to anything one might properly call an 'ecclesiology'. I keep here fairly narrowly to the eschatological perspective on ecclesiology to which my examination of Augustine's views in this field was also confined in Chapter 5.

[1] M. Wiles, *The making of Christian doctrine*, 173 and *passim*.

ESCHATOLOGY AS HISTORY

Outside dissenting or schismatic circles Augustine was the only thinker of any stature who was deeply disturbed by the developments of the fourth century towards a sacral conception of the Empire. He rejected the identification of the Church's destiny with that of the Empire, implied in this conception. If the Empire was the God-willed vehicle of Christianity, then either the Empire must have an eternal destiny and a universal mission, or the Church, in being so tied to a temporal structure, was dangerously at the mercy of the Empire's vicissitudes. If the Empire should turn out to be anything less than everlasting and all-inclusive, then the Church has failed in its mission. But neither implication was acceptable to Augustine, and his whole theology of history came to a focus in the rejection of the fundamental assumption behind this dilemma: the assumption that any slice of secular history, of any nation, institution or society, could have an indispensable place in the historical realisation of God's purpose. The *mysterion* of the divine purpose had been revealed in Christ, and faith compelled the believer to await in hope the return of the Lord in glory to gather his faithful from the ends of the earth into his kingdom. The time and shape of that coming no man could tell; meanwhile the Church would continue to bear witness to its Lord until the end. But the shape of this witness and the historical form of the Church's existence, the human structures within which its life is carried on, were changeable. It was vital not to tie the Church to anything temporary that might be discarded. The Empire, for instance, may have served the Church's mission; but lest its service assume too much importance in the eyes of churchmen, Augustine reminded them that it had served the Church when it immolated its martyrs as much as in persecuting pagans and heretics. Christian rulers might bring their subjects to the worship of Christ: but the Gospel continues to be betrayed in these 'Christian times', as it always must continue to be betrayed. The Empire, as any secular structure, always has its contribution to make to the Church's life. But nothing essential to the Church's mission can be lost if any particular structure were to collapse and disappear.

Augustine thus liberated the Church from dependence on any secular framework. Contrary to what is sometimes said, he did so not solely because he saw in the Sack of Rome in 410 a portent of a threat to a Church too closely identified with the Empire, but because his reflection on history had already led him to withhold from the Empire—and from any other secular institution since Christ—any ultimate, sacred significance. Within universal history he distinguished a privileged strand which we have called, taking our cue from Augustine, 'sacred'. This strand was uniquely privileged in virtue of our having been given a clue to its eschatological meaning. The clue was the prophetic vision in which this particular strand of history became a part of the history of God's saving acts. This was the sense in which Augustine accepted the biblical canon as 'prophetic': on its authority the biblical history was uniquely distinguished from all other human history. We have rendered this distinction in terms of 'sacred' and 'secular' respectively (Chapter 1).

Outside the limits of the history told in the Bible we have no way of assessing the meaning of any action, event, of any person or institution, of any culture, society or any epoch in the unfolding history of salvation. The Christian believer has no privileged insight and the Christian Church no norms in terms of which to judge historical developments on which the Bible is silent. The whole period since the Incarnation until the return of the Lord in glory at the end is radically ambiguous. We know, to use Augustine's language, that all that is done and all that is suffered here goes into the building of the two eschatological 'cities'. But we are not to deceive ourselves into thinking that we can ever detect the *locus* of the two cities in secular history, for here their careers are 'inextricably intertwined'. This does not, of course, mean that a Christian believer may not exercise ordinary human judgement in history. In recoiling from monstrous wickedness or admiring heroism, in deploring the collapse of a great culture or applauding an advance to a more humane society he is drawing on the normal resources of the human mind. His evaluations possess both the validity and the uncertainty to which this is subject, and they fall short of reaching insight into the ultimate eschatological significance of the events and objects judged.

Augustinian agnosticism about secular history involves an uncompromising refusal to read its course in terms of this ultimate significance: but it does not exclude all 'prophecy' from the period since the Incarnation. We are not taught that the prophetic charisma has been withdrawn from the Church, but that the closing of the biblical canon represents the conclusion of the process of interpretation of the history of salvation in a 'total interpretation'.[1] Prophetic charisma will always be active in the Church; but it can add nothing to the achieved totality of sacred history concluded in Christ. Its exercise since the end of the Apostolic age is, in the first place, fraught with deep uncertainty. No prophet since Christ can claim an authority other than the inherent force of his message and of the words which proclaim it. The message which may have compelling power here and today, may lack all force elsewhere, tomorrow. In the second place, the prophetic charisma can now, since the end of the Apostolic age, no longer bear on the pattern and development of the history of salvation, for that is— except for the final *dénouement* in the Parousia—concluded, and to it there can be no addition. Prophetic interpretation of history is now bound to be something more fragmentary. It bears essentially on the present. The demand to read the 'signs' of the times is a challenge to the believer to see his present as containing the hidden drama of the ultimates of divine judgement; and such a vision must inevitably seek embodiment in the imagery of the Bible.[2] The vision and the imagery have a tendency to expand; and a besetting temptation of Christian prophecy, in its most varied forms such as that of Joachim of Floris or of Teilhard de Chardin, has always been to allow the biblical imagery to develop on a grand historical

---

[1] On this, see O. Cullmann, *Salvation in history*, 296, and Appendix D.
[2] Von Balthasar, *Man in history*, 144.

or cosmic scale, and thus to compromise the unique completeness of the sacred history as concluded in the biblical canon.

Post-canonical prophecy is concerned with 'history' only in the sense that it bears upon the time of its present: on acts, events and things with which the Christian community is faced in its own time and place. It is a summons to decision and to action. Prophecy is linked to an immediate task. Its reference to 'history' is to 'history' understood as a complex of acts and events in time, not as the record and the interpretation of these events. This is the fundamental respect in which prophecy now differs from the 'prophecy' contained in the scriptural canon: the prophetic quality of the inspired writer consists precisely in the fact that he is authorised to integrate his narrative within the framework of a 'total interpretation' of God's saving action. His prophecy bears upon 'history' understood not as events and deeds but as their interpreted record (Chapter 1). The post-biblical prophet, however, has to forgo integrating his prophetic vision into the pattern of a 'total interpretation'. As soon as it loses its reference to the immediacy of the present upon which it bears, and projects its commitment back into the past or forward into a historical or cosmic future, it runs the risk of infringing the uniqueness of a completed 'sacred' history. It is therefore in no way paradoxical that a prophetic commitment in the present, even a vision of the present in the stark imagery of apocalyptic, should, in retrospect, as soon as the present has become past, become an anachronism. Obsolescence is built into post-canonical prophecy: as soon as its present passes into history (the past as recorded and interpreted), the prophetic quality of the vision in which that present has been seen also passes into history. Its perpetuation as 'prophecy' would constitute a blasphemous anachronism.

The Christian is bidden to arm himself with the sword of the Spirit, which is the Word of God (Eph. 6:17); and the Word of God is 'living and active, sharper than any two-edged sword, piercing to the division of soul and spirit, of joints and marrow, and discerning the thoughts and intentions of the heart' (Heb. 4:12).

How could a prophet, charismatically proclaiming this Word to his present, fail to cut deep into its substance? But his present will become past, and the Word addressed to the present has nothing to say to the past.

> We cannot revive old factions
> We cannot restore old policies
> Or follow an antique drum.
> These men, and those who opposed them
> And those whom they opposed
> Accept the constitution of silence
> And are folded in a single party.
>
> T. S. Eliot, *Little Gidding*

Even the prophet of his day must accept the 'constitution of silence' imposed upon the past when his day is done. This is how he differs from the prophets who are responsible for the 'sacred history' of the biblical narratives. For they, in interpreting events prophetically, linked them with a whole history of earlier events and a whole history of earlier prophetic interpretations, thus continually showing the old in the light of the new and the new in the light of the old, and progressively building up a 'total interpretation'.[1] But this totality of interpretation is now closed. The prophetic judgement now bears solely on its present. In becoming history, it no longer adds to 'sacred history'.

Augustine's agnosticism about the historical developments of his own time, and, more fundamentally, about all 'secular' history, was perhaps his most 'prophetic' challenge to his contemporaries. √ It was certainly an almost unique protest against the direction which had come to dominate fourth-century theology. Even his own disciple, Orosius, who wrote his *Seven books of histories against the pagans* at Augustine's suggestion, had wholly failed to understand his master's mind.[2] Orosius once more reverted to the tradition of Origen, Eusebius, Prudentius and the rest. The Empire founded by Augustus was the providentially established vehicle of

---

[1] Cullmann, *Salvation*, 88 f.
[2] See primarily Mommsen, 'Orosius and Augustine'. On Orosius, cf. also Patterson, *God and history*, 130 f.; Lacroix, *Orose*, 200 f., and Markus, 'The Roman Empire'.

Christianity, and the history of the period since the Incarnation (under Augustus!) could be read as the progressive realisation of divine purpose. The spreading and establishing of Christianity over the world, inaugurated under Augustus, was being completed under the Christian emperors of the fourth century. The divine purpose was written plainly in the course of events, and could be diagnosed from their direction. In Orosius's scheme of history there was room for set-backs on the road; but there was no room for reversal, disaster or tragedy. Thus, he argued, the world was now Christian, and there could be no more persecutions of the Church (except for the final persecution just before the *eschaton*); and even volcanoes were more sleepy now than they had been in the past.

This was the kind of theology of history which Augustine had come to reject, and the kind of historical optimism which he repudiated specifically as transgressing the required agnosticism about divine purpose.[1] But Orosius's perspective, in one way or another, continued to dominate the imaginations of late Roman Christians. The barbarian invasions and settlements of the fifth century were seen as part of God's plan. For Orosius the Germans had been brought within the orbit of the Roman Empire in order that they might be assimilated into Christendom. 'We ought to praise and extol God's mercy, which has brought the nations—even at the cost of our weakness—to the knowledge of so great a truth, which might otherwise have remained inaccessible to them.'[2] Augustine's protest against such an identification of the Church with a social order, merged in a 'Christendom', went almost unheeded until the Roman Empire was itself a distant memory in Western Europe. Then, two centuries and more after his death, the great Dark Age historians of their own nations, Isidore of Seville, Paul the Deacon, and, above all, the English Bede, could write their histories in a totally different perspective: for them the Roman Empire was a state among many, which had had its day and its greatness. The Goths, the Lombards, the English had their own Christian destinies, and it was a history which could be

---

[1] Cf. Ch. 3 above, p. 54, n. 4. [2] *Hist.* VII, 41; cf. Ch. 2 above, p. 40, n. 3.

written without their being brought into any essential relation with the Empire. Its existing remnant in the East, 'the Empire of the Greeks', had no universal mission or claims in their eyes.

The historical developments brought about what Augustine's theological protest failed to bring about: men could think of Christianity without thinking of it within the framework of a Roman Empire as its God-willed political and social *milieu*. In the West the Empire had slowly disappeared, a mosaic of German kingdoms taken its place, and the Church had emerged, if not unchanged, at any rate with a consciousness of uninterrupted life and identity. But it had not learnt the lesson of Augustine's historical agnosticism. For the Church, instead of being identified with the social order in which it had grown and taken shape, the Roman, now became identified with an order which it helped, in very large measure, to create, to mould and to dominate.

In the ancient world, and throughout the period of late antiquity, the Church had been placed in the midst of a world from which it had to learn and to receive almost everything except its own peculiar saving message. If there was a risk of its becoming too closely identified with the Roman Empire, as there was by the end of the fourth century, at least the society to which it was linked was one of great cultural variety, a world of sophisticated intellectual life with its own independent origins and some surviving momentum. Some of this world the Church came to terms with and made its own, and in doing so made itself the medium through which much of the legacy of the ancient world was passed on to medieval Europe. Historians, especially some Roman Catholic writers, have sometimes been too ready to applaud uncritically the Church's role in civilising Western Europe and in transmitting much of classical culture to Germanic barbarians. They have failed to see the enormous cost to the Church that this civilising mission entailed. The Latin Church became gradually cut off from the Greek East, and North Africa, and ended by being identified with Western Europe. Here it helped to create a culture and a society over which it exercised a dominating influence for centuries.

It became identified with a culture and a society which did not even possess the degree of independence due to largely independent origin. Too much in it was the Church's own contribution. There was little left for the Church to learn and much to teach; little to receive and much to give. The developing barbarian nations soon came to form a recognisable 'Western Christendom', with which the Latin Church became more intimately and more disastrously identified than it had ever been with the Roman Empire. As its political vehicle it created a medieval empire. In the course of the middle ages the Church's destiny became inextricably tied up with secular forms, institutions and a culture largely of its own making but no less constricting than bondage to secular structures of alien origin. By a supreme paradox, it was a writer who took—or thought he took—his inspiration for his great panoramic vision of universal history from Augustine's *City of God*, Otto of Freising, who, in the twelfth century, saw the process of human history as a growing together of the heavenly and the earthly cities. Since the time of Constantine, and especially since Theodosius, 'not only the peoples, but even their rulers, for the most part, have become Catholics. From then on, it seems to me', he wrote, 'that I have been writing the history not of two cities but, almost, of one, which I call "Christendom".'[1] Augustine's conception of history as the careers of two interwoven, eschatologically opposed cities has here become the very thing which it was designed to undermine: the theological prop of a sacral society, of a Christian political establishment in which the divine purpose in history lay enshrined. It was the Emperor Frederick Barbarossa, Otto of Freising's nephew, or someone in his circle, who first called the German Empire the 'Holy Roman Empire'.

Otto envisaged as a possibility, indeed as a possibility fast being actualised, what would for Augustine have constituted a piece of meaningless nonsense: the growing together of the two cities, with their radical and ultimate conflict. Otto's vision of history owed

[1] *Chron.* v, Prol. On the meaning of *ecclesia*, here rendered by 'Christendom', cf. Lammers, Introduction to *Otto von Freising*, xii and xlvi–l.

almost everything to Orosius, almost nothing to Augustine. There were, throughout the middle ages, apocalyptic thinkers, writers and groups, often on the edges of the ecclesiastical establishment, who rejected this kind of ratification of the existing order. The ideal of a pre-Constantinian 'Apostolic' Church, poor, persecuted, and at odds with its world, remained a symbol which often reasserted its power. (There are traces of it even in Otto of Freising, especially when he writes on monasticism.) But the medieval Church did not possess the intellectual and imaginative resources with which it could really have liberated itself from the 'Christendom' of its making. It belonged too much to this setting to be capable of belonging to the world which was coming into being in the course of the political, social, intellectual and religious upheavals which followed each other unremittingly, especially from the sixteenth century onwards. The cost of belonging to the future is readiness not to belong to the past.

The social order and the intellectual world in which the Church found itself at home disappeared. The various fragments into which Christendom became split faced the problem created by this transformation in various ways. Of the apocalyptic consciousness of being set apart from a hostile world and gathered into a holy community of the elect, the Anabaptist movement is the most striking example. Calvinism and Roman Catholicism, in their different ways, both manifested the urge to create a new 'world' for themselves. Calvinism, especially in Geneva and in New England, showed much of the energy which generates a sacral political community appropriate to the life of the elect in the world. Roman Catholicism, perhaps less consciously and more dangerously, embarked on the creation of an intellectual world alternative to the real world of Western Europe since the sixteenth century. The emergence of this alternative intellectual and spiritual world is what made a man like Friedrich von Hügel feel that since the Counter-Reformation a Roman Catholic was condemned to inhabit an intellectual world quite alien to the real intellectual world of Western Europe. It is really only very recently that

Christians have widely begun to see the present as an opportunity to break the fetters of the past; to recognise that if the world in which they, as Christians, are 'at home' collapses, the response should not be an attempt to create or to find another world in which the Church may thus find itself 'at home', but rather a determination to enter into the much more ambiguous relation with the world which Christian eschatological hope demands.

ESCHATOLOGY AS POLITICS

The great discovery which lies like a deep gulf between Augustine and Orosius (and all their intellectual progeny) is the eschatological dimension of Christian hope. The fulfilment promised to man is revealed as a unique possibility given in Christ and only achieved in His kingdom. No historical conditions can provide so much as a shadow of this fulfilment, no historical process can lead either towards or away from it. It is an act of God, or rather a history of God's acts concluded in Jesus, that fully revealed the promise; and it is only God's act that will, finally, fulfil it. Augustine knew that the Christian hope was too radical to require the buttress of any optimism about the future. There must be room in history for the sharpest reversal of all that one could discern as 'progress'. The darkest tragedy could not shake Christian hope. Historical optimism and pessimism are equally alien to its eschatological transcendence, and to the historical agnosticism which is its correlative. Christian political commitment is no less and no more than the operation of this eschatological hope in present society.

Augustine's assessment of the Roman Empire and of the state in general coheres, not unnaturally, with his views on secular history; for a secular institution, such as a state, is quite simply a localised and temporally circumscribed slice of secular history. The ambivalence in his theology of the Roman state, as of the state in general, is the political corollary of the ambivalence he saw in all secular history. The roots of this ambivalence may be seen in Augustine's rejection of the two opposed assessments of the Roman state in fourth-century theology: the one found in the current fashions of sacralisation of the Empire, the other found in the Donatist repudiation of the Empire as profane, if not diabolical. Alternatively stated, they are seen in the recognition, with the Donatists, that the true Christian is always and necessarily at odds with the world, and the recognition, with the 'establishment' Catholic of the imperial Church, that the social order does not constitute an irrelevance to the Christian life and that political engagement and commitment are inescapable duties laid upon the Christian by the exigencies of his social existence. The two sides of this attitude are equally essential to Augustine's understanding of political life, and equally essential consequences of his eschatological understanding of the Christian hope. For this hope is necessarily both critical and creative; and this duality is the fundamental reason for the Augustinian ambivalence of politics. It will be as well to take its two facets in turn.

In his rejection of the Constantinian, or more exactly, the Theodosian, establishment of Christianity in the Roman Empire, and of the theology behind the 'Christian Empire', Augustine devised the charter for a critique of all sacral conceptions of society. The Christian cannot be 'at home' in the world, as the Donatists were insisting, along with the old African tradition which Augustine shared with them. But, unlike the Donatists, Augustine (and his ex-Donatist mentor, Tyconius) saw the Christian's homelessness in the world not in sociological but in eschatological terms (Chapter 5). There was no need for Christians to be set apart, sociologically, as a community separated from the 'world', hated and persecuted, uncontaminated by it and visibly 'over against the world'. On the contrary: the Christian community was, quite simply, the world as redeemed and reconciled. What defined it over against the 'world' was not sociological separation, but its eschatological orientation. What prevented the Christian from being at home in his world was not that he had an alternative home in the Church, but his faith in the transformation of the world through Christ's victory over sin and death and his hope in the final sharing of this victory in His kingdom. His sense of identity in the world comes not from membership of a closed group, but from the eschatological posture of his hope: 'by whom our nothing has a definition!...Our absent Presence, and our future Now' (RICHARD CRASHAW, 'Answer for hope'). The quality of the Christian's strangeness to the world was, on Augustine's premises, bound to be something very different from the simple hatred and opposition characteristic of men for whom being set apart from the world meant being taken out of it, set over against it in their own social *milieu*, in a holy community. It is a strangeness to the world which appears in the perspective in which the Christian sees and handles his world. Worldly values cannot, for him, be simply endorsed and ratified, nor rejected; they must be given a more complex assessment in eschatological terms. The characteristically Christian assessment of all human values is structured in an eschatological perspective. This is what defines the peculiarity of Augustine's 'pilgrim city' in this world: its members, unlike those of the earthly city, who are fully at home in their temporal concerns, refer these concerns to the enjoyment of 'eternal peace' (Chapter 3). Thus when a Christian, from such an eschatological perspective, affirms some secular value, some human enterprise or achievement, his affirmation will not be any simple self-identification. His peculiar posture in the world precludes identifying himself with its values without some reservation. The fullest endorsement of secular value is tinged with criticism. What others may affirm simply as 'good', the Christian has to subject to a more exacting standard. His 'good' must survive the more deeply penetrating questioning from an eschatological perspective.

It should be clear from the summary of Augustine's eschatological assessment of all human enterprise that 'political Augustinianism'[1] is, of its nature, politically radical. It is bound to be unremittingly critical of all and any human arrangements, any actual and even any imaginable forms of social order. Seen in an

---

[1] I am here using the phrase in a very different sense from that given it by Arquillière, *L'Augustinisme politique*, 4, quoted above (Ch. 6), p. 153, n. 1, to mean the political theory implied in Augustine's theology of the *saeculum*.

eschatological perspective, there can be no existing or possible
society in which there is nothing to criticise. The reference to the
eschatological Kingdom, the fully human community of love
promised by God, discloses injustice and inhumanity in the best of
social structures. The Christian hope is of its nature a searchlight
which, turned on its social *milieu*, seeks out the opportunities for
protest. The Gospel can never be at home in the world, and cannot
fail to bring a true believer into conflict with any existing order of
things. It is in essential and permanent tension with the world.
This tension should be a fruitful one, from which awkward
questions are continually being put to the world. Hope is a
permanently unsettling force, seeking to prevent social institutions from becoming rigid and fixed, always inclined to treat
the *status quo* with suspicion. No one has given more powerful
expression to this radicalism of Christian hope than Jürgen
Moltmann:

...faith, wherever it develops into hope, causes not rest but unrest,
not patience but impatience. It does not calm the unquiet heart, but is
itself this unquiet heart in man. Those who hope in Christ can no
longer put up with reality as it is, but begin to suffer under it, to
contradict it. Peace with God means conflict with the world, for the
goad of the promised future stabs inexorably into the flesh of every
unfulfilled present. If we had before our eyes only what we see, then
we should cheerfully or reluctantly reconcile ourselves with things as
they happen to be. That we do not reconcile ourselves, that there is no
pleasant harmony between us and reality, is due to our unquenchable
hope. This hope keeps man unreconciled, until the great day of the
fulfilment of all the promises of God. It keeps him *in statu viatoris*,
in that unresolved openness to world questions which has its origin in
the promise of God in the resurrection of Christ and can therefore be
resolved only when the same God fulfills his promise. This hope makes
the Christian Church a constant disturbance in human society, seeking
as the latter does to stabilise itself into a 'continuing city'. It makes the
Church the source of continual new impulses towards the realisation
of righteousness, freedom and humanity here in the light of the promised
future that is to come. This Church is committed to 'answer for the
hope' that is in it (I Peter 3.15). It is called in question 'on account of

the hope and resurrection of the dead' (Acts 23.6). Wherever that happens, Christianity embraces its true nature and becomes a witness of the future of Christ.[1]

If his eschatological hope keeps a Christian restlessly critical of his society, it also, and at the same time, provides the impulse for innovation, improvement and advance. Eschatological restlessness in the present is not mere unshaped discontent or unrealistic perfectionism. There is no place for such politically sterile withdrawal in the Christian hope. Rather, it is realistically constructive:

The believing hope will itself provide *inexhaustible resources* for the creative, inventive imagination of love. It constantly provokes and produces thinking of an anticipatory kind in love to man and the world, in order to give shape to the newly dawning possibilities in the light of the promised future, in order as far as possible to create here the best that is possible, because what is promised is within the bounds of possibility. Thus it will constantly arouse the 'passion for the possible', inventiveness and elasticity in self-transformation, in breaking with the old and coming to terms with the new.[2]

The critical and the creative aspects of Christian hope combine to define the peculiarly Christian posture in politics. It is one which is bound to be subversive in that it must subject the existing social order—whatever it is—to a questioning more radical than that to which it may be exposed from any political party or programme. In this sense the Gospel is 'revolutionary', and a theological ratification of the Constantinian establishment constitutes a betrayal of the Gospel by the Church in the course of its history. But more caution is needed in attaching the label 'revolutionary' to the Gospel than is sometimes realised, for instance among the 'Catholic left'. The revolutionary is a man with a programme or an ideology, which he seeks to realise. It is very easy to slip from eschatological hope directed to the coming Kingdom into revolutionary strategy directed to the establishment of a socialist society, without being conscious of the gulf between the divine act which alone establishes the one and the human work which builds the

---

[1] *Theology of hope*, 21-2.   [2] *Ibid.* 34-5; italics in original. Cf. *ibid.* 288-9.

other. Augustine's repudiation of the classical 'politics of perfection' was, in effect, a repudiation of any hope of resolving the tensions inherent in fallen society through human means (Chapter 4). In contrast to the revolutionary with his programme and his strategies for realising it, the man whose hope is eschatological has no programme, no ideology, and no strategy. His hope is set on a resolution of tension and conflict far beyond any ideology. In so far as an ideology commits a man to a vision of an ultimately desirable form of social order, eschatological hope is the very negation of ideology. It asserts that the Gospel is in radical conflict with the world, and must be so until the end, whatever shape 'the world' may assume—even if the 'world' were one shaped by the Gospel itself, even if the society were permeated by Christian inspiration and formed under Christian impulse. The Christian hope is radically revolutionary in that it must question at its roots all forms of social order. But it is also anti-ideological and anti-utopian in that it cannot hold out any positive ideal or utopia as an alternative.

Outwardly, therefore, a revolutionary hope of this kind may look very like a liberal reformism, or like 'social engineering', and it is compatible with a widely ranging political eclecticism. Living with a transcendent hope but without a unifying political ideology, political discernment and action must become fragmentary, *ad hoc*, piecemeal. It may well be that this involves a denial of a 'genuine and true response to an aspiration which is ineradicable in man—the aspiration to understand, explain and unify his experience';[1] but eschatological hope forces the Christian to renounce such an aspiration, and at the same time it reconciles him with the fragmentary, piecemeal and *ad hoc* character of his political enterprise. The human urge for a total and unified response must be seen as an eschatological objective, not to be anticipated in the present world of politics. Christian hope deflates all ideologies and utopias: in their place it sets provisional goals, to be realised piecemeal, and to be kept flexible and perpetually subject

[1] Wicker, *First the political kingdom*, 63.

to revision and renewal in the light of political experience seen in an eschatological perspective. It resists political programmes which seem to make an ultimate claim on men, for programmes belong, of their nature, to what Dietrich Bonhoeffer called the 'penultimate'.[1] Bonhoeffer's 'penultimate' is the almost exact equivalent of Augustine's *saeculum*, the temporal reality of the two eschatological ultimates in their present inextricably confused and interwoven state. Like Augustine, Bonhoeffer resisted any attempt to bring the ultimate categories into play prematurely: 'Does one not in some cases, by remaining deliberately in the penultimate, perhaps point all the more genuinely to the ultimate, which God will speak in his own time?'[2]

The radically revolutionary character of Christian hope makes it, in practice, compatible with almost any political programme which does not set itself up as an ideology with absolute claims upon men's ultimate loyalties. Christian political commitment not only permits but demands intelligent planning for the future, for meeting the needs of society; and it will reinforce the impulse behind such planning by the recognition that it is a duty laid upon Christians as a demand of love. But it must resist the confusion of levels which comes of erecting political objectives into absolutes. It protects men from the willingness to sacrifice one another to a programme, an ideology, a political vision. Indeed the most pressing and urgent social tasks, seen in the light of eschatological hope, assume the features of circumscribed problems, capable of being dealt with on a restricted canvas, without raising ultimate questions. This highly pragmatic posture is one of the chief characteristics attributed by Harvey Cox to modern, secular, 'technopolitan' man:

He approaches problems by isolating them from irrelevant considerations, by bringing to bear the knowledge of different specialists, and by getting ready to grapple with a new series of problems when these have been provisionally solved. Life for him is a set of problems, not an unfathomable mystery. He brackets off the things that cannot be

---

[1] *Ethics*, 84 f. For an interpretation, cf. Markus, 'A relevant pattern'.   [2] *Ibid.* 85.

dealt with and deals with those that can. He wastes little time thinking about 'ultimate' or 'religious' questions. And he can live with highly provisional solutions.[1]

Christian hope, just because it is eschatological, resists the investing of immediate projects, policies and even social ideals, with any absolute character. It draws the believer into participation in political life and into full membership of his society without tethering him to any ideology or any final political vision. In the political process he stands on the same ground as all others, with whatever divergent ultimate beliefs and values. In the *saeculum* we must be content with the provisional, the ultimately ambiguous, the 'secular'; for the ultimates are here inextricably intertwined, and must not be prematurely unravelled.

Augustine's attack on the 'sacral' conception of the Empire liberated the Roman state, and by implication, all politics, from the direct hegemony of the sacred. Society became intrinsically 'secular' in the sense that it is not as such committed to any particular ultimate loyalty. It is the sphere in which different individuals with different beliefs and loyalties pursue their common objectives in so far as they coincide. His 'secularisation' of the realm of politics implies a pluralistic, religiously neutral civil community. Historically, of course, such a society lay entirely beyond the horizons of Augustine's world. After centuries of development it has begun to grow from the soil of what has been Western Christendom; but it is still far from securely established in the modern world. It is assailed from many sides. Even Christians have not generally learned to welcome the disintegration of a 'Christian society' as a profound liberation for the Gospel. Augustinian theology should at least undermine Christian opposition to an open, pluralist, secular society.

We have seen that Augustine gradually realised that the final resolution of the tensions endemic in the human situation could not be achieved in this life on earth. The sphere of politics belongs irrevocably to the realm infected with sin. Politically organised

[1] *The secular city*, 63.

life was itself a consequence of the Fall. Political arrangements had as their *raison d'être* the safeguarding and fostering of a lowly form of 'peace': the public order and security which human sin has made unstable in society. This view gave political structures and political action a comparatively modest, though vital role in society. The tendency of Augustine's theology of the *saeculum* was to restrict the area of politics to what Aristotle referred to as the realm of 'the goods men fight about'.[1] The greater goods, those from which men could expect real fulfilment and ultimate satisfaction, were beyond the scope of politics. Politics, in Augustinian terminology, occupy the area in which human contrivance secures a living space for society in the midst of strife and conflict (Chapter 4).

In contrast with this sense of the precariousness of human order secured and maintained in the teeth of chaos and perpetually threatened by deep human forces poised delicately between civilisation and savagery—a sense so powerfully explored by William Golding[2]—the Aristotelian tradition in Christian political thought saw human social order as part of an overarching cosmic order. This tradition eclipsed the Augustinian during the thirteenth century (Appendix C), and has enjoyed a great vogue, especially in forming the theoretical background of much papal political teaching, and widely among Roman Catholic political writers, until very recent times.[3] Like the Augustinian view, this, too, had its roots in the New Testament insistence on the state as divinely ordained. But it rejected the distinction which we have seen to be fundamental to Augustinian political theory between

---

[1] *perimacheta agatha—Eth. Nic.* IX, 8, 1169a 21.

[2] I am thinking not only of the exploration of the 'schism in the soul' in terms of the break up of a society in *Lord of the Flies*, but also of the powerful image in *The Inheritors* of a community of pre-human innocents, at home in their world and living in concord among themselves, under the unquestioned authority of their elders accepted as a fact of nature, and Golding's confrontation of it with a human political community, with fear, tension, conflict and power. The Christian Aristotelian tradition would invite us to see the civil community in terms of something like Golding's 'People', the innocent pre-humans; on the Augustinian approach the more appropriate of Golding's images would be that of the 'Men'.

[3] The great exception among Roman Catholic thinkers is Newman. Cf. Kenny, *The political thought*, esp. 75.

divine ordinance in natural forms and processes, and divine ordinance in human institutions and actions (Chapter 4 and Appendix B), and assimilated the latter to the former.[1] Order in society was to be understood on the model of natural order in the *cosmos*. This way of thinking gave less weight than the Augustinian tradition to the eschatological perspective of the New Testament 'doctrine' of the state.[2] It is cast in cosmological rather than in historical and eschatological categories. Thomas Aquinas, who must be seen as the father of this tradition in Christian political thought, conceived the political order as part of the natural order and political subordination among men as a form of natural subordination of inferior to superior. Political government was analogous to God's government of the world, to the soul's rule over its body or to a father's over his children. Such analogies—all deliberately rejected by Augustine—express the fundamental conviction behind this model of political authority: that government is part of the chain of natural agencies provided by God for the realisation of human purposes, and exists in order to bring men to their ultimate fulfilment.

Just as the functions of natural agents proceed from the way they are constituted, so the activities of human agents proceed from human will. But among natural agents it is necessary that the higher should move the lower to their activity, by means of the superiority of natural powers divinely assigned to the higher. Hence it is necessary that among human agents, too, the higher should move the lower, through his will, in virtue of the divinely ordained authority of the higher.[3]

The subordination of subject to ruler is one instance of the natural subordination of lower to higher, part of a hierarchically ordered universe in which every being has its appropriate level, below some, above others, in an order of agents acting upon one another and being acted upon in accordance with their proper place in the

---

[1] Aquinas distinguished between two modes of subjection to the eternal law, one for rational and one for irrational creatures: *S. T.* I–II, 93.5, but he thought of a single order in which both participate, though in their different modes.

[2] On this see especially Cullmann, *The state in the New Testament*.

[3] Thomas Aquinas, *S. T.* II–II, 104.1.

hierarchy. This was a very Greek vision of the *cosmos*, one that had entered deeply into the minds of medieval Christians. It found a supreme expression in the 'great sea of being' of the first Canto of Dante's *Paradiso*, in which each being has its natural bent bearing it in its assigned direction towards its goal. Man had his own place in the hierarchy, somewhat above the beasts of the field, a little lower than the angels. Furthermore, the human community was itself stretched out, so to speak, vertically, along a number of grades of the cosmic hierarchy, bridging the gap between the angels and the beasts. Men were far from equal by nature, and would not have been so even in the state of primal innocence from which Adam fell. Political authority, and its converse, the subject's duty of obedience to its bearers, were based on this natural in-equality among men. Just as a child, subordinated by nature to its father, needs to be ruled by him in order to realise its natural potentialities, so men need to be subject to their rulers to realise theirs. Man is by nature a political animal, and politically organised community exists to promote the achievement of ultimate human purpose, the good life and its heavenly consummation. Man's final end is only to be attained through the ministry of the Church. The task of government is to act in partnership with it to direct men's footsteps on the way towards eternal life:

Since the goal of a good life lived here is blessedness in heaven, it pertains to a king's office to promote the good life of the people in such a way that it is fitted for the acquisition of heavenly blessedness; that is to say, he must command those things which lead to heavenly blessedness and prohibit, as far as possible, what is inconsistent with this.[1]

This is no model for a pluralist society. Its social cosmology springs from an assurance about the existing order of things, both in the *cosmos* and in society, in which there is little doubt about aims and directions. Man knows his place in the general scheme of things, and men know their place in society. There is room for rebellion, but not for revolution.

[1] *De reg. princ.* I, 15.

By contrast, the Augustinian vision springs from a sense of conflicting purposes, of uncertainties of direction and of tensions unresolvable in society. In place of the Aristotelian confidence in the established order, the Augustinian tradition is inspired rather by a sense of its precariousness, and by an awareness of the perpetual proximity of disintegration. The Jewish rabbis and Christian Fathers who saw the function of the state in terms of preventing men from devouring one another like fish, were writing, like Augustine, from a consciousness of conflict, of upheaval and insecurity. It is no accident that among modern theologians it is Karl Barth to whom we owe, especially in his post-war writings, the most powerful re-statement of this tradition of political theology:

The civil community embraces everyone living within its area. Its members share no common awareness of their relationship to God, and such an awareness cannot be an element in the legal system established by the civil community. No appeal can be made to the Word or Spirit of God in the running of its affairs. The civil community as such is blind and ignorant...[It] can only have external, relative and pro-visional tasks and aims...

The Christian community is aware of the need for the civil com-munity, and it alone takes the need absolutely seriously. For—because it knows of the Kingdom and grace of God—it knows of man's presumption and the plainly destructive consequences of man's pre-sumption. It knows how dangerous man is and how endangered by himself. It knows him as a sinner, that is, as a being who is always on the point of opening the sluices through which, if he were not checked in time, chaos and nothingness would break in and bring human time to an end.

[The civil community] serves to protect man from the invasion of chaos and therefore to give him time: time for the preaching of the Gospel; time for repentance; time for faith.

...The Christian community participates—on the basis of and by belief in the divine revelation—in the human search for the best form, for the most fitting system of political organisation; but it is also aware of the limits of all the political forms and systems which man can discover (even with the co-operation of the Church), and it will beware of playing off one political concept—even the 'democratic' concept—as *the* Christian concept, against all others. Since it proclaims the Kingdom of God it has to maintain its own hopes and questions in the face of all purely political concepts.[1]

Here, once more, we encounter the neutral, pluralist society of the Augustinian tradition, excluding ultimate commitments from its sphere of interest, content with securing a living space against chaos. On this Karl Barth could take his stand against the diabolical pretensions of Hitler's state; on this, too, he could take his stand against the theologians, such as Emil Brunner and Reinhold Niebuhr, who, at the time of the Amsterdam Assembly of the World Council of Churches in 1948, could not support his refusal to condemn Communism as anti-Christian. Like Augustine, Barth knew something of the precariousness of human order in society, and of the proximity of chaos. Like Augustine, he recognised the civil community as a human work, blessed and commissioned by God, for keeping chaos and disintegration in check. Like Augustine, he rejected all attempts to compromise the transcendence of the Kingdom which is the object of Christian hope: 'It belongs to the very nature of the state that it is not and cannot become the kingdom of God.'[2]

ESCHATOLOGY AS ECCLESIA

The Donatists of Augustine's day considered that their own religious communities constituted the true Church. They were the representatives of the old Christian tradition, especially lively in Africa, for which the true *ecclesia* was the eschatological community, gathered out of the world, called forth into the wilderness, there to await the coming of the Lord, unspotted by the worldliness of secular society and its culture. In their eyes 'sacred' and 'secular' were two separate spheres, each contained within their own sociological *milieu*. Between the two there could be no overlap. Outside the pure Church there lay an unredeemed, profane world (Chapter 5).

[1] Barth, 'The Christian community', 16–17, 20, 21, 25.   [2] *Ibid.* 31.

For Augustine the *ecclesia* was the eschatological community in a very different sense. For the Donatists' sociological interpretation of the Church's holiness and apartness he substituted an eschatological one. The Church was holy not because it was here and now the congregation of the holy, the unspotted or elect, but because as a community it had an essential relationship with the heavenly city. Only in that community, as finally constituted by God's predestining choice, will the elect be gathered together to form a community free from all contamination. Here and now the *ecclesia*, though 'holy', must always be a mixed body. In it, as in the 'world', the two cities are inextricably intertwined. From this point of view, there is no difference between 'Church' and 'world'. Augustine, as we have seen, deliberately upheld against the Donatists the appropriateness of speaking of the Church in 'worldly' terms, and indeed defined the Church as 'the world reconciled'. The Church is no more 'sacred' than the world is 'profane': they are both 'secular'. In this final section I begin by exploring the meaning and some of the implications of Augustine's 'secularisation' of the *ecclesia*, and I conclude by considering how, in Augustine's eschatological perspective, it is possible to distinguish the *ecclesia* in the world at all.

For Augustine the *ecclesia* must always be 'secular' in the sense that it is, during its earthly career, like any other human grouping, part of the *saeculum*. Its membership embraces citizens of both the heavenly and the earthly cities. It cannot be identified, *tout court*, with the body of the elect, those predestined to be saved. In this sense it is in an eschatological perspective ambivalent: like all human institutions, the Church comes under the Judgement. Only that one Judgement can discern in its midst what is destined to be saved and what reprobate. The history of the Church is no more sacred than the history of anything else between the Incarnation and Parousia (Chapter 1). The divine oracles alone provide the clue with the aid of which 'sacred' history may be distinguished from 'secular', and on the history of this interim period they are silent. What place any episode of the Church's history plays in the unfolding of the divine purpose in history we can no more know than we can know this about any episode of secular history. We do know the meaning of the Church's continued existence throughout the period, for to that the scriptures have provided the clue, in the same way as we know the meaning of the secular history of the period as a whole: it is the gap in the sacred history, between Incarnation and Parousia, the age of the Church. But beyond this, the history of the Church must be subject to as stark an agnosticism about its ultimate significance as the history of anything else. The Church's mission to preach the Gospel to all men until the end, and perhaps some of the structures through which this commission is to be carried out, are indeed laid down within the New Testament. It is true, of course, that the implications of the New Testament are themselves far from simple, and that to establish the relevance of its witness to one or other ecclesiastical institution or function can be a task of considerable delicacy. It is no part of my present purpose to discuss what part of the Church's life and structure can be grounded, directly or indirectly, upon the New Testament. Whether it is much or little, the essential kernel of the Augustinian 'secularisation' of the Church is that beyond its limits ecclesiastical institutions and their history are in no way privileged above the 'secular'. They share the same ultimate ambivalence, the same relativity, the same liability to infection with sin and distortion through betrayal; also, the same possibilities of creative holiness and redeeming love.

God's work in the world is only in part carried on by and in the *ecclesia*. On the one hand, the *ecclesia* is always capable of falling away, indeed is in part bound to constitute a standing betrayal of the Gospel simply because it is a *corpus permixtum*. On the other hand, the vehicle of God's work is the City of God in its earthly pilgrimage: the part of mankind whose hearts are invisibly ruled by God, whose love, hope and faith are shaped by this ultimate loyalty, perhaps obscurely and implicitly. And this City is not the Church, though it will exist within the Church as well as outside it. The path of its pilgrimage is hidden, its working is anonymous:

only at the last will they appear for what they were. Christ's presence in the world cannot be simply identified with the Church.

We are in the presence here of the paradoxical relationship of the Church's mission to the salvation of the world. This relation lies in the mystery of the divine purpose: 'God our saviour desires all men to be saved...' (1 Tim. 2:4): the object of Christ's redemptive work is the world. The Church, Augustine had said, *is* the world—the world redeemed and reconciled. Yet, it is also, in some sense, not identical with the world but *in* the world. Even a 'worldly' Church is in some way 'set apart', recognisable as an institution among others, as something distinct in the world—as 'visible', in the traditional vocabulary of theology. Are we then to say that salvation is somehow confined to the empirically circumscribed thing which we can recognise in the world as 'Church'? Although Augustine was, as a matter of fact, inclined to answer in the affirmative, though with some important qualifications, few theologians, even of the Roman communion, would now accept such a solution. If then we refuse, on the one hand, thus to confine salvation to a visible grouping and, on the other hand, to jettison the visibility of the Church as a distinct entity in the world, there is a wide gap between the visible Church and the Kingdom in which the redeemed world is to be consummated. What is the visible Church in relation to this Kingdom, on the one hand, and in relation to the world on the other?

The Church proclaims the inauguration of God's Kingdom by Jesus, it is not identical with it. The Church is not this Kingdom, even in its germ or chrysalis. For there is no continuous development, no growth or maturation of the Church into the Kingdom. The Kingdom is established by God's act alone. Man can only wait in hope, with faith and repentance. The Church lives still as a pilgrim Church, waiting for the final fulfilment of the promises made to it. Hans Küng has expressed this in a fine passage:

While ekklesia is something essentially of the present, something finite, basileia is something which, although it has irrupted into the present, belongs fundamentally to the future. Ekklesia is a pilgrimage through the interim period of the last days, something provisional; basileia is the final glory at the end of all time, something definitive. Ekklesia embraces sinners and righteous, basileia is the kingdom of the righteous, of the saints. Ekklesia grows from below, can be organised, is the product of development and progress and dialectic, in short is definitely the work of man; basileia comes from above, is unprepared action, an incalculable event, in short is definitely the work of God.[1]

The Kingdom is the final consummation of God's creative intention: not the Church. The Church is an interim institution, whose distinct existence in the world is itself provisional. The very duality of Church and world will be overcome in the eschatological kingdom.

'Jesus announced the Kingdom, and it was the Church that came', as Alfred Loisy once observed.[2] Shorn of its irony, the statement is a precise expression of the state of affairs during the period between the first and second Advents. Jesus announced the presence of the Kingdom in his own person. In him all things were made new, the promises of God made to his people were fulfilled. And yet all things seemed, and still do seem, to continue unchanged, and will so continue until the end. During this period, the 'last age', the Church is set in the midst of the world to bear witness to its Lord and to his coming Kingdom. The Church is not Christ's presence in the world; it is the sign of that presence. The provisional distinct existence of the Church in the world during this epoch as an empirical, sociological fact derives not from any need to embody holiness in a social structure (as for an ecclesiology of the Donatist or Cyprianic type), but from its being a sign. It is a sign because it is constituted as what it is by the mission laid upon it by the Lord: to bear witness to him and to his Kingdom. If it is to be a sign, it must be visible, that is to say it must be in some way perceptible as distinct from other things in the 'world'. Though part of the world and not taken out of it, it is given a special status within it as the sign of something still to come, a Kingdom whose

---

[1] *The Church*, 93. [2] Quoted in Peterson, 'Die Kirche', 411.

advent is based on a coming which has already taken place once and for all. As a sign, the Church points both into the past and into the future. In preaching its Lord and his Kingdom the Church actualises itself as the sign instituted by its Lord pointing to the consummation of his work. The meaning of the Church is not something that resides in itself, that it has as a possession: it is to be found in its relation to something of which it is the herald, an 'anticipatory sign'.[1]

Augustine came near to working out a theology of the Church in terms of its being a sign in his sacramental theology, but he did not in fact elaborate an ecclesiology on such lines. He did have at his disposal a sophisticated theory of signs and meaning,[2] which, though not devised for this purpose, could have done full justice to his conception of the Church. A sign, as he defines it, is 'something which, in addition to being what it is perceived to be, also brings something else to mind'.[3] Anything that can function as a sign is thus capable of treatment either in its own right as a *res*, without considering it in its signifying function, or in its function as the bearer of a meaning, as a *signum*. This is true even of things such as words, in which we would have little or no interest but for their meaning.[4] A word treated as sign (*signum*) is an element in meaningful communication; treated as a thing (*res*) it would be an optical pattern of marks on paper or a sound pattern, a system of vibrations or perhaps of anatomical functioning. A sign, then, generally, may be considered either from the point of view of what it is in itself, prescinding from its significance, or from the point of view of what it is as used meaningfully, with significance.

Augustine formulated his theory of signs for the purpose of expounding the method to be employed in the study and exposition

---

[1] Küng, *The Church*, 96. Despite some profound insights in F. D. Maurice's work, it is among theologians of the Roman communion that a theology conceived in such terms has been furthest developed in modern times. Cf. Schillebeeckx, *Christ the sacrament*; Rahner, 'The Church and the sacraments'; McCabe, *The new creation*, among some stimulating essays.

[2] For an account, Markus, 'St Augustine on signs'.

[3] *signum est enim res praeter speciem quam ingerit sensibus aliud aliquid ex se faciens in cogitationem venire*—De doctr. chr. II, 1.1.   [4] *Ibid.* I, 2.2.

of scripture, particularly for the purpose of relating scriptural figures or 'types' which pointed beyond themselves as anticipations of future 'anti-types'. The theory could be given wide applications; its bearings on sacramental theology, in particular, have been much explored. I am not aware that Augustine ever used it to expound a conception of the Church as a sign. But there is at least one close approximation to this to be found in his work. In the *City of God* a famous passage represents the Holy City of the Old Testament as prefiguring the heavenly city:[1]

A certain shadow, or prophetic image of this City [the heavenly] served here on earth to signify rather than to present this City...

It [the earthly Jerusalem], too, was called a holy city, on account rather of its symbolic meaning than of any factual truth, whose realisation still lay in the future...

...A part therefore of the earthly city is here made into an image of the heavenly city, signifying not itself [the earthly Jerusalem] but another [the heavenly Jerusalem]...

Thus we find in the earthly City [i.e. the pre-Christian world] two forms, one presenting itself, the other serving to represent the heavenly City which it manifests by the significance of its presence.

Jerusalem, the physical city, is given symbolic reference to the heavenly Jerusalem; but it does not on that account cease to be what it is, a city of the Jews of the Old Covenant. The identical treatment could be applied to the Church: a part of the world reconciled in Christ is distinguished within this world by its special signification; the Church is the world set apart for signifying and pointing to the coming Kingdom. Taken by itself, without its dimension as sign, the Church is not distinguished from the world. Taken with its signification it anticipates the Kingdom as its herald. Although it cannot be identified with the eschatological Kingdom, yet it may be called 'the Kingdom of God' or 'of Christ'[2] just as

---

[1] xv, 2, somewhat freely translated. The correct interpretation of this passage has been established, definitively in my view, by Cranz, '*De Civitate Dei*, xv, 2', against Leisegang, 'Der Ursprung'.

[2] As Augustine does call it, e.g. *De civ. Dei*, xx, 9.

the old Jerusalem could be called the 'holy City' on account of its symbolic reference. As *res* the Church is lost in the 'world'; as *signum* it has distinct being as the world's pointer to the Kingdom.

A theology of the Church elaborated in terms of its being a sign is not to be found in Augustine's work. But he does provide a theory of signs with the aid of which such an ecclesiology may be constructed, and an Old Testament model to show how the concept of 'sign' might be applied to the case of the Church. Moreover, and this is of more fundamental importance, a theology conceived in such terms alone seems to offer the possibility of doing full justice to the duality deeply embedded in Augustinian theology: it would allow us to give full weight, on the one hand, to Augustine's insistence on the 'secular' character of the Church, on its identity with the 'world', on the anonymity of Christian presence in the world, the uncertainty and ambivalence of human institutions to which the Church is not immune, its perpetual liability to betray the Gospel which it must proclaim and the Lord whom it must serve. On the other hand such an ecclesiology would safeguard the notion of the Church as visible, as an institution with a distinct form, with a specific task and a mission. In so far as it is not actualised as *signum*, the Church is a *res*: as such, its mission is to be formless, merging into the human historical and cultural context in which it exists, to be 'lost' in and identified with the 'world'. In so far as it is actualising itself as *signum*, the whole of the Church's essential being is concentrated in its business of becoming visible as a sign.

In its mission of functioning as a sign, the Church is seen for what it is principally in three kinds of activity: first, in the work of proclaiming the Gospel, preaching the message of the Kingdom established by the crucified Lord. Second, in sacramental worship, wherein the Christian community becomes an anticipatory sign of the fully human community of love whose coming we are required to await in hope. Third, in its ministry the Church serves the world in the redeeming love whose presence in the world it proclaims in its preaching. In this ministry the Church does not transform societies into the Kingdom of God—though it must support, and sometimes inspire, creative initiatives for their transformation into better societies—but it subjects all worldly institutions as well as all programmes to a critical scrutiny in the perspective opened by the hope of that Kingdom. Seen in this way, everything essential in the Church's life, everything that constitutes it what it is, as a sign (which is nothing unless it does its work of pointing), is shot through with a tension between what is already accomplished in Christ and what is still awaiting fulfilment at the end: 'The pilgrim, if he walks in faith, is not yet at home; he is on the way...Our joy is not yet achieved: it is held in hope...Yet, let us even now place ourselves in that victory which is still to come...'[1]

[1] *Enarr. in Ps.* 123.2, 4.

HISTORY, PROPHECY AND INSPIRATION[1]

The controversies of more than half a century concerning Augustine's intellectual development have brought us to a clearer appreciation of the authority with which Augustine endowed the holy scriptures from the very first days of his conversion to Christianity.[2] The works of his maturity and old age supply ample testimony to the growing submission of his mind to the *auctoritas divinarum scripturarum unde mens nostra deviare non debet*.[3] Even in his thirties, however, the young Augustine, with his adventurous mind giving its assent to the Christian faith, shared this basic conviction with the simplest piety of traditional, popular Christianity. Life within the Christian community and pastoral responsibility only deepened the hold of the scripture on his mind. Not unnaturally, he came to devote some thought to its status as the word of God.

The first of the works in which he was brought face to face with questions concerning the inspiration of the scriptures is his *De consensu evangelistarum*, written in the first year or two of the fifth century. Hermann Sasse has seen in this work the beginnings of a new idea of inspiration. The language which Augustine uses here, speaking of the evangelists writing their stories on the basis of God's *suggestio*,[4] Sasse remarks,[5] certainly allows more scope to the free creative work of the human author than did the cruder image of God using the writer as a tool or dictating the words, so widely current in the earlier tradition. Further, when Augustine refers in this work[6] to the evangelists as the 'hands' by means of which Christ wrote what he wished to be recorded about himself, the thought is very different from the simple

---

[1] Originally published in *Augustinus* [Essays in honour of V. Capanága], ed. I. Oroz-Reta (Madrid 1967), 271–80.

[2] Any remaining doubts on this score can scarcely survive the distinguished and immensely thorough work of Holte, *Béatitude et sagesse*. The authority of the *regula fidei* used in interpreting the scriptures and the exact relation of this to the authority of the scriptures are matters I do not wish to consider here.

[3] *De Trin.* III, 11.22.   [4] II, 21.51.

[5] 'Sacra scriptura'. Cf. also the useful survey by Costello, 'St Augustine's concept of inspiration'.   [6] I, 35.54.

traditional image of a tool and its user. As the context in the whole paragraph shows, Augustine is not concerned to provide a model for the working of inspiration; what he is concerned to stress is that inspiration is one instance of the action of Christ, the Head, in his members. The office of evangelist is one among the *charismata* of the division of sacred labours, undertaken within the Body, for the benefit of its members. The paragraph is revealing as an indication of the strongly 'ecclesial' approach to the problem of inspiration—an emphasis almost forgotten since Augustine until its revival in our own days by Karl Rahner—and tells us nothing about what is special about inspiration as distinct from any other action of the Head in his members.

Nor is the idea of biblical inspiration one to which Augustine seems to have felt it necessary to devote explicit thought at any stage of his career. He appears to have been ready to accept the fact without feeling any need to analyse the meaning of 'inspiration', when applied to the biblical writers or their work. All the same, there are elements in his work from which something very like a 'theory of inspiration' can be put together. These elements occur in his account of the nature of prophecy. I shall argue that his idea of inspiration should be understood in terms of what he says about prophecy. To establish the propriety of this procedure, I begin by noting an important feature about the meaning of 'prophecy' in Augustine's writings.

Repeatedly in his early works, Augustine contrasts prophecy with history. The key to this conceptual pair is a passage in the *De vera religione*[1] in which he discusses the manner in which God's purposes are disclosed to men. They may be disclosed *quasi privatim*, in God's dealings with individuals; his purposes for the human race as a whole are disclosed *per historiam* and *per prophetiam*. God's ways, whether in the past or in the future, are revealed as temporal realities. They are known to us through faith rather than through understanding. It is clear in this passage that Augustine is relating *historia* to *praeterita*, and *prophetia* to *futura*; this is also asserted in a passage of somewhat later date.[2] It is in the light of this disjunction—history referring to the past, prophecy to the future—that we must understand other passages such as: *huius religionis sectandae caput est historia et prophetia dispensationis temporalis divinae providentiae*...[3] History must refer to the past, prophecy to what is (or was) to come. This juxtaposition of narratives

[1] 25.46.   [2] *De Trin.* IV, 16.21.
[3] *De vera rel.* 7.13.

of the past and of predictions of the future is a fundamental and re-current theme in Augustine's earlier work.[1]

An element of complexity appears with a related but quite different distinction which Augustine also used at this stage of his career, largely dominated as it was by the concerns of anti-Manichaean controversy. This was the distinction between various ways of expounding the scriptures: *secundum historiam*, or *secundum prophetiam*, as Augustine states it in one place.[2] According to this way of distinguishing exposi-tions, 'the exposition *secundum prophetiam* foretells things to come'.[3] It is important to note that the distinction here made is between different ways of expounding the scriptures, not between different kinds of text contained in them. A text may itself be a historical narrative in form and substance, but may nevertheless be read either 'historically' or 'prophetically',[4] that is to say as referring either to the past or to the future: a *story* about past events could be read as *prophecy* prefiguring things to come.

But these two distinctions, the one between two kinds of text, the other between two kinds of exposition, tended to merge in Augustine's mind. Thus, in another work,[5] he enumerates four modes of expound-ing the scriptures. The first of these is exposition *secundum historiam*, which Augustine goes on to describe: not, as we should expect, as the kind of exposition which treats the text in terms of its historical, narrative meaning; he suddenly changes direction, and instead of offering us an explanation of the historical mode of exposition, what he actually gives is a definition of *historia*. *Historia*, he writes, is the record of *sive divinitus sive humanitus gesta*.[6] This is a revealing passage: it shows the ease with which Augustine could move from ideas of the different kinds of thing contained in the scriptures to ideas about different ways of expounding the scriptures. This easy transition had two important consequences. First, it defined and restricted the meaning which *history* and *prophecy* bore in his language at this stage. By defini-tion, 'historical exposition' referred to the past; 'prophetic' to the future. Identifying the one with 'history', the other with 'prophecy' thus implied the notions of 'history' and of 'prophecy' which Augus-tine held in his earlier writings: 'history' as *res gesta*; 'prophecy' as *res gestura*.[7] This is not, of course, far from the normally current

---

[1] *De lib. arb.* III, 21.60–2; *De agone chr.* 13.15; *De fide r.q.n.v.* 5.8; *De cons. Ev.* I, 35.54.
[2] *De Gen. c. Man.* II, 2.3.
[3] '*Secundum historiam facta narrantur, secundum prophetiam futura praenuntiantur.*'—*ibid.*
[4] Elsewhere, of course, Augustine also uses other terms which do not concern us.
[5] *De Gen. lib. impf.* 2.5.   [6] *Ibid.*   [7] This phrase is used in *De agone chr.* 13.15.

meaning of the words; but it is not in fact the meaning they bear, as we shall see, in Augustine's later work.

The second important consequence of Augustine's identification of the two dichotomies is that it moves the emphasis from the content of the scriptures to their interpretation. Already at this stage of his career he was obscurely feeling his way towards another conception of history and prophecy in the scriptures. He was still saying that there are both history and prophecy within the scriptural canon; but he came very near to saying that more important than this duality of content within the Bible is the possibility of reading the whole Bible either as history or as prophecy. This, again, is on the verge of the view which emerges with great clarity from his later work: that the whole scriptural canon is simultaneously historical and prophetic. As the preoccupations of anti-Manichaean controversy ceased to press on his mind, Augustine became less interested in distinguishing and tabulating the different ways of expounding the scriptures. But it had been precisely defining these that, spilling over into his conception of history and of prophecy, had established *historia* and *prophetia* in the restricted senses they bore. The limitation of 'history' to the past and of 'prophecy' to the future thus came to be deprived of the very grounds on which it had originally rested. *Historia* is less rigidly confined to the past and tends to embrace all that is in the scriptures; and *prophetia*, as I shall show, becomes equally wide.

In the idiom of the *City of God*, within the scriptures, 'history' and 'prophecy' are almost synonymous. A frequently recurring theme in this work is the contrast, exploited with fine rhetoric, between the sacred scriptures and the pagan authors.[1] One would not expect the distinction between different kinds of text represented among the biblical books to loom at all large in this context; prophets, historians, poets and the rest of the scriptural authors are joined in a total confrontation with pagan antiquity. Their differences are blurred, no weight is now placed on the question as to whether they deal with past or future. Indeed one of the qualities, we are now told,[2] which may predispose us to believe an author's reports about the past is his success in foretelling the future. The biblical writings are referred to as *divina historia, nostrae religionis historia*,[3] as *sacra historia*,[4] irrespective of whether they are 'historical' or 'prophetic' in the sense these terms bore in Augustine's older language. Indeed Augustine could now speak[5]

---

[1] I may refer to *De civ. Dei*, XVIII, 40 for one of the finest examples.
[2] XVIII, 40. [3] *Ibid.* [4] XV, 8.1. [5] XVI, 2.3.

of the Bible as *prophetica historia*, thus joining in one phrase two terms that had been antithetical.

Two chapters of the work are of particular interest in this connection. In XVIII, 38 Augustine considers why the biblical canon does not contain certain ancient writings to which canonical texts allude, such as, for instance, the writings of prophets mentioned in the 'histories of the kings of Judah and the kings of Israel'. These, we are told, were the works of prophets; yet, they are not in the canon. Augustine confesses himself baffled by this. He does, however, offer a conjecture to account for this, and it is, for our purpose, a highly significant one: he distinguishes in these authors' output 'some things which they wrote as men, with historical investigation (*historica diligentia*)', from what they wrote 'as prophets, with divine inspiration'. The first category comprises their own work, the second is attributed to God, speaking through them. The first may have its uses in the enrichment of learning, but only the second pertains to the authority of religion; and the canon of scripture is concerned only with the latter. Nothing outside it is to be trusted as endowed with prophetic authority. Now in this chapter 'inspiration' is coextensive (though not quite synonymous) with 'canonicity'; and canonicity has become the criterion of prophetic inspiration. 'Prophetic' writings are excluded not because of any failure to predict the future, but simply on account of their extra-canonicity. Prophetic inspiration has become identified with scriptural inspiration, and both are attested by canonicity. Prophecy has lost its previous reference to foretelling of the future.

In another chapter of the work, XVI, 2.3, Augustine again remarks that the scriptures may omit much true historical material which has no bearing on the pattern of divine redemptive action which forms their true subject-matter. For it is certain to the eyes of faith that the things done (*gesta*) and recorded (*conscripta*) in scripture are to be referred to Christ and his Church, which is the City of God. Anything that the sacred writers leave aside may find its place in the realm of historical investigation (*historica diligentia*) but does not belong to prophetic foresight (*prophetica providentia*). Sometimes, to be sure, the 'prophetic history' (!) includes material which is not in itself significant for the future; the stories told (*gesta*) may include material which is linked with narratives of prophetic significance, as part of the necessary context of such narratives, without necessarily containing any hidden future reference; just as only the ploughshare turns the earth but nevertheless the whole plough does its work.

At first sight this is reminiscent of Augustine's older way of linking history to the past, prophecy to the future. But he is not concerned here to distinguish prophecy and history within the sacred text as much as to establish that the text as a whole is prophetic, whether its ingredients are 'prophetic' or 'historical' if taken in isolation; and that to interpret the text as a whole prophetically one is not committed to the absurdity of finding recondite meanings for each of its parts. In terms of this approach the distinction between historical and prophetic texts loses its importance within the biblical canon. It is all prophetic, all inspired, all authoritative, all has a reference beyond itself to the future, a significance within the total pattern of redemptive history.[1] The difference between the realm of 'historical investigation' and of 'prophecy' is the difference between what is canonical and inspired on the one hand, and what is extracanonical and non-inspired on the other; it is not primarily a difference between what refers to the past and what refers to the future. In the Bible the past as a whole has a reference to the future. The old distinction between history and prophecy had been applicable within the scriptural canon; the dichotomy in the *City of God* is between the Bible and all else. Perhaps it was in recognition of this change in perspective that Augustine now no longer spoke of *historia* when he wanted to contrast something with prophecy, but used a circumlocution referring to stories belonging to the sphere of *historica diligentia*. *Historia* has become a new category, which, far from being exclusive of prophecy, may be either *prophetica* (or *sacra* etc., see p. 190, nn. 3–5 above) or not. The meaning of 'prophecy' has correspondingly widened to mean the work of the Holy Spirit in inspiring not only 'prophets', but biblical authors and even their translators.[2]

If the scriptures belong, as a whole, to the *genre* of prophecy, we ought to be able to get some light on the manner in which Augustine conceived them to be inspired from what he says about prophetic inspiration. There is in fact a good deal of material in the twelfth book of his *De Genesi ad litteram* concerning prophetic visions and insight. This last book of the Commentary must have been written in or about the year 414, soon after Augustine had embarked on the

[1] ... *ipsa scriptura, quae per ordinem reges eorumque facta et eventa digerens, videtur tamquam historica diligentia rebus gestis occupata esse narrandis, si adiuvante Dei Spiritu considerata tractetur, vel magis, vel certe non minus, praenuntiandis futuris quam praeteritis enuntiandis invenietur intenta, De civ. Dei*, XVII, 1.

[2] On the LXX, as a translation 'prophetically inspired', cf. *De civ. Dei*, XV, 23.3; XVIII, 43.

vast project of the *City of God*. Many of the ideas first elaborated in the Commentary are put to good use in this great work. The language in which Augustine speaks of inspiration in it is entirely in line with his treatment of prophetic inspiration in the Commentary on Genesis. It may well be that we should account for the change in his language as a result of the application of the ideas developed here. In any case, everything points to the need to take his theory of prophetic insight into consideration in seeking to trace his views on the inspiration of scripture.

Book twelve of the Commentary is a treatise on visions. Visions like Paul's in the third heaven, or that of Moses on Mount Sinai, the visions of Old Testament prophets and of the seer of the Book of Revelation are discussed here in relation to an elaborate theory of perception and imagination.[1] In the course of it Augustine distinguishes three kinds of *visio*, 'corporeal', 'spiritual' and 'intellectual'.

The first of these is what the eyes are engaged in when we see. As Augustine describes the process, it is a physical interaction engendered by the encounter of the bodily sense-organ with its object. It does not amount to *seeing* unless we are at the same time aware of what we see; seeing is more than the physical interaction of eye and object, and involves the mind.

This more is what Augustine calls 'spiritual sight' and it consists of the mind's awareness of images, the likenesses of objects. What the mind 'sees' is of the same nature as itself, created by the mind out of its own substance, not external realities, but their likenesses. When this 'spiritual sight' accompanies 'corporeal sight', these likenesses will, in some manner, correspond to their external counterparts.[2] 'Spiritual sight' is not, however, tied to bodily perception. It also occurs in its absence, when the mind contemplates the images before it in states such as imagination, dreams, trances, hallucinations and ecstasies.

The third kind of 'seeing', 'intellectual sight', is the mind's activity in interpreting, judging and correcting the material furnished to it by the lower kinds of 'sight'. This is the specifically intellectual component of experience. This is the level at which the crude data of sense and imagination are interpreted, images referred to external objects, meaning discovered or created.

This last is the kind of 'seeing' which Augustine singles out as the

---

[1] Cf. Markus, 'Augustine', 85–6; what follows is a brief résumé of that analysis, where fuller references are given.
[2] The notorious philosophical difficulties of such a theory do not concern us here.

essential constituent of prophecy. Whether 'images' or 'visions' are vouchsafed to a prophet or not, he must have insight into the meaning of his experience. The prophet is a prophet in virtue of his judgement, not in virtue of the material on which it is exercised. Thus we should rather call Joseph the prophet, who understood the meaning of Pharaoh's dreams, than Pharaoh himself: for Pharaoh's 'imagination was activated so that he had visions, whereas his [Joseph's] mind was illuminated that he might understand'.[1] This, however, is the simplest kind of prophecy. He who merely perceives in his imagination or sense signs without being vouchsafed an understanding of their meaning is less worthy of being called a prophet than he who has insight into their meaning; but most of all does he deserve the name of prophet who is given both the visions and an understanding of them: like Daniel, who could tell the king both the dream he had dreamt and its meaning. In this earthly life the prophet is tied to his experience of sensuous nature: either to that obtained through his bodily senses, of the public world open to everybody's experience, or to the private, imaginative experience specially vouchsafed him by God in a state of trance and abstraction from the world of public experience.[2] This second constitutes a higher kind of prophecy than the first; foretelling the course of future events, of course, belongs here. Nevertheless, God-given insight into the meaning of ordinary, publicly accessible facts, whether of the present or of the past, is enough to constitute a man a prophet in a wider sense. The essential activity of prophecy which a 'prophet' in this wider sense shares with the 'prophet' in the narrower (and superior) sense is the prophetic judgement on the meaning of his experience.

Augustine always speaks of this prophetic judgement or insight as achieved with divine assistance, under divine illumination,[3] in much the same terms as he uses to describe the illumination of the mind by the divine light in its work of rational understanding. The language of illumination had the great virtue that it enabled Augustine to treat in its terms a wide range of mental activity, from ordinary rational understanding to the achievement of wisdom by special grace. The illumination of the prophet's mind has a place somewhere in the wide spectrum over which the language of illumination is applicable. Augustine did not feel any need to have a special theory to account for God's activity in inspiring the prophet. This could be explained in the

---

[1] *Illius enim spiritus informatus est ut videret; huius mens illuminata ut intelligeret.*—XII, 9.20.
[2] On this cf. *ibid.* XII, 26.53.   [3] E.g. *ibid.* XII, 26.53; 30.58; 31.59.

same terms as God's activity in anybody's mind, as one of the many modes of his presence to the human mind; more specifically, as one of the many modes of his intellectual presence, that is to say of illumination, in the mind. We may note that Augustine refers to divine illumination not only to account for prophetic insight, but also in the larger context of the scriptures in general.[1]

I have already argued that by the time Augustine came to write the *City of God*, he had come to think of 'prophecy' and the 'scriptures' as near-synonymous. Although he does not discuss the case of the inspired author as such in the course of his analysis of prophetic inspiration in *De Genesi ad litteram* XII, it is clear that the theory there elaborated can easily be applied to this case. This fact may indeed have helped to pave Augustine's way towards the identification of scripture and prophecy. In terms of the theory of prophecy worked out there, the biblical writer—say, an evangelist, or the author of one of the historical books of the Old Testament—would be a prophet in the wider (and inferior) sense: a prophet to whom God makes no special private revelation, who is given no visions, but whose mind is enlightened by a special *charisma* to interpret a particular slice of ordinary, publicly available experience; in this case an episode in the national history of the Jews, or in the biography of Jesus. The insight imparted by such illumination will reveal to the prophet the hidden, inner meaning of the events, the meaning they bear within the overall pattern of God's saving work. His narrative will be historical in its form and substance, and prophetic in the manner in which the meaning of the historical narrative is displayed. It will be precisely what Augustine came to call it: *prophetica*, or *sacra historia*. The prophetic quality of such a piece of history is what distinguishes it from an ordinary piece of history, as it might be told by any historian.

To an ordinary historian the history of the Jews, or some episode of it, or the life of Jesus, may be totally devoid of significance. They may be no more than minor incidents in the history of the ancient Near East; and if they are more, their further significance derives from the fact that they already had been endowed with prophetic significance before he ever came to write of them. The meaning of the narrative derives from the activity of interpretation; without it its constituent facts would be a meaningless mass of information about the past, lacking even such coherence as is required to incorporate them in a narrative, lacking direction.

[1] *De civ. Dei*, XI, 3.

On this mass any historian must impose a shape to tell a story; the prophetic, inspired historian differs from others only in that the shape he imposes on his story is the shape God wishes to give it:[1] in this strand of history God reveals himself. The prophet (i.e. the inspired writer) allows the events to speak. To borrow Augustine's terms, the prophet is the man who transforms the *facta* of history into *verba*[2]—events become God's communication to men through his deeds.

[1] Augustine's theory of inspiration could easily be extended to do justice to the interpretative work present in the community's tradition prior to the text being written down, or receiving its final form. These distinctions did not, of course, arise for Augustine.

[2] *Ep.* 102.6.33. Cf. also *Sermo Mai* 94.2 (Morin, 335.2 f.); 98.3.3; *In Joh. Ev. Tr.* 25.2; 44.1, discussed by Strauss, *Schriftgebrauch*, 109–10. Cf. above, p. 12.

'DE CIVITATE DEI', XIX, 14–15 AND THE ORIGINS OF POLITICAL AUTHORITY[1]

Augustine never discusses the question of the state's origin both directly and in detail. The fullest remarks on this theme occur in these two chapters of his *De civitate Dei*, and, as we shall see, even these are not wholly centred on the problem with which we are concerned. Allusions and quotations by later writers, when debating our problem, are most frequently to these two chapters. They make a suitable focal point to our enquiry.

Chapter 14 of the *De civitate Dei* begins with a statement about the ends which the two 'cities' pursue, the main theme under discussion in Book xix. 'In the earthly city the use of temporal things is referred to the enjoyment of earthly peace; whereas in the heavenly city it is referred to the enjoyment of eternal peace.' Augustine now goes on to expound what the peace is which is desired by all men. As he describes it, it is identical with what he has called 'eternal peace'; this alone ultimately satisfies all human longings. He continues with an account of how man is to conduct himself so as to attain this eternal peace. He is to obey the two chief commandments of God: to love God and to love his neighbour as himself. The latter must include having consideration for one's fellow men, encouraging them to love God,[2] and being prepared to be thus encouraged by others. In this way only can men achieve 'peace' with their fellows; first with those close to them 'either by the order of nature, or by the bonds of society', their families and households, then with others more remote in so far as life brings them into contact with them. The chapter ends with a picture of the 'domestic peace', defined as the 'ordered harmony of authority and obedience of the household'.[3] This is the point in the chapter at which 'authority' (*imperare, imperium*) is brought into the discussion. Hitherto Augustine had been speaking of the duties of the

---

[1] Originally part of a paper published in *JTS*, NS 16 (1965).
[2] The range of meanings and overtones brought into play by Augustine's use of *consulere* can seldom be rendered adequately without more than one equivalent in English. I use 'have consideration', 'care for', 'guide', 'encourage'.
[3] *ordinata imperandi obediendique concordia cohabitantium*; cf. also *De civ. Dei*, XIX, 13.1.

head towards his household in terms of 'care for' and 'guidance' (*consulere*). This duty is now defined in terms of authority: 'to guide is to exercise authority (*imperant enim qui consulunt*)...and to be guided is to obey (*obediunt autem quibus consulitur*)...'. Authority and obedience (*imperare–obedire*) are a wider notion, to which giving and receiving guidance (*consulere–consuli*) are assimilated, a little arbitrarily, as a special case of the wider pair of concepts. Authority and obedience may present a very different face from the idyllic harmony sketched here; but in the household of the just man who lives by faith, those who rule in reality serve the subjects whom they appear to be ruling; and they rule 'not through a craving for power but in virtue of their obligation of caring for and guiding [their subjects] (*neque enim dominandi cupiditate imperant, sed officio consulendi*); nor with pride in lordship, but with merciful concern'.

The burden of the chapter is an exhortation to men in a place of authority, and particularly a place of authority in household and family, how to conduct themselves in relation to their subjects. In the heavenly city the exercise of authority must be conceived as service. Augustine does not discuss the origin of social institutions at all in this chapter. He is concerned solely with how a man is to live within social institutions, particularly of family and household, as a citizen of the heavenly city. To this extent the chapter is concerned with two ways of exercising power within any social grouping.

The following chapter shows that the fact that in any institution power can be exercised on the model of a *paterfamilias* or otherwise has no implications for Augustine concerning the origins of institutions. The opening sentence of this chapter refers back to the previous chapter: 'this is what the order of nature prescribes, this is how God created man'; and referring to Gen. 1:26, Augustine explains that God did not wish man, whom he made rational and in his own image, to rule over any but irrational creatures. Man was given dominion or authority not over other men, but over beasts. Thus the first just men of old were shepherds rather than kings. The condition of servitude is rightly imposed on sinners. The origin of the servitude in which man is subjected to another in virtue of the bondage of his condition, is sin. Only in this chapter does Augustine begin to speak about the origin of any social institution, and the institution he discusses, that of slavery, is unambiguously traced to sin as its origin. Augustine stresses that it is nevertheless a just enactment of God; for although 'nobody is the slave either of man or of sin by nature, as God first created man, nevertheless penal servitude is ordained by the same law as the one which enjoins the order of nature to be kept and forbids its transgression: for if nothing had been done against that law in the first place, there would be no need for the coercion of penal servitude'. The chapter concludes with an exhortation to slaves to behave so as to achieve freedom, after a manner, in their servitude, by serving their masters with loving fidelity 'until iniquity shall pass away and all domination and human power shall be emptied and God shall be all in all'.

It is generally not noticed that Augustine is insisting on two things in these chapters: that, on the one hand, servitude is a condition or institution whose origin is not to be found in man's nature as created; and, on the other hand, that there is a way of exercising authority—and subjection—either in accordance with the order of nature or otherwise. Augustine explicitly includes the relation between master and slave among those in which he asserts that 'this [way of conducting oneself in it] is prescribed by the order of nature'.[1] Although, then, the institution itself originates in sin, the exercise of authority in it need not be and ought not to be sinful but in accordance with the order of nature. We must conclude that these chapters give no ground for the opinion that for Augustine the state and political authority are, or can be, an institution of nature. Chapter 14 asserts nothing about institutions, and speaks only about the exercise of authority, and Chapter 15 indicates that he thought that the natural order could be observed within an institution—slavery—belonging to the order of fallen nature.

---

[1] Schilling, *SSLAug*, 46, n. 1, gratitutously inserting a phrase in his footnote, takes *hoc* to refer to *officium consulendi ac providendi*. This clearly cannot be the case; *hoc* must refer to the whole of the last sentence of Chapter 14, or to the argument as a whole, of which it serves as the conclusion. It is noteworthy, however, that despite this, Schilling did not interpret the passage as asserting that political authority was an institution derived from the *ordo naturae*. Although he thought that this was in fact Augustine's view, his arguments for this are based on other passages, to be considered in due course. Schilling interpreted the two chapters under discussion as making a distinction between two ways of exercising power: either despotically, or as 'sympathetic guidance' (*teilnehmende Fürsorge*), *ibid.* 55. What he failed to notice is the shift in Chapter 15 to a discussion of institutions, that of slavery. Gustave Combès, in his *La doctrine politique*, 76 f., also appears to be clear that these passages exclude political authority from the state of man's innocence. He bases his opinion that political authority is nevertheless a natural institution for Augustine on 'the intervention of a second law of nature', which impels men to associate with each other. Their original freedom, in his view, is cancelled out by this law, and characterised men only in *une vie errante et solitaire*, in which men were alone with their consciences before God. His arguments are rarely more than assertions based on quotations torn from their context and linked by innuendo. An attempt to refute them would contribute little to an understanding of Augustine's views.

Apart from this general principle, our two chapters assert nothing explicitly about the nature of political authority. There is a phrase in Chapter 14 which suggests that Augustine would have distinguished it from the kind of authority enjoyed by a father over his family; for he distinguishes within the household over which the *paterfamilias* presides those who are close to him 'by the order of society' (i.e. his household slaves etc.). The impression given—it is no more—is that the 'order of nature' is thought of as coextensive here with the family. There is nothing specific in the text to show whether political authority is to be taken, with slavery, as originating in sin or, with the family, as arising from the order of nature. None the less, in the absence of positive grounds for excepting political authority, the most natural way of reading what Augustine says about the subjection of man to man is to take it quite generally, including within its scope the subjection of men to their rulers. The verse quoted from Genesis (1:26), 'Let them have dominion over the fish of the sea and over the birds of the air and over every creeping thing that creeps upon the earth', and Augustine's comment that God did not wish man to rule over other men, taken in its most immediately natural sense, would exclude any kind of dominion of men over other men; and the observation in the following sentence that for this reason just men were at first shepherds rather than kings clinches the appositeness of interpreting Augustine as wishing to include political dominion within his meaning. Finally, the conclusion of the chapter also suggests that Augustine thought of all institutions of human domination and power as on a level with slavery, at least in respect of their final destiny. It is at least striking that he does not dissociate political from other forms of authority, as one might expect him to have done if he had thought of it as different in origin and kind. A long passage,[1] which recalls *De civitate Dei*, XIX, 15 at a number of points, gives a similar impression. Here Augustine discusses the dominion exercised by the bad over the good. What is interesting for our purpose about this passage is not Augustine's defence of such a state of affairs, which rests on his view that it is God's dispensation *ad tempus*, and will be done away with at the end; it is the equivalence between slavery and all political authority, secular power, and dignity on which some stress is laid. Though the origins of the institutions are, again, not under discussion, the effect of the passage is to reinforce the impression that slavery and other

[1] *Enarr. in Ps.* 124.7–8.

institutions of human subjection are not fundamentally distinguished in Augustine's mind.

Augustine clarifies his position to some extent when he explains[1] that a harmonious social existence is natural to man, and a desire for such an existence implanted in man by nature. His account of such a state implies that in it men are equal before God, until perverse imitation of God disrupts the social harmony. Rejecting equality with his fellows, man wishes to impose dominion on them. Three assertions are clearly made here: that man's nature is social, not solitary; that by their original nature men are equal and subject to God, not to one another; and that subjection to one another is the consequence of sinful pride. The last assertion, we may note, is made without particular reference to slavery; and a similar argument[2] involving political subordination suggests that this should be taken as included among the results of sin. Augustine sometimes refers to man's dominion over lower creatures as *potestas naturalis*, and traces this to man's superiority to other creatures in virtue of being made to God's image and likeness.[3] Gen. 1:26, invoked here as in *De civitate Dei*, XIX, 15, gives no grounds for including any form of subordination of man to man within the range of this *potestas naturalis*.

None of this, however, would suffice for a conclusive refutation of the view that for Augustine the state is natural. The case for this view rests almost entirely on the twin assertions[4] that Augustine admitted a natural subordination of men to men, notably in the family, and that the state is in this respect homogeneous with the family and therefore belongs to the order of nature. It is important, therefore, to examine more closely the manner in which Augustine distinguished natural from non-natural forms of subjection between man and man, and whether political institutions really do belong with those of the family, or, rather, with slavery.

That Augustine did not exclude all forms of subjection from the order of nature in the state of primitive innocence there can be no doubt. He asserts this quite explicitly in commenting on Gen. 1:26 in a work of 419.[5] It gives us to understand, he argues, that reason is to have dominion over irrational life; this subjection is just, whereas

---

[1] *De civ. Dei*, XIX, 12.2.
[2] *Ibid.* XVIII, 2.2: *hinc factum est ut non sine Dei providentia...quidam essent regnis praediti, quidam regnantibus subditi...* [3] *In Ep. Ioh. Tr.* 8.6–8.
[4] Cf. Schilling, *SSLAug*, 57–60; Combès, *La doctrine politique*, 79–80.
[5] *Qu. in Hept.* I, 153.

iniquity and adversity subject men to the service of others. But, Augustine goes on to observe, the verse does not exclude 'a natural order [of subjection] in mankind, too, such that in virtue of it women should be subject to men and sons to their fathers; for in these cases, too, it is right that the weaker in reason should be subject to the stronger'. How little inclined Augustine was to extend this 'natural order of subjection' to include political subjection we may gauge from the opening remark, which began this train of reflections. There Augustine commends the patriarchs, *à propos* of Gen. 46:32, for being shepherds—and one recalls the comparison of shepherds and kings in *De civitate Dei*, XIX, 15—for 'this sort of dominion and subjection, whereby beasts are subjected to men and men put in charge of beasts, is undoubtedly right'. It is clear that the oft-invoked text cannot serve to justify the opinion that political authority is based on a natural order of subjection among men. An analysis of the antecedents of this text, however, reveals the structure of ideas in Augustine's mind of which this theme forms a part. The view that there is a natural subordination among men is, of course, not by any means expressed here for the first time in his work. It is clearly asserted in his great Commentary on Genesis, written *c*. 401–14. Commenting in this work[1] on the verse 'To the woman [God] said "I will greatly multiply thy pain in childbearing...and thou shalt be under thy husband's power and he shall have dominion over thee"',[2] Augustine observes that the text clearly speaks of what woman's condition is to be as a punishment for her sin. All the same, he insists, we are not to doubt that even before sin woman was so made that she should be under man's dominion. The punishment should therefore be understood as consisting in that kind of subjection (*servitutem*) 'which belongs to a certain condition rather than to love (*quae cuiusdam conditionis est potius quam dilectionis*); so that we should understand that this kind of servitude, too, whereby men afterwards began to be servants of each other, has its origin in the punishment of sin'. The servitude which Augustine identifies with loving subordination belongs to the nature in which man and woman were originally created. In their fallen state, however, this mutual service in charity is overlaid by the kind of subjection by which one person owes service and obedience to another in virtue of his condition or status. And this kind of subjection is a result of sin. Within it, service and dominion can be exercised as an office of charity; but the partnership may fall

[1] *De Gen. ad litt.* XI, 37.50.
[2] *ad virum tuum conversio tua et ipse tui dominabitur* (Gen. 3:16), in Augustine's text.

short of this and be a case of one being dominated by the other. The Apostle, Augustine says, exhorts married partners to the former (Gal. 5:13), and absolutely forbids woman to dominate over man (1 Tim. 2:12). The distinction between service as required by the natural order of subordination and service as owed in virtue of status and condition is identical with the distinction alluded to in *De civitate Dei*, XIX, 15.[1]

This extensive Commentary on the book of Genesis contains the first germs of many of the ideas which we meet later in the *De civitate Dei*. It is important therefore to note that it gives no countenance to the suggestion that Augustine linked the institutions of marriage and the state as belonging to the natural order as created. On the contrary: it is clear that the service and subjection which a man owes another in virtue of being subject to him as to his legitimate ruler is an instance of subjection in virtue of status only; it has nothing to do with any possible moral or intellectual superiority of the ruler over his subject. This emerges with all clarity from the theory of divine providence which Augustine elaborates in Book VIII of the Commentary, which stands, like so many of these seminal ideas, behind the applications they find in the *De civitate Dei*.

His theory of divine providence led Augustine to dissociate the authority of man over woman, and other forms of natural subordination, from purely institutional forms of subjection to authority, such as exist in the state. With the insertion of man (and angels) into the universe, an element of freedom and rational agency is introduced: as Augustine expresses it in a fine and untranslatable image, with man 'the bud (*oculus*) of reason is grafted on to the world, as on to a great tree of things'.[2] With this grafting, the divine gardener's operation becomes twofold. His providence operates in two channels, through the processes of nature and through the acts of wills. In his grand catalogue of the works of man which fall under the operation of providence, Augustine mentions 'the administration of societies' specifically as under God's *providentia voluntaria*. A few paragraphs later[3] he returns to the same duality of God's providence, and enumerates examples of natural subordination which God's providence secures among natures thus: 'he first subjected all things to himself,

---

[1] Cf. above, p. 198: *rationalem...noluit nisi irrationalibus dominari* and the consequent duty (Ch. 14) of the just man to serve those whom he rules; and the subjection of man to man *conditionis vinculo*, rooted in sin.

[2] *De Gen. ad litt.* VIII, 9.17. [3] *Ibid.* VIII, 23.44.

then he subjected corporeal to spiritual creatures, irrational to rational, earthly to heavenly, female to male, those of lower value to those of higher, the more restricted to the more comprehensive'. Neither slavery nor political subjection is mentioned here. From the two passages taken together we may infer that the subjection of woman to man, as of those inferior in some relevant respect to those superior, derives from the order of nature; whereas the subjection of men to political authority (and slavery) does not.

It is in this great Commentary on Genesis that Augustine first came to grips with the idea of nature. The distinction here developed, under the impulse of that reflection, between the twin channels of providential order lies behind the later discussions of the *De civitate Dei*. It underlies, for instance, the fine chapter[1] devoted to providence in which Augustine describes, in a passage of sweeping rhetoric, the all-embracing range of God's providence in nature, and then adds that 'the kingdoms of men, their dominations and their subjections (*regna hominum eorumque dominationes et servitutes*)' are in no way to be thought remote from 'the laws of his providence'. These laws are obviously identical with the law Augustine refers to in *De civitate Dei*, XIX, 15, the law which ordains penal servitude on the one hand, and enjoins the order of nature to be observed and forbids its transgression on the other.[2] There is a clear reference embedded here to the dual operation of divine providence elaborated in the *De Genesi ad litteram*. Augustine's view that the institutional subjection of man to man is rooted in human sin and is part of a divine dispensation for sin, has deep roots in his thought about the operation of divine providence in the world. The subjection of wives to their husbands and of children to their parents is not, in the relevant sense, institutional; it is clear and generally agreed that Augustine held these to be ordinances of nature. Nor, it is also clear, is society itself institutional in this sense. For, as we have seen,[3] a social existence was in Augustine's view natural to man. God had created man with a view to social existence,[4] and the saints shall live in sociable union.[5] Men are driven 'by the

---

[1] *De civ. Dei*, v, 11.

[2] Cf. above, p. 92: *poenalis servitus ea lege ordinatur quae naturalem ordinem conservari iubet, perturbari vetat*...; Augustine is not speaking of a natural law, as some commentators suggest, but of a law (that of divine providence) which enjoins the observance and forbids the disturbing of the order of nature.

[3] Cf. above, pp. 95 f.

[4] *De civ. Dei*, XII, 21 (22, Dombart and Kalb); and 27 (28, Dombart and Kalb).

[5] *Ibid.* XIX, 3.2; 5.

laws of their nature' to enter a social existence; but Augustine conceives this 'natural' society as a society of equals living in concord and subject only to God.[1] That he envisaged a wide variety of grades of intelligence and ability among men we need not deny. But he was certainly not so naïve as to assume that political authority and subjection were in fact often based on such a hierarchy of ability, and he certainly did not seek to justify the claims of political authority on grounds of any alleged natural superiority of ruler to subject, such as he attributed to the husband or the father over his family. He did think that the superior abilities of the wise man should find expression in concern for and guidance of the less wise. This is in accordance with the order of nature, displayed by the *paterfamilias*,[2] and it should be the pattern for the conduct of anyone in a position of authority. But the institutions of government, coercion, and punishment are brought into human society by sin. They are God's just punishment for man's transgression, and they are also his providential dispensation for coping with its consequences, disorder, strife, and lack of concord. Like society, the family, too, can be disordered by sin; here, too, disobedience may require coercion and punishment.[3] The parallel between society and the family is, indeed, important to Augustine. But it does not imply that political authority is grounded in the order of nature, as is paternal. A ruler or magistrate should behave like a *paterfamilias*; but the analogy between the two men holds only in respect of family life in the fallen state of man. For the coercive power which is part of the very substance and meaning of political authority also exists in the family; it enters the family, as it enters society, through sin and disorder. But a family is a family without it—we may conceive, even in a sinful world, of a family in which paternal authority is an exercise of care and guidance without coercion. But coercive power is part of the essence of political authority. Without it the state is not a state, though we may imagine lesser societies without it. Political authority, coercive

---

[1] *De civ. Dei*, XIX, 12.2. This section is in fact only indirectly concerned with this question. Harald Fuchs's fine analysis of the chapter in *Augustin*, 17–36, shows that Augustine is here primarily interested in the universal drive towards *pax* operative throughout nature, human and non-human. The sociable nature of man is only an illustration of this general principle. The final sentences of section 2 of the chapter, on the *perversa imitatio Dei* which seeks to subject others naturally and originally equal with oneself under God to one's own rule, give a further illustration of the natural drive towards peace operative even in this disordered state.

[2] *Ibid.* XIX, 14, 16. This commonplace is frequent in Augustine's correspondence, e.g. in *Epp.* 104.2.7; 130.6.12; 133.2; 138.2.14 etc.

[3] *De civ. Dei*, XIX, 16; 12.1.

power and its apparatus are what transform society into a state. Society, so we may summarise Augustine's view, has its origins in the order of nature; the state is a dispensation rooted in sin.

It remains to consider the analogy between the authority enjoyed by the soul over its body and that enjoyed by the ruler over his subjects. The application of this analogy would clearly point away from the view I have ascribed to Augustine. It would suggest that the relations of political authority are based on a natural order of command and obedience such as Augustine undoubtedly thought obtained between soul and body. Gustave Combès, indeed, saw the force of the analogy, and quoted[1] a passage from Augustine's *Contra Julianum* to clinch his interpretation of Augustine's theory of the state as natural. As this work is likely to be not very much earlier in composition than the later books of the *De civitate Dei*, it is worth examining its use of this analogy with some care. In the passage adduced by Combès[2] Augustine is quoting Cicero's *De re publica:*

Is it not clear that nature always gives authority (*dominatum*) to the better, for the great profit of the weaker? Why else should God rule over men, the mind over the body, reason over lust and anger and the other vicious parts of the soul?...But we must advert to the different forms of rule and subjection. The mind is said to rule both its body and its lusts; but it rules its body as a king rules his subjects or a parent his children, whereas it rules its lusts as a master rules his slave, with coercion and repression. Kings, emperors (*imperatores*),[3] magistrates, fathers and victorious nations have authority over their subjects in the way that mind has authority over its body...

Undoubtedly, Cicero here links political authority with paternal and likens them both to the natural authority of superior over inferior, such as the mind has in relation to its body; and Augustine quotes the passage with approval. Nevertheless, Cicero's view is not Augustine's. We may begin by noting the evident reserve with which Augustine quotes Cicero against his Pelagian opponent. Secular letters are no ground—Julian had himself appealed to Cicero—on which to refute bishops charged with expounding the holy scriptures; rather should such literature be deemed to be mad ravings if such a conflict appears.[4] All the same, since worldly literature sometimes contains 'traces of the truth' (*vestigia veritatis*), Julian's arguments can be answered from the very source of his own[5]—this is how Augustine introduces his

---

[1] *La doctrine politique*, 80.
[2] *C. Iul.* IV, 12.61. The same analogy is used by Ambrosiaster, *Q. Vet. & Nov. Test.* 115.35.
[3] Whatever Augustine's historical knowledge, *imperatores* here could scarcely have made him think of anything but emperors.
[4] *C. Iul.* IV, 12.61.   [5] *Ibid.* IV, 12.60.

appeal to Cicero. We need not lay too much weight on the view expressed in it; Augustine makes it only too clear that the passage is introduced as a polemical device. He wishes to confute Julian on his own ground, rather than by theological argument from the scriptures. Augustine's use of this Ciceronian analogy is, however, of considerable interest and repays elucidation.

Cicero is concerned with distinguishing two kinds of authority among men, one which is in accordance with nature, and one which is despotic. The analogy with the two ways in which the mind rules its body and its passions is intended to throw light on the two ways of ruling men. Augustine reverses the application of the analogy: he is concerned with the soul and bodily passions, especially in their disorganised state in man's fallen condition. It is to illuminate this relation of mind to body that he uses the analogy with political authority. Cicero's analogy would have been just as useful to him for this purpose had it contrasted only paternal authority with despotic, omitting royal authority.[1] But since Augustine was not directly concerned with discussing the nature of political and despotic authority, as Cicero had been, he saw no harm in quoting the whole passage as it stood.

The origin of royal authority was in fact one of the issues over which Augustine sharply disagreed with Cicero.[2] For Cicero, ancient kingship was wielded, in accordance with the order of nature, by the justest and wisest of men; whereas one of the themes which appear in the *De civitate Dei* with almost monotonous frequency is the theme of the origin of kingship in conquest, domination, and lust for power. And repeatedly Augustine dwells on the significance of the fact that the Old Testament patriarchs were shepherds rather than kings.[3] There can, therefore, be no justification for inferring from Augustine's use of the passage from Cicero's *De re publica* that he grouped kingship—

---

[1] In *De civ. Dei*, XIV, 23.2 Augustine, in the course of a similar argument, merely refers to this passage of Cicero's *De re publica* without quoting it in full. It is significant that in his summary he omits mentioning royal authority, and reduces the dichotomy between the two types of authority to the basic form in which it was acceptable to him. Cicero, he writes, 'when discussing the varieties of authority (*de imperiorum differentia*), took an analogy from human nature: the limbs of the body are ruled like sons, on account of their readiness to obey, whereas the vicious parts of the soul are coerced, like slaves, by a harsher kind of rule'. Nothing could give a clearer indication of the sense in which he understood the analogy, and what really mattered to him in its application. The idea of a hierarchy of God–mind–body recurs e.g. in *Sermo Morin* 11.12 (Morin, 633) without any mention of political authority. Cf. *De serm. Dom.* I, 2.9.

[2] This is noted by Schilling, *SSLAug*, 53–4. Schilling refers to Cicero, *Leg.* III, 2; *Off.* II, 12 and, by way of pointing the contrast, to *De civ. Dei*, XVI, 4; 17; XVIII, 2; V, 12 etc.

[3] *De civ. Dei*, XIX, 15; *Qu. in Hept.* I, 153.

and other non-despotic forms of political authority—with paternal and other natural forms of authority. Once in the *De civitate Dei*[1] Augustine refers to Cicero's argument, using it, on this occasion, in its original sense, that is to say, as an argument to justify political authority on the analogy of the natural rule of the mind over its body, rather than in the reverse direction. But in doing so, Augustine takes every care to evacuate the argument of all its force. In earlier parts of his *De re publica*, as Augustine summarises Cicero, he had argued the case for injustice, and suggested that a commonwealth could not exist without it, for the rule of one man over others is unjust, and yet, there can be no dominion over nations without it. Now, Augustine says, Cicero changes his standpoint, and meets this argument by asserting that this subjection is justified by the fact that 'it is good for such men to be subjected, for subjection is to their benefit', in that by removing from the wicked the power to hurt, they will be better off when tamed than they had been untamed. Augustine passes over this classical piece of imperialist dogma without comment—he had plenty to say about it earlier in his work—and goes on to note Cicero's further justification of such rule by invoking the analogy of nature: 'Why else should God rule over men, the mind over the body, reason over lust and the other vices?' But his answer to the rhetorical question drastically deflates its Ciceronian implications, and turns its significance in another direction. Cicero's examples show, he says modestly, that for some people subjection is good,[2] and that subjection to God is good for all. For the mind which is justly subject to God rules justly over its body; and with the Ciceronian claim for political authority and subjection quietly by-passed, Augustine returns to the point with which the present excursus had begun: the meaning of justice and the need for it in the *res publica*, defined as Cicero had defined it. His handling of Cicero's argument shows profound reserve about Cicero's aligning of political authority and subjection on the side of natural authority and subordination.

---

[1] XIX, 21.2.

[2] This view, too, is anticipated in *De Genesi ad litteram*, where Augustine notes the value to be set upon the *ordo reipublicae in cuiusdam pacis terrenae vinculum coercens etiam peccatores* (IX, 9.14). This is, of course, a commonplace of patristic literature, and finds its classical expression in Irenaeus, *AH*, V, 24.2. There are good grounds for thinking that Augustine was acquainted with Irenaeus's work; cf. Altaner, 'Augustin und Irenaeus'. Schilling quotes (*SSLAug*, 46 f.) several passages from other writers containing similar views on the origins of political authority; but he does not admit that the apparent similarity entitles us to infer that Augustine derives 'the whole political order from sinfulness as its source' (*ibid.* 51).

The views on the origin of political authority which I have traced in Augustine's works appear to be his settled views from about 401 onwards. Before this time he does not appear to have devoted much thought to this question. From remarks scattered through his earlier works a somewhat different view of the nature of political authority can be pieced together.[1] The strand in Augustine's reflection on society which we have been studying is only one among several which shaped his views on the state and its functions; views which sometimes gave rise to tensions in his mind, some of which he never fully resolved. In so far as our present theme can be isolated as a coherent theme in his thought, it seems very likely that his deepened study of Paul in the mid 390s helped to give it shape. This is the source of his consciousness of the power of sin over human nature. The shift from an early optimism is nowhere more marked than in his reflection on society. The whole complex cluster of themes which go into the making of this reflection is too wide for study here. From a wider point of view, the revolutionary effect of thirteenth-century Aristotelianism could be summed up quite simply as lying in the assertion of the innate value of the natural order as a positive force for good, as against Augustine's refusal to assign value to the things of nature, *per se*, in a sinful world. But here I am concerned with a narrower question: just how, precisely, did Augustine[2] think of political society in relation to the natural order? Stating the question in these terms, one does, of course, run the risk of giving Augustine's own treatment of the theme an air of spurious terminological precision. The looseness of his conception of 'nature' is too notorious to require comment; and the extent to which one should speak of his conception of 'political' authority, let alone of the 'state', is open to debate. But we may, at any rate, summarise the result of the present enquiry by saying that the terms in which Augustine came to formulate his views on politically organised society (that is to say, on society articulated within the framework of government and its agencies, law, enforcement and the machinery of their administration: roughly what we should nowadays call the 'state') were those which he thought appropriate to the treatment of the institution of slavery, rather than those which he applied to the human family.

The crucial point at stake in the theological discussions of the origins

---

[1] Cf. Ch. 4, above, pp. 73–9.
[2] On his thirteenth-century interpreters, cf. Appendix C, below.

of political authority is the question as to whether it is to be treated on the model of the authority of a master over his slave, or on that of a husband and father over his wife and family. These are the paradigm cases which give us a clue to the senses in which the concept of 'nature' is applied to social groupings. What is meant by asserting—or by denying—that political authority belongs to the natural order depends on the meaning attached to 'natural': it will clearly be something very different according to whether, and in what sense, the 'natural order' is held to include or to exclude the institution of slavery. If there is a sense in which political society was, for Augustine, 'natural' —and we shall see that some of his medieval interpreters thought that there was such a sense—it is a sense very different from that in which he thought the family to be 'natural'. We may, therefore, conclude, without fear of distorting his view, though in a language slightly more formalised than his own, that after *c.* 400 Augustine continued to think, with Cicero,[1] that man was a social animal by nature, but that he came to reject the view that he was also naturally a political animal.[2] Of this latter view there is no trace in the two chapters of the *De civitate Dei* which we have examined; and, interpreted in the context of the ideas with which they belong in Augustine's thought, and particularly in the light of his *Auseinandersetzung* with Cicero's views, they clearly assert the contrary.

---

[1] *duce natura congregabantur homines—Off.* II, 21.73.

[2] *Ibid.* and *Fin.* V, 23.66: human nature has *quiddam ingenitum quasi civile atque populare quod Graeci politicon vocant.*

AUGUSTINE AND THE ARISTOTELIAN REVOLUTION OF THE THIRTEENTH CENTURY[1]

Thirteenth-century scholastics were addicted to quoting statements of Augustine's, as of other *sancti*, as *auctoritates* in support of their opinions. The conventions of the scholastic employment of *auctoritates* are now tolerably well known. A modern scholar will not be surprised by frequent divergences between the meaning of such statements in their original setting and the meaning given them by one or other thirteenth-century theologian. Thirteenth-century theologians would have been even less worried by such divergences. Their analysis can, nevertheless, be illuminating. In this Appendix I examine the use made by a number of thirteenth-century writers of Augustine's statements about the origins and nature of political authority and subjection, mainly in the *De civitate Dei*, Book XIX, Chapters 14 and 15. This is one of the points at which we should expect the impact of Aristotelian ideas to show itself most clearly on political thought. It is here that we may best test the validity of the rival claims that the impact of these ideas revolutionised medieval political thought or, alternatively, that they stood in direct continuity with traditional, patristic and especially Augustinian thought-forms.

A. J. Carlyle may serve as representing the more widely held view:

> To the Stoics and the Fathers the coercive control of man by man is not an institution of nature. By nature men, being free and equal, were under no system of coercive control. Like slavery, the introduction of this was the result of the loss of man's original innocence, and represented the need for some power which might control and limit the unreasonable passions and appetites of human nature...It was not till Aristotle's *Politics* were rediscovered in the thirteenth century that Saint Thomas Aquinas under their influence recognised that the State was not merely an institution devised to correct men's vices, but rather the necessary form of a real and full human life.[2]

This generally current view has been controverted by scholars such as Otto Schilling and Gustave Combès, who, relying on their peculiar

---

[1] Originally part of a paper published in *JTS*, NS 16 (1965).
[2] Carlyle, *A history*, vol. 3, 5. Cf., among more recent discussions, Ullmann, *Principles*, 231 f.

interpretation of Augustine's thought in this sphere,[1] have represented Aquinas's political thought as standing in direct continuity with Augustine and the patristic tradition. We have already seen (see Ch. 4 and Appendix B) that in fact Augustine's thought was very different in its orientation, and increasingly so in the course of its development. In this respect the thesis of a continuity between the Augustinian and the Thomist traditions cannot be maintained.

The purpose of this Appendix is not to study the contrasts and the opposition between the two traditions. It is a much more modest one, which nevertheless lies at the centre of the larger question. Having defined the meaning of Augustine's statements about the origin of political authority in Appendix B, I now turn to some thirteenth-century interpretations of the key passages by a number of writers of both the Aristotelian and what is traditionally referred to as the 'Augustinian' schools. Anything like a full study of their theories of political authority is beyond my scope here. An examination of their various attempts to come to grips with the Augustinian view of the foundations of this authority will, however, enable us to watch at close quarters what Augustine meant as seen through thirteenth-century pre-occupations, and how far this meaning was modified by Aristotelian preoccupations. If in doubt about the meaning of a statement, it is in any case good policy to ask what would be involved in its denial: the Aristotelian denial of Augustine's views on the origin of political authority may help to clarify the meaning of these views.

Although *De civitate Dei*, xix, 14 and 15 find no place in the exposition of Gen. 1:26–7 in the *Glossa Ordinaria*, or in the discussion of political authority in the *Sentences* of Peter Lombard, they were nevertheless common property to medieval theologians and were often invoked in debates about the origins of authority and subjection. The purpose of this Appendix is to shed some light on the interpretation of Augustine's views on this subject primarily by St Thomas Aquinas. Thomas's first work, his commentary on the *Sentences*, though written before Aristotle had made his full impact on his political thinking with the Latin version of the *Politics*, was already marked by strong Aristotelian influence, especially of the *Ethics*. In his *Scriptum super Sententiis* we can observe Thomas in dialogue with the tradition of the schools on the one hand, and with his contemporaries, notably

---

[1] Schilling, *SSLAug*, and Combès, *La doctrine politique*, contain their interpretations of Augustine (discussed above, Appendix B, pp. 199 f.). On these Schilling bases the continuity-thesis developed in his study of Saint Thomas. Cf. *SSLThom*, 238 f. and *passim*.

St Albert the Great and St Bonaventure, on the other.[1] To throw Thomas's views into sharper relief, I shall begin by comparing them with Bonaventure's and Albert's, referring, incidentally, to one or two other writers. The comparison with Bonaventure serves to assess Thomas's views in relation to a theologian less intoxicated with the new learning and more reserved about its results than was Albert, Thomas's teacher and one of the leaders of the Christian Aristotelian revival of the thirteenth century.

Of the three writers it is Bonaventure whom we should expect to follow Augustine's teaching most closely. We may begin with his comments on Distinction 44 of the second book of the *Sentences*. Bonaventure makes an important distinction here[2] between two ways in which we can speak of something being against the *ius naturae*: either absolutely (*simpliciter*) or within the limits of nature in a particular condition (*secundum aliquem statum*). The statement that authority (*potestas dominandi*) is against natural right, Bonaventure says, is true only if understood in the second sense; that is to say, it is not true of nature as such, in all its states, only of nature in its state of original integrity 'in which there was no place for servile subjection (*subiectio servitutis*) or authority (*praelatio potestatis*)'. The conclusion is Augustine's, and a commonplace of medieval theology; but there is a refinement introduced in the distinction between 'nature' taken *simpliciter* and 'nature' taken *secundum aliquem statum*, a distinction which tends to be notoriously blurred in Augustine's language. The distinction is of some importance in Bonaventure's discussion of our problem in the next *quaestio*.[3] Here he distinguishes three ways in which we may take *potestas dominandi vel praesidendi*: first, we may take it, *largissime*, to include a man's power to use something as his possession. Secondly, we may take it to mean, *communiter*, a man's power to command someone else who is capable of reason and obedience. Finally, we may take it, *proprie*, to mean the power to coerce subordinates. Authority taken in its first sense obtains in nature in all its states. The second kind exists in nature *in via*, both in its original integrity and in its fallen state. Bonaventure illustrates this second type of authority by that which a man has over his wife or a father over his child, both of which, in his view, exist in nature, whether in its original

[1] Cf. Chenu, *Introduction*, 235.

[2] *In Sent.* II, D. 44, a. 2, q. I, ad 4 m.

[3] *Ibid.* q. 2. The treatment and phraseology of Richard of Middleton (*In Sent.* II, D. 44, a. 2, q. 2) are very closely parallel.

or its fallen state. Authority in its third sense, however, understood as coercive power, exists in fallen nature only; *servitus* is to be reckoned as *poena peccati*, or, as he puts it in his reply[1] to an objection, men possess dominion over other men *quodammodo praeternaturaliter, in punitionem peccati*, whereas their dominion over lower creatures belongs to them by nature. Bonaventure concludes his analysis with the remark that it is authority in its third sense, as coercive power, that is under discussion now; and this concluding remark indicates how completely he is in agreement with Augustine. For what is under discussion is political authority; and, like Augustine, Bonaventure cannot divorce this from coercive power, and, like Augustine, too, he refuses to assimilate it to the sort of authority enjoyed by a husband over his wife or a father over his child. Bonaventure's refinement of the vocabulary of 'nature' and his care in applying it here has enabled him to define a sense in which political authority can be said to be 'natural'. But it is a sense in which its status is 'natural' in the way that slavery is 'natural', not in the way that the human family is. Bonaventure's profound fidelity to Augustine's thought is scarcely concealed by the greater precision of his terminology.

One phrase, however, of Augustine's chapter which Bonaventure adduces in support of his view gave him some trouble. This is the statement[2] that dominion and subjection are ordained by the same law as that which bids the observance of nature and forbids its transgression. Like many more careless readers, Bonaventure misunderstood Augustine's statement. He took it to mean that dominion and subjection were ordained by the order of nature, whereas Augustine had asserted the quite different position that the same eternal providence stands behind human subjection as operates in the natural order. Even in its misunderstanding of Augustine's text Bonaventure's argument is revealing. The statement, he says, applies only to fallen nature, 'so that the wicked might be restrained and the good protected': for otherwise man's corrupt nature would make social life impossible. In the state of innocence, however, there would have been no need for such dominion and subjection, for here all would have remained equably *in gradu et statu suo*.[3] Bonaventure was anxious not to allow Augustine's statement —erroneously understood—to call into doubt his view of authority. The distinction between nature *simpliciter* and nature *secundum aliquem*

[1] *Ibid.* ad 3 m.
[2] *De civ. Dei*, XIX, 15. Cf. above, Appendix B, p. 204 n. 2.
[3] *Loc. cit.* ad 4 m.

statum enabled him to avoid this neatly: it was only necessary to identify the 'order of nature' in Augustine's statement with that of nature in its fallen state. Thus notwithstanding his misunderstanding of Augustine at this point, Bonaventure succeeded in bringing the statement into line with the theory of political authority which he had learnt from Augustine. Like Augustine, he saw human subjection to rulers—even to non-Christian rulers—as a human institution sanctioned by a dispensation of divine providence,[1] but not as an ordinance of nature.

Bonaventure's treatment of our theme is clearly a great advance on the cursory remarks given it by Alexander of Hales.[2] If one considers it together with St Thomas's comments in his *Scriptum super sententiis*,[3] and another text of the mid or late 1250s, from the *Summa* attributed to Alexander of Hales,[4] it is not easy to escape the impression that the new approach to this question owed something to perplexities aroused by quite recent intellectual movements. Perhaps it was such perplexities that prompted the author of the article in the *Summa fratris Alexandri* to a meticulous re-reading of Augustine's key texts. In his article he is concerned with the question whether Adam had dominion over other men before his fall. The authorities cited against an affirmative answer are, significantly, identical with those used by Bonaventure in the article I have discussed. They are: (1) the statement that freedom is part of man's original condition (here fastened on to Isidore, *Etym.* v, 4.1); (2) Augustine, *De civitate Dei*, XIX, 15; and (3) the famous passage of distinctly Augustinian inspiration from Gregory the Great, *Moralia*, XXI, 15.22-3. The argument begins by distinguishing two forms of *dominium*, that of superiority by reason of higher excellence on account either of origin or of priority in time, or by reason of superior knowledge or virtue; and *dominium* as *auctoritas praesidendi*,

---

[1] *Loc. cit.* a. 3, q. 1.

[2] His comments on *Sent.* II, D. 44 in his *Glossa* take a different direction and do not discuss *dominium*. He touches on the theme of *dominium* in the *Summa*, P. III, q. 48, m. 1 (the passage may well be from his pen). Here he is content to affirm (ad 3m) the commonplace taken from Gregory's *Moralia*, XXI, 15.22, cited here, that men are equal and not made to dominate each other by nature but have fallen into this state through their perversity.

[3] Cf. below, pp. 219 f.

[4] P. II, q. 93, m. 1, 521. V. Doucet, in the *Prolegomena* appended to the Quaracchi edition of the *Summa* (vol. 4, p. ccclvi), assigns the block of which it forms a part to the years 1255-7, and is inclined to attribute it to William of Milton or to somebody working under his supervision. The possibility that it may be the work of a pupil of St Bonaventure's is not proven, but cannot be discounted.

immo potius possidendi. In language very similar to Bonaventure's, the former is referred to as *dominium* understood *communiter, sive nomine extenso,* the latter as *dominium* taken *proprie.* Corresponding to the two kinds of *dominium* there are two kinds of subjection (*servitus*): *obsequium reverentiae et libertatis,* the freely given service and respect of the natural-ly inferior to his acknowledged superior, and the servile subjection owed in virtue of condition and necessity (*necessitatis, conditionis, scilicet servilis*). The passage from Augustine's *De Genesi ad litteram*[1] which we have considered above is invoked, and interpreted, rightly, as distinguishing 'the service of generosity or love (*servitus liberalitatis sive dilectionis*)' from that of enforced, unwilling service owed in virtue of condition (*servitus contradictionis sive violentiae*); and in conclusion the author asserts, with a reference to Augustine's *De civitate Dei,* XIX, 15, that only the first kind of authority could have existed in nature before the Fall.

This is entirely within Augustinian horizons. The only thing that the author fails to make clear, in contrast with Bonaventure, is whether he considers political authority as an instance of the authority of natural superiority, or as to be classified with the *auctoritas praesidendi, immo potius possidendi,* along with authority over slaves. The author can scarcely have failed to realise that it was in fact political authority that his enquiry was about; for Bonaventure makes this clear, and the two discussions have so much in common—the authorities used, the frame-work of thought, the whole *Problemstellung*—that we may suspect either a direct relation between them or, at least, a fairly well crystallised approach to debating the theme in the schools. In these circumstances it is difficult to envisage the possibility that two Franciscan theologians could have given as radically opposed answers to the question as would be implied by interpreting the present article as asserting a natural origin for political authority.

Be this as it may, the author of the article shows an exact and penetrating understanding of Augustinian passages often misunder-stood, not only by his contemporaries. We have already noted his very relevant comments on Augustine's distinction between the service of 'generosity or love' and the enforced 'subjection of condition'.[2] His remarks[3] on the final sentences of *De civitate Dei,* XIX, 14 and the first of chapter 15, though they take some liberty in interpreting the text,

---

[1] XI, 37.50; cf. above, Appendix B, pp. 202 f.
[2] Cf. the previous note.   [3] *Loc. cit.* ad 1 m.

are equally penetrating. Augustine's words do not imply, he says, that men are by nature made to dominate other men, but that men in a position of authority have the twofold duty of instructing their subjects (*officium consulendi*) and of caring for them (*providendi misericordia*). He appreciated that Augustine was here speaking not of the origins of authority but of conduct in authority. Further, he shows quite remarkable insight into Augustine's conception[1] of a twofold providential order, working through nature on the one hand and through human actions on the other. It is with a perceptive paraphrase of this doctrine and a reference to *De civitate Dei*, xix, 15 that he answers[2] the objection that if men were not naturally subordinated to each other, this would constitute a breach of the principle seen operating throughout nature. In conclusion, he denies the force of the argument that things are made by nature to form a hierarchy in which some are subordinated to others: for inanimate things are, so to speak, made to be 'pushed around' by each other, whereas man, being made in God's image, is directly related to him without intermediaries. Wherefore, his argument continues, God had made man in such a condition of freedom that he was not bound to serve anybody in order to attain his own good, which he was to pursue freely and unhindered. So long as he remained subject to God, he was subject to no one else, as are other creatures which are not themselves responsible for their actions but act on impulse. The writer shows little originality; but his understanding of Augustine's texts is impressive. His way of facing the perplexities raised by current debate was the scholar's way, by returning to the authentic source of the tradition he was representing.

The most striking contrast between these Franciscan writers and St Albert the Great is that his ideas on political authority are not worked out in the context of a theory of *dominium* at all, and that his theory of *dominium* is elaborated without reference to the standard choice of texts, from Augustine and Gregory. Thus in his early commentary on the *Sentences*, he shares the simple, untheoretical approach which marks Alexander of Hales's treatment of the corresponding themes. There is no attempt here[3] to relate what is said about the duty of obeying ecclesiastical or secular authorities to any theoretical framework; there is no talk whatever of *dominium* or *servitus*, of nature and sin. When he returns, perhaps some twenty-five years later, to the same theme in his *Summa*,[4] the theoretical framework of the discussion

---

[1] Cf. above, pp. 87, 203 f. [2] *Loc. cit.* ad 3 m.
[3] *In Sent.* II, D. 44, a. 6. [4] P. II, q. 141, m. 3.

is provided by Aristotle's *Politics*. By the time he came to write his *Summa*, Albert had come to see the institutions of human society in Aristotelian terms. And although he does devote an article[1] to the theme of *dominium*, it has no application to political authority. Even the very definition of what constitutes *dominium* excludes in advance the possibility of treating political authority as a case of *dominium*. For one of the factors essential to 'perfect *dominium*' (the only kind discussed) is the supremacy of someone worse than or inferior to the subject. Such subjection to somebody (or something) inferior in rank or value will constitute a restriction of a rational being's freedom. Of the ways enumerated by Albert, in which such servitude occurs, only one is of interest to us, the *servitus conditionalis* 'whereby a man is subjected to another in such a way that all his actions and possessions are referred to that person, and that whatever he does or possesses he does and possesses in the other's name... This subjection originates in sin, for it is just that he who has sinned against his superior by nature, against the Father, should be subjected to his equal by nature...' Although the argument follows the Augustinian lines, there is no reference to any of the Augustinian passages which Albert might have invoked to confirm his view. The similarity with Augustine's view is, however, deceptive—and it may be that it was an awareness of this that kept Albert from appealing to Augustine. Albert may be in full agreement with Augustine on the origins of slavery; but he holds a very different view of subjection to political authority. His precise, almost legal description of *servitus conditionalis* indicates that his remarks on it refer to slavery only, and are not intended to embrace other forms of subjection of man to man. Nothing is said here about political authority, for the very good reason that *dominium*, defined in the unusual way as it is by Albert, excluded political authority by definition.[2] He saw the state through Aristotle's eyes[3] and appears to have felt no need to relate this vision to traditional patterns of debating the nature of authority.

[1] P. II, q. 39, m. 2, a. 1, p. 1, q. 1.
[2] There is an extended discussion in *Sum. theol.* p. II, q. 26, m. 1, again on quite traditional lines, of two forms of subjection, the servitude which has its origin in sin, and subjection to those wiser or better, in accordance with the order of nature and reason. The latter has nothing in common with servitude, for one is freely subject to the other. Albert calls this form of subjection *subiectio providentiae et regiminis*. Although he is speaking of the angelic hierarchy of subordination, he clearly wishes to assimilate political authority to this form.
[3] Cf. ... *de numero eorum quae sunt natura homini, id est quae sunt naturalia homini, civitas est, et communicatio civilis sive politica. Comm. in lib. Pol. Arist.* L. I, c. 1.

The only reference I have discovered to any of the relevant passages from Augustine is one to *De civitate Dei*, XIX, 15. This occurs, however, in a context only remotely and indirectly related to the problem of authority, in the course of an objection in a question concerned with the providential order in the universe.[1] Here Albert quotes the opening sentences of the chapter, and concludes from them that 'if a man rules over a man or a sinner over a just man, which frequently happens in the world, then there is confusion, not order'. He answers[2] by saying that 'the rule of man over man or of sinners over just men confounds the *ordo particularis*; but the order of universal justice is thereby made the greater and the more beautiful'. We may well doubt if Albert would have allowed that political authority as such amounted to a disturbance of the *ordo particularis*. Augustine's distinction between the two modes of providence is, likewise, identified[3] with his own distinction between the two senses of 'order'. Albert's interests lay elsewhere, and he felt no need to be more than perfunctory here. He relied on traditional, Augustinian, ideas for his views on slavery, on Aristotelian ideas for his views on politics; and the pressure to clarify their relations by-passed him.

His pupil, St Thomas Aquinas, appears from the start to have been much more anxious to relate his Aristotelian ideas on society to the Augustinian views on subjection generally current in the schools in the 1250s. Although he had not yet a complete translation of Aristotle's *Politics* at his disposal, he could learn Aristotle's view of man as *animal politicum* from the *Ethics*,[4] a work already well known to him when he composed his *Scriptum super Sententiis*. In this, his earliest work, he already shows a concern to relate the two sets of ideas within a single framework.[5] That his way of dealing with the problem owes something to the current debates we may guess from his very selection of texts: they include the texts from Augustine and from Gregory which we have seen being repeatedly invoked. In his answer to the question whether there would have been authority (*praelatio seu dominium*) in the state of innocence, Thomas begins with distinguishing two 'modes' of authority: one is for the sake of government (*ad regimen ordinatus*), the other for the sake of domination (*ad dominandum*). With a reference to Aristotle's *Ethics* (apparently 1161 a 30–b 10), he remarks that the

---

[1] *Sum. theol.* p. II, q. 63, m. 1, ob. 3.   [2] *Ibid.* ad 3m.
[3] *Ibid.* ad ult. qu. 1, referring to *De Gen. ad litt.* VIII, 23.44, discussed above, pp. 87, 203 f.
[4] E.g. 1097 b 11, 1162 a 17–18, 1169 b 18.
[5] *In Sent.* II, D. 44, q. 1, a. 3.

second mode is analogous to a tyrant's authority over his subjects, the first to a king's: for the former dominates over his subjects for his own benefit, the latter rules them for their good. The authority of domination could therefore exist in the state of innocence only over creatures made to subserve human purposes, not over other men; for men are not made to serve human ends. This subjection comes about only in so far as their condition is assimilated, as a consequence of sin, to that of irrational creatures. Only the authority of ruling men in their own interests could have belonged to man in his creational integrity.

The distinction between two 'modes' of authority is quite at home within a fundamentally Augustinian context. In *De civitate Dei*, XIX, 14 Augustine had been speaking of two ways of exercising power; what Aquinas says about two 'modes' of *dominium* can be translated into Augustine's less formal speech without difficulty. He uses traditional material to state the distinction between tyrannical rule (assimilated naturally to the rule of a master over his slaves) and non-tyrannical. It is essentially the same distinction as Augustine had made between the ruler who rules *dominandi cupiditate* and the ruler who rules *officio consulendi*. On the matter of the exercise of power, and its harmony or lack of harmony with the order of nature, there is no disagreement between Aquinas and Augustine. A strain begins to show as soon as Aquinas turns to answering objections based on the Augustinian view of the institutions of human subjection. To reconcile this with his views, Thomas has to confine their significance by interpreting them as referring to the exercise of authority. Thus one objection[1] is based on Augustine's *dictum* that since man was made in the image of God, he was placed only above other creatures, not above his fellow men, over whom he would have no dominion but for sin; another,[2] based on the same chapter of *De civitate Dei*, asserts that since *dominium* implies *servitus* as its correlative and since the latter, as all the Fathers agree, was introduced on account of sin, there could have been no *dominium* or *praelatio* in the absence of sin. Aquinas answers both together,[3] remarking that these statements refer to the second mode of authority, that of domination. This, of course, had been far from Augustine's intention; but it was a means that lay ready to hand to effect a reconciliation. But Aquinas was not content with as perfunctory and superficial a reconciliation as satisfied Albert. In the article we are considering, he goes on to examine political authority explicitly; and

[1] *Ibid.* ob. 2.   [2] *Ibid.* ob. 3.   [3] *Ibid.* ad 2m and *similiter* ad 3m.

his procedure shows a real attempt to clarify in his own mind how far the Augustinian assessment of political authority is acceptable.

Having distinguished the two modes of *dominium*, of which only the one 'ordained for the sake of government' could have belonged to nature in its original integrity, he further considers this mode of authority in respect of three functions (*usus*) enumerated as follows: first, the direction of subjects in 'what is to be done'; second, the providing for needs such as common defence of the people against enemies; third, the correction of morals, 'so that the wicked may be coerced to perform the actions of virtue' by punishments. Of these functions, Aquinas says, only the first would have had a place in the absence of sin, for there would have been no need for the others. Thus, to secure agreement with Aristotle, Aquinas has driven a wedge into the substance of political authority. For Aristotle, as, indeed, for Augustine, political authority was not conceivable without coercive power. This belonged to its very essence, and this was one of the reasons why Augustine thought that all earthly kingdoms were, as institutions, rooted somehow in the dispensation of sin. Aquinas wished to concede this, and he also wanted to speak, with Aristotle, of the political order as an ordinance of nature. In his attempt to reconcile the two ways of thought, he left what Augustine would have regarded as the distinctive features of political authority in the world of fallen man; but he dissociated them as in some way adventitious to the essence of political authority, which could have existed without such features. He did not notice that in doing this he was in effect rejecting Augustine's protest against assimilating political to paternal authority. What Aquinas left on the side of nature, Augustine would not have recognised as 'political'. For Augustine the institutional life of the Roman Empire was still a daily reality. That he thought more readily of governmental institutions in concrete terms than Aquinas need cause no surprise. Even with the great acceleration in the growth of governmental institutions in his own century, Aquinas could readily break down their institutional character into a series of 'functions' which could be isolated in this way.

If Thomas purchased agreement with Augustine by almost evacuating 'political authority' of meaning, his agreement with Aristotle was purchased at the same price. This appears from his manner of dealing with the objection that according to Aristotle[1] kings and other rulers had to be instituted in order to make laws with coercive power, a

[1] *Eth. Nic.* 1179 a 33 f.

power lacking to mere exhortation by wise men; and that there would have been no need for this if men had remained in their original state of justice. Aquinas answers[1] this argument with the simple assertion that in respect of 'that function' (he refers to the coercive function) there would have been no authority in man's original state; whereas there would have been in respect of the other governmental functions.[2] It would have been just as unreal to Aristotle as to Augustine to drive a wedge into the substance of government in this way. He would no more have recognised political authority in the guise of a citizens' advice bureau than would Augustine.

There are many signs that Aquinas was dissatisfied with this manner of solving his problem. With his deepening appreciation of Aristotle, he came to see the full force of Aristotle's view that man is by nature *animal politicum*.[3] The view that man was by nature *animal sociale* was, by itself, entirely traditional, and could be found—on occasion in almost the very words—in Augustine.[4] With growing understanding of Aristotle, Thomas came to see that Aristotle's views on man as *animal politicum* were more far-reaching than the traditional view of him as *sociale*,[5] and he was clear that from the Aristotelian point of view there could be no distinction between *politicum* and *sociale*, as if the former were no more than a particular form or species

[1] *Loc. cit.* ad 4 m.

[2] Aquinas speaks of these in the plural. This must be a slip, as the article only allows one *usus* in the original state of innocence.

[3] Thomas's terminology and its development could be investigated with profit. A cursory and far from exhaustive study of his language suggests to me that he began with an appreciation of Augustine's view of man as social by nature, and then came to see that Aristotle meant more than this by asserting that man was naturally *animal politicum* (or *civile*); and that as he came to see man in more thoroughly Aristotelian terms, he tended to expand the meaning of *sociale* so as to make it effectively synonymous with *politicum* (or *civile*). He uses the terms *civile*, e.g. *In Pol.* I, lect. 1, *In Pol.* III, lect. 5, or *politicum*, e.g. *Sum. theol.* I–II, 61.5; *In Eth.* I, lect. 9; IX, lect. 10; but he speaks more often of man as *animal sociale*: e.g. *Sum. theol.* I, 96.4; I–II, 95.4; II–II, 109.3, ad 1; *Sum. c. gent.* III, 117, 128, 129, 147; *In Eth.* I, lect. 1. Sometimes he uses *sociale et* (or *vel*) *politicum*, e.g. *Sum. theol.* I–II, 72.4; *Sum. c. gent.* III, 85; *De reg. princ.* I, 1. Schilling asserts (*SSL Thom.* 80–1) that Aquinas distinguished the two concepts and only used them as synonymous where this did not affect his argument. I can find no support for this view in the references he gives. I am inclined to agree with I. T. Eschmann's judgement: 'unless special reasons suggested to Aquinas the exact textual reproduction of the Aristotelian principle [that man is a *political* animal] he prefers to say that man is a *social* animal' (*St Thomas on Kingship*, 4, n. 2). Generally speaking, the terms appear to be used interchangeably.

[4] Cf. above, Appendix B, pp. 204–5.

[5] One of the many indications of his increasing appreciation of the far-reaching implications of Aristotle's view has been noted by Fr Eschmann, *St Thomas on kingship*, 4, n. 3, who draws attention to the fact that Thomas gradually came to the view that Avicenna's

of the latter. Social existence, in Aristotle's perspective, was identical with political existence. The *polis* was not society plus political structure, and a 'society' without political structure would have been even less than chimerical in his eyes: for at least a chimera could be imaginatively constructed from elements experienced separately. If for Aristotle a society which[1] was not political was meaningless, it was not so for Augustine and the Christian Fathers. For Aristotle the archetypal society was the *polis*; for them it was the family of the saints in heaven. For them there could be a real distinction between that kind of society and the politically organised society which they knew in the Empire. From their point of view 'social' and 'political' were by no means synonymous concepts, as they had to be for Aristotle. As Thomas came to regard society increasingly from an Aristotelian standpoint, it is not surprising that in his vocabulary, too, *sociale* and *politicum* should have tended to lose their distinctive features. The profound significance of Thomas's Aristotelian view of society is entirely beyond the scope of this study, though its growth in his mind could still profitably be mapped with more precision than it has yet received. We must return to his understanding of Augustine's view, and consider how he interpreted it later in his career, after the Aristotelian vision of society had established itself more deeply in his mind.

The one occasion when Aquinas returns to consider our two chapters of Augustine's *De civitate Dei* is in connection with his re-statement of his views on the origins of authority in his *Summa theologiae*. The framework within which he places his article[2] on man's dominion over man in the state of innocence is entirely traditional. It follows articles devoted to man's authority over the lower creation, original equality of men, and so forth. His answer to the question about dominion over men is also, at first sight, impeccably traditional. It begins with a distinction between two kinds of *dominium* reminiscent of, but not identical with, the early distinction we have considered. Where the early work contrasted two mutually exclusive modes of authority, one exercised for the benefit of the master, the other for that of the subject, we now find the distinction drawn between authority as a general concept (*secundum quod communiter refertur ad subiectum qualitercumque*),

---

arguments for man's being naturally a social animal ceased to satisfy Aquinas because they were incapable 'of demonstrating the conclusion that man is a *political animal*' (italics in text).

[1] I am, of course, excluding, for this purpose, lesser groupings such as the household or small community.   [2] I, 96.4.

related to any form of subjection, and authority in a special sense, understood as the correlative of servitude. This latter could not have existed in the state of innocence; the former could. This way of stating the distinction between two sorts of *dominium* may be logically equivalent to the earlier manner of speaking; but it creates a much firmer impression that Thomas wishes to affirm, in the first place, that *dominium* does belong to the state of nature before the Fall. Instead of asserting that in one mode it did and another it did not exist in the state of innocence, he now says that *dominium* belongs to this state, except for one form of it, the form found in slavery. Another difference between this and the earlier treatment is noteworthy: whereas the two 'modes' of authority distinguished had been two ways of exercising authority, the contrast is here drawn in institutional terms: it is between authority as existing in slavery and authority as existing, among other institutions, in the 'office of governing free men'.

The crucial difference, however, between this and the earlier treatment of the same theme is the greater simplicity and assurance with which Thomas now speaks. The hesitations and qualifications which he had found necessary are now gone; most significantly, the further enumeration of the three 'functions' of authority is omitted. The purpose of that enumeration had been to discuss the extent to which authority *ad regimen ordinatus* could be found in the institutions of political authority. Aquinas was, at the time, still too much of a traditionalist to be prepared to throw to the winds Augustine's insistence that these institutions, with their necessarily coercive character, were infected with the dispensation of sin. He had sought to reconcile Augustine and Aristotle by dividing political authority into three functions and allocating one of these to nature, the others to sin. Now he treats political authority as all of a piece; and it belongs to the institutions grounded in nature. What Aquinas had come to discern in the course of the ten years or so between the two works was that coercive power belonged indivisibly to the stuff of political existence. There can be no doubt that this insight came to him with his growing understanding of Aristotle's political theory.[1] The insight excluded the

---

[1] The extent to which the unitary conception of political authority is derived from Aristotle appears strikingly in *Sum. theol.* I, 92.1 and 2m, where *subiectio civilis* is coupled with *subiectio oeconomica* and contrasted with *subiectio servilis*. References to passages in which Aquinas can be seen to assume that the power of coercing refractory subjects belongs to the essence of political authority could be multiplied. The following must suffice here:

possibility of compromise on the lines that he had experimented with in his youth.

In his explanation of the reason for his opinion Aquinas remarks that a subject is ruled in servile fashion in so far as he is ruled for his master's benefit; and this conflicts with the primitive order of nature. A subject is governed, however, as a free man, in so far as he is directed to his own good or the common good; and this sort of dominion must have existed before the Fall, for man is by nature a social animal, and social life, according to Aristotle, would be impossible without a directive authority. The appeal to Aristotle underlines what is in any case clear: Aquinas is thinking in terms of genuine political authority with the full apparatus of governmental machinery and the power of enforcement. This is what is now traced, unambiguously, to an origin in nature. The break with the Augustinian theory of the origins of political authority appears to be complete. But Aquinas invokes *De civitate Dei*, XIX, 14–15 in the course of a second argument added to prove that authority over free men would have existed in the state of innocence. It would have been inconvenient, he says, if those with a superabundance of wisdom and justice could not have devoted their superior gifts to the service of others less well endowed. 'Wherefore Augustine says that "the just rule not through a desire for power but through an obligation to give guidance; this is what the order of nature prescribes, this is how God created man".'[1] Augustine's admonition to people occupying a position of authority has been finally turned on its head: the obligation to act as a *paterfamilias* rather than as a tyrant is turned into a justification of precisely the thing Augustine wished to deny: that political society is, like a family, a natural institution. Augustine's wholesale exclusion of all human dominion of man over man from the state of innocence is quoted as an objection;[2] Aquinas's imperious reply to all the objections, that they are valid only against the first mode of authority—authority over a servile subject—conceals a radical change of attitude to political authority. It is scarcely

---

Sum. theol. I–II, 95.1; *In Eth.* X, lect. 14; *In Pol.* I, lect. I. It is most explicitly argued in *In Pol.* III, lect. 5. Most revealing, perhaps, is the surprising presence of the idea in as unhospitable a context as that provided by the pseudo-Dionysius's speculations on the angelic hierarchy; cf. *In div. nom.* ch. 12. Schilling, *SSL Thom*, 48 recognised that coercive power was for St Thomas included in political authority; he refers to *Sum. theol.* I–II, 105.2 and *In Pol.* III, lect. 9 to substantiate the view that judicial and penal systems belong to the essence of the state as conceived by St Thomas. It is Schilling's attempt to father on Augustine the view that all this belongs to the order of nature (*ibid.* 101) which must be rejected.

[1] *Sum. theol.* I, 96.4, quoting *De civ. Dei*, XIX, 14–15; cf. above.   [2] *Loc. cit.* ob. I.

surprising to find Thomas using, among his favourite models for political authority, the analogies rejected by Augustine. Without misgiving he returns, time and again, to the image of political authority as modelled on the relation of soul and body, or of God and the world.[1]

Augustine and the tradition which he helped to inspire may not have been always wholly clear about the meaning of 'nature'.[2] But both Augustine and some, at least, of his followers were clear enough about a radical difference they detected between the kind of authority and subjection to be found in the family and the kind found in slavery. In its essentials, this basic dichotomy was retained by Aquinas. The real problem lay in answering the question as to which side of the dividing line political authority was to be placed. Aquinas's first answer to this question had been, in effect, to evade its force. He had tried to split political authority by drawing the line across its very substance. Later, with increasing insight into the meaning of 'political authority', acquired through Aristotle, he came to discern the unsatisfactory character of his compromise. He now opted unambiguously for what, from the Augustinian standpoint, was a revolutionary view. He was too clear-sighted to be unaware of this revolution in political thinking. He had understood the Augustinian theology of society clearly enough, and loyalty to its tradition made him wish to fit his Aristotelian views into its framework. His understanding of Augustine's views Thomas shared with Bonaventure; with Albert he shared the fascination of the new Aristotelian vision of human society. Without a very much fuller study of contemporary debates, his originality in the way he accomplished the revolutionary transition from the one to the other tradition cannot be assessed. It is clear, however, that of the writers here considered, at any rate, he alone combined an appreciation of the real significance of Augustine's views with a growing, and in the end

---

[1] E.g. *De reg. princ.* I, I; 12 (= II.I, Eschmann); *Sum. c. gent.* III, 78. The analogy between political authority and the two ways in which the mind rules its body: *Sum. theol.* I, 81.3 ad 2 m; I–II, 58.2; 17.7 etc. *In Pol.* I, lect. 3 reveals its principal source. Interestingly, Aristotle's application of the analogy differs slightly from Cicero's version found in and rejected by Augustine.

[2] This consideration has been given more weight, I believe, than it deserves in this context by Dr W. Ullmann, *Principles*, 238 f. Whether Augustine had an adequately clear conception of 'nature' or not, he was as clear as he was emphatic that subjection was of two kinds, typified by servile subjection and by subjection to parental authority respectively. Aquinas certainly drew the line more carefully in giving the concept of 'nature' greater precision (as Bonaventure had also done); but the crucial break with Augustine's theory lay in transferring political authority from one side of the line to the other (as Bonaventure had refused to do).

triumphant, commitment to Aristotle's ideas on man as *animal civile*. As the new ideas took a deeper hold in his mind and served to crystallise his fundamental thought about man in society, the tensions proved insurmountable. He knew he had in effect broken with the old tradition, that the whole perspective of his thought had altered. It was no longer a matter of interpreting Aristotle within a traditional framework, but of fitting Augustine—by manhandling him, if need be—into the Aristotelian scheme.

The new preoccupations of political thinkers of the age of Boniface VIII, and the fourteenth-century controversies about dominion by grace,[1] were soon to eclipse the problem with which we have watched Aquinas grapple. New calls were made on Augustine's theology of authority, which are not our concern here.[2] We may, however, catch a last glimpse of Augustine's two chapters in a writer who stands on the confines of the intellectual world of Aquinas and of the world of the papalist theologians of the fourteenth century, Ptolemy of Lucca, his disciple and the continuator of his work on kingship, which has come down to us, completed by Ptolemy, as *De regimine principum*. Both in his continuation of Thomas's work[3] and in his *Determinatio compendiosa de iurisdictione imperii*[4] Ptolemy refers to *De civitate Dei*, XIX, 14–15. It would be out of place to consider his arguments—such as they are—in this study. The transition from Augustine's words to Aristotle's *Politics*, effected in both passages without the slightest misgiving, is part of his inheritance from St Thomas and was only made possible for him by his master's work. There is no trace here of any sense of tensions of thought, no trace of an inward struggle to reconcile a cherished tradition with new insight. Without scrutiny, all roads can now be assumed to lead in the same direction. Ptolemy of Lucca was the herald of a comfortable obliviousness to a profound cleavage in the tradition of Christian political thought.[5]

[1] An early appearance of our theme within the new context of debate can be seen in James of Viterbo, *De reg. chr.* II, 3.

[2] The most stimulating discussion of these known to me is Wilks, *The Problem of Sovereignty*.

[3] *De reg. princ.* III, 9.   [4] Ch. 17.

[5] The same assumption can be seen at work in the treatment of this theme by Giles of Rome. Political authority is essentially bound up with man's social existence, as Giles insists, in entirely Aristotelian language, equating *vita politica* with *vita socialis*. This being, in his view, natural to man, he interprets the opening statements of Augustine's *De civ. Dei*, XIX, 15 as excluding only despotic rule. See his *In Sent.* II, D. 44, q. 1, a. 2–3. The assumption that Aquinas and Augustine were asserting the same view of the origins of political authority and subjection had a long future. Its history in Christian political thought of Aristotelian inspiration and its effects on some of the social attitudes encouraged by it would make a fascinating study.

That the cleavage between Augustine's theology of political existence and the teaching of Christian Aristotelians is a matter of political thought perhaps requires some defence. Speculations about the kind of authority which might have existed in the Garden of Eden are not obviously and immediately relevant to an assessment of political life and institutions as experienced by actual human beings. Even such fine scholars as R. W. and A. J. Carlyle could altogether by-pass the political significance of the patristic and Augustinian denial that the state is a natural institution with a contemptuous reference[1] to 'these curiously unhistorical and infelicitous interpretations of human institutions', and their replacement by 'the sane and penetrating conceptions of Aristotle'. In a general way, of course, the assertion that political authority belongs to nature obviously serves to heighten its importance and dignity.[2] But to be content with this observation is to fail to appreciate the fundamental divergence between the two conceptions of political authority. What is involved is a radical disagreement, expressed in perhaps quasi-mythological terms, about the purpose of political authority and the meaning of freedom in society.

The older tradition which Augustine took up had perhaps been clearer in its insistence than was Augustine himself that to regard the Roman state as a divine dispensation for sinful men was at once an endorsement of its legitimate authority and a reminder of the restricted sphere of its competence. That state, like all others, originated in sin, and its purpose was both punitive and remedial. Political authority and its coercive agencies exist for the purpose of coping with the consequences of man's sin, with the disorganisation and conflict endemic in the human condition.

This particular strand of Augustine's political reflection is one which allies him with Christian thinkers of a period before the official recognition granted to Christianity by the Empire, and with Donatist and other schismatic writers opposed to the imperial state-Church. There is, of course, much in Augustine's political thought that dissociates him sharply from this tradition of thought.[3] If Augustine was

---

[1] *A history*, vol. 5, 6.

[2] Thus E. Lewis, for instance, rightly remarks that 'the Aquinist view of the state obviously implies a more positive view of the functions of government within the state' (*Medieval Political Ideas*, vol. 1, 151). Even Otto Schilling, notwithstanding his resolve to effect a far-reaching *rapprochement* between Augustine and Aquinas, notes that the Augustinian approach lays greater stress on the limitations of state-power than does the Aristotelian (cf. *SSLThom*, 60–1).

[3] See Ch. 6, above.

compromised on the subject of the range of legitimate political authority, on the scope to be allowed it in enforcing morality and orthodoxy, Aquinas saw the issues at stake with greater clarity. It is neither necessary nor possible to sketch here the systematic coherence between his views on its functions as an agency of enforcing Christian morality and orthodoxy, and his views on the state as a natural institution. It will scarcely be questioned that these views form, by and large, part of a single systematic exploration of the implications of his Aristotelian theory of political authority. He perceived the radical divergence between his own views on these subjects and the views implied by Augustine's theology of authority and subjection. Nothing illustrates this divergence better than the two different conceptions of freedom involved.

Augustinian and Aristotelian theologians were agreed that any subjection which restricts the subject's liberty cannot have belonged to nature in its original state. The Augustinian tradition, in excluding political authority from this state, implied that any interference with a subject's activities constitutes a restriction of his freedom. It may be a salutary and necessary restriction; but for all that, a man is unfree to the extent that he is coerced against his will. Political authority conceived as grounded in human nature implies a totally different conception of liberty. It becomes an agent of men's true interests, which only their shortcomings conceal from them. In securing the true goal of man, authority may override his actual wishes without thereby restricting his freedom, for it will express the 'free' choice of what Sir Isaiah Berlin has called[1] 'his "true", albeit submerged and inarticulate self'. Thomas had, of course, no difficulty in agreeing that slavery was incompatible with freedom,[2] but the grounds on which he establishes this are not that this kind of subjection is a curtailment of the range in which men can act as they wish, unhindered by other men, but that it curtails it without regard to their own good. The subjection of free men to their ruler implies no diminution of their freedom, so long as they are ruled for their own or for the common good. In exercising this kind of dominion over his subjects, a ruler 'rules over another *ut libero*',[3] and such a ruler 'is appropriately called the servant

---

[1] In *Two Concepts of Liberty*, 18.

[2] The argument of *Sum. theol.* I, 96.4 on slavery is anticipated in *In Sent.* II, D. 44, q. I, a. 3, ad 1m, in reply to the famous passage of Gregory's *Moralia* (XXI, 15.22), which asserts man's original freedom.

[3] *Sum. theol.* I, 96.4. The phrase by itself does not, of course, imply that a man is free even though coerced. It can be taken to mean that he is free in no more than a legal sense, i.e.

of his subjects'.[1] Augustine had exhorted rulers to act thus; but he had no illusions about political authority, even when exercised in accordance with the order of nature, amounting to a restriction of men's freedom. His account of the origins of political authority brings into play what Sir Isaiah Berlin has called the 'negative concept of freedom': the sense according to which any coercion implies a diminution of liberty. Thomas's conception relies on the 'positive sense', according to which the purpose for which a man is coerced determines whether his freedom is being restricted or not. What is at stake between the two conceptions of political authority, in the end, is the meaning of freedom.

that he is not a slave. But Thomas's argument does in fact presuppose that a man remains free in being coerced, provided that it is for his own or the common good.

[1] *In Sent.* II, D. 44, q. 1, a. 3, ad 1m.

'SACRED HISTORY' AND 'SALVATION HISTORY'

The conception of 'sacred history' used here and defined in Chapter 1 above is an attempt to render explicit and precise what is implicit in Augustine's view. It will be clear that this conception is both very closely related to, and not exactly identical with Cullmann's notion of 'salvation history' (*Heilsgeschichte*). The vital difference is that Augustine's conception presupposes a clear distinction between 'history' as what has happened ('the past') and 'history' as the record of what has happened. In the phrase 'sacred history', 'history' is used in the second of these senses, and 'sacred history' is defined by the special character of the record. This special character derives from the privileged status of the writers and of their interpretative judgement on the events recorded by them. This is the 'prophetic' quality of inspiration in the biblical canon (see Appendix A).

Cullmann does not make the distinction between the two senses of 'history' presupposed in the Augustinian conception of 'sacred history': i.e. that as past events, there is nothing distinctive about any part of history in virtue of which some history is 'sacred', whereas, understood as 'record', some history is 'sacred' in virtue of the distinctive status of its authorship and the authors' distinctive judgement on their past. In so far as Cullmann's language allows us to guess, 'history' (*Geschichte*) as used in the phrase 'salvation history' (*Heilsgeschichte*) seems to mean 'what has happened' rather than its record. Thus he writes: 'Salvation history itself continues but only as the unfolding of the Christ event. However, the revelation of the divine plan presented through event and interpretation, according to which salvation history has developed and will continue to develop up to the end, is concluded.'[1] The Augustinian 'sacred history' would coincide with Cullmann's 'revelation' here, and the Augustinian insistence on its completion within the biblical canon has its exact counterpart in Cullmann's assertion that 'if the temporality of salvation history is taken seriously, the *history of the revelation* of the saving plan must stand as concluded with this event...'.[2] Cullmann's statement that salvation history continues,

---

[1] *Salvation*, 294.   [2] *Ibid.* 295; italics in original.

indeed that since Christ all history has become salvation history,[1] would be represented in the Augustinian vocabulary by the affirmation that salvation continues in history since Christ and is, indeed, being worked out in a hidden manner in all history, but, as there are no properly authorised historians to discern its pattern, its history cannot be written. It is thus undistinguishable from all other ('secular') history.

This last insistence of Augustine's has its equivalent in Cullmann's —slightly hesitant—affirmation[2] that 'the crucial distinction has to do not with the saving process but with our *knowledge* about it. We know precisely in what way the saving process developed in biblical times. We know about the relationship between this process and ancient history, for we possess the Bible. On the other hand, the Bible tells us about our present time only the fact that it continues, and the direction in which it continues; we are not told the individual events and interpretations in which it is developed.' The distinction between 'the saving process' and 'our knowledge about it' made in this passage is roughly equivalent to the two senses of 'history' distinguished above. If one makes that distinction clear in the way one defines 'history', and if the phrase 'sacred history' is understood in the sense defined, the need for this distinction of Cullmann's vanishes. German theological writing seems to me to have been prevented from reaching a satisfactory clarity of usage, largely as a result of being bewitched by the attention that it has paid to the problem of distinguishing *Geschichte* from *Historie*. Thus even as clear-minded a theologian as Oscar Cullmann labours under the heritage of an insufficiently clarified vocabulary. I would wish, however, to pay tribute to him as the most distinguished of the modern theologians who have helped us to recover—in a number of books on varied themes, yet with a singularly impressive consistency of vision—the true eschatological perspective of Christian belief.

[1] *Salvation*, 325–6. [2] *Ibid.* 299–300.

BIBLIOGRAPHICAL NOTE

AUGUSTINE'S WORKS: The edition by the Benedictines of St Maur (1679–1700) is still the only serviceable complete edition. It is reprinted in J. P. Migne's *Patrologia latina*, 32–47, and is used in many of the volumes of *Bibliothèque augustinienne*, where the Latin text may be read with French translation, introductions and notes. Other standard editions of individual works are given by E. Dekkers & A. Gaar, *Clavis patrum latinorum*, 2a ed. (Bruges, 1961). English translations of individual works, where available, are listed in the appendix by J. J. O'Meara to Marrou's *Saint Augustine* and by Brown, *Augustine of Hippo*.

GENERAL WORKS ON AUGUSTINE: The best expositions are G. Bonner, *St Augustine of Hippo: Life and controversies* (London, 1963) and Peter Brown, *Augustine of Hippo: a biography* (London, 1967). On a much smaller scale, H.-I. Marrou, *Saint Augustine and his influence through the ages* (E. tr., London, 1957) is good. His *Saint Augustin et la fin de la culture antique* (Paris, 1938) [and *Retractatio*, Paris, 1949] is indispensable for Augustine as a late antique man of letters. F. Van der Meer, *Augustine the bishop* (E. tr., London, 1961) is a lively account of Augustine's life and work as a North African churchman.

AUGUSTINE ON HISTORY AND SOCIETY: the best short introductions are: P. R. L. Brown, 'Augustine', Ch. 1 in *Trends in medieval political thought*, ed. B. Smalley (Oxford, 1965), 1–21 and N. H. Baynes, *The political ideas of St Augustine's 'De civitate Dei'* (London, 1936). R. H. Barrow, *Introduction to Saint Augustine, 'The City of God'* (London, 1950) is useful both for its select passages in translation and its comments. For a detailed and conscientious account, see H. A. Deane, *The political and social ideas of Saint Augustine* (N.Y. and London, 1963). J. N. Figgis, *The political aspects of St Augustine's 'City of God'* (London, 1921) is a classic which keeps much of its value. On history, the only useful study is A. Wachtel, *Beiträge zur Geschichtstheologie des Aurelius Augustinus* (Bonn, 1960). For a short survey, see L. G. Patterson, *God and history in early Christian thought* (London, 1967), Ch. 5 and my chapter on this theme in *Cambridge history of later Greek and early medieval philosophy*, ed. A. H. Armstrong (Cambridge, 1967), 406–19.

ON DONATISM AND THE AFRICAN THEOLOGICAL TRADITION:
P. Monceaux's great though unfortunately never completed work, *Histoire littéraire de l'Afrique chrétienne*, 7 vols. (Paris, 1901-23) remains fundamental. On the Donatist movement a new era opens with Dr Frend's studies, especially his *The Donatist Church* (Oxford, 1952). Among the discussions provoked by his work the most important is P. R. L. Brown, 'Religious dissent in the later Roman Empire: the case of North Africa', *History* 46 (1961), 83-101. Of lesser importance are some of the studies, especially of the Circumcellions, gathered in H. J. Diesner, *Kirche und Staat im spätrömischen Reich* (Berlin, 1963) and the criticism in E. Tengström, *Donatisten und Katholiken: soziale, wirtschaftliche und politische Aspekte einer nordafrikanischen Kirchenspaltung* (*Studia Graeca et Latina Gothoburgensia* 18, 1964). On the continuity between Donatism and earlier African tradition (especially Cyprian), J. P. Brisson, *Autonomisme et christianisme dans l'Afrique romaine* (Paris, 1958), especially 33-239; on the continuity of Augustine's ecclesiology with previous African tradition, J. Ratzinger, *Volk und Haus Gottes in Augustins Lehre von der Kirche* (*Münchener theol. Studien*, II, 7, 1954) and a succinct survey by Y. M. J. Congar in his introduction to *Œuvres de saint Augustin*, 28: *Traités anti-Donatistes*, t. 1 (Bibliothèque augustinienne, Paris, 1963). On the later phases of dissent, and on the continuity of the tradition of African dissent, see my papers 'Donatism: the last phase', *Studies in Church history* 1 (1964), 118-26 and 'Reflections on religious dissent in North Africa in the Byzantine period', *ibid*. 3 (1966), 140-9. There are many accounts and discussions of the theological problems concerned with the Church, orders and sacraments. Among the general accounts see P. Batiffol, *Le catholicisme de saint Augustine* (Paris, 1920), F. Hofmann, *Der Kirchenbegriff des hl. Augustinus* (München, 1933), and S. J. Grabowski, *The Church: introduction to the theology of Saint Augustine* (St Louis, 1957). For a fuller discussion cf. my paper in *Bull. of the Soc. for African Church history* 3 (1969), 1-16.

BIBLIOGRAPHIES: There is a useful select bibliography, arranged by theme, in C. Andresen, ed., *Zum Augustin-Gespräch der Gegenwart* (*Wege der Forschung*, 5; Darmstadt, 1962), 459-83. An exhaustive bibliography covering a field adjacent to and largely overlapping that of the present study is E. Lamirande, 'Un siècle et demi d'études sur l'ecclésiologie de saint Augustin; essai bibliographique', *Revue des études augustiniennes* 8 (1962), 1-125.

WORKS REFERRED TO IN
THE FOOTNOTES

A. SOURCES

Details of editions have been given only in the case of works not in any of the standard series (*PL*, *PG*, *CC*, *CSEL*, *GCS*, *MGH*).

AMBROSE	*Ep.*	Epistolae. *PL* 16
	Expl. s. ps.	Explanatio super psalmos. *CSEL* 64
	Expos. in Luc.	Expositio evangelii secundum Lucam. *CC* 14
AMBROSIASTER	*Q. Vet. & Nov. Test.*	Quaestiones veteris et novi testamenti. *CSEL* 50
AMMIANUS MARCELLINUS		ed. J. C. Rolfe, 3 vols. (Loeb, 1935–9)
ARISTOTLE	*Eth. Nic.*	Ethica Nicomachea, ed. I. Bywater (OCT, 1894)
	Pol.	Politica, ed. W. D. Ross (OCT, 1957)
AUGUSTINE	*Brev.*	Breviculus—cf. De civitate Dei
	Brev. Coll. Don.	Breviculus collationis cum Donatistis. *CSEL* 53
	Conf.	Confessiones. *CSEL* 33.1
	C. Acad.	Contra Academicos. *CSEL* 63.3
	C. Cresc.	Contra Cresconium. *CSEL* 52
	C. ep. Parm.	Contra epistolam Parmeniani. *CSEL* 51
	C. Faust.	Contra Faustum Manichaeum. *CSEL* 25.1
	C. Gaudent.	Contra Gaudentium. *CSEL* 53
	C. Iul.	Contra Iulianum. *PL* 44
	C. litt. Pet.	Contra litteras Petiliani. *CSEL* 52
	De agone chr.	De agone christiano. *CSEL* 41
	De bapt.	De baptismo contra Donatistas. *CSEL* 51

AUGUSTINE *De cat. rud.* *De catechizandis rudibus. PL* 40

De civ. Dei *De civitate Dei. CC* 47–8

[*References have throughout been given according to the chapter numbering of the Benedictine editors, PL* 41. *Dombart & Kalb's text divisions have been shown where they differ.*]

De cons. Ev. *De consensu evangelistarum. CSEL* 43

De corr. et gratia *De correptione et gratia. PL* 44

De cura *De cura pro mortuis gerenda. CSEL* 41

De div. qu. LXXXIII *De diversis quaestionibus LXXXIII. PL* 40

De div. qu. ad Simpl. *De diversis quaestionibus ad Simplicianum. PL* 40

De doctr. chr. *De doctrina christiana. CSEL* 80

De fide r.q.n.v. *De fide rerum quae non videntur. PL* 40

De Gen. ad litt. *De Genesi ad litteram. CSEL* 28.1

De Gen. lib. impf. *De Genesi ad litteram liber imperfectus. CSEL* 28.1

De Gen. c. Man. *De Genesi contra Manichaeos. PL* 34

De gratia et lib. arb. *De gratia et libero arbitrio. PL* 44

De lib. arb. *De libero arbitrio. CSEL* 74

De mor. eccl. *De moribus ecclesiae et de moribus Manichaeorum. PL* 32

De ord. *De ordine. CSEL* 63

De perf. iust. *De perfectione iustitiae hominis. CSEL* 42

De quant. an. *De quantitate animae. PL* 32

De serm. Dom. *De sermone Domini in monte. CC* 35

De Trin. *De Trinitate. CC* 50, 50 a

AUGUSTINE	*De Urb. exc.*	*Sermo de Urbis excidio.* PL 40
	De vera rel.	*De vera religione.* CC 32
	Enarr. in Ps.	*Enarrationes in psalmos.* CC 38–40
	Ep., Epp.	*Epistolae.* CSEL 34.1, 34.2, 44, 57, 58
	Ep. ad Gal.	*Epistolae ad Galatas expositio.* PL 35
	Exp. prop. Ep. Rom.	*Expositio quarumdam propositionum ex epistola ad Romanos.* PL 35
	In Ep. Ioh. Tr.	*In Iohannis Epistulam ad Parthos tractatus.* PL 35
	In Joh. Ev. Tr.	*Tractatus in Johannis Evangelium.* CC 36
	Qu. in Hept.	*Quaestiones in Heptateuchum.* CC 33
	Retr.	*Retractationes.* CSEL 36
	Sermo	*Sermones.* PL 38–9 (1–50: CC 41)

	Sermo bibl. Casin. ⎫
	   Caillau
	   Denis ⎬
	   Frangip.
	   Mai
	   Morin ⎭
		Sermones post Maurinos reperti, ed. G. Morin (*Miscellanea Agostiniana,* 1, Roma, 1930)

CICERO	*Fin.*	*De finibus bonorum et malorum.* ed. H. Rackham (Loeb, 1914)
	Leg.	*De legibus.* ed. C. W. Keyes (Loeb, 1928)
	Off.	*De officiis.* ed. W. Miller (Loeb, 1913)
	Pro Milone	ed. N. H. Watts (Loeb, 1913)
	Rep.	*De Re publica.* ed. C. W. Keyes (Loeb, 1928)
CLAUDIAN	*De bello Gild.*	*De bello Gildonico.* MGH. AA. 10
	De bello Goth.	*De bello Gothico.* MGH. AA. 10

COUNCILS AND CANONS	{ C. Carth. { Cod. eccl. Afr.	Concilium Carthaginense ⎫ Codex canonum ecclesiae ⎬ Africanae ⎭ ed. H. T. Bruns, Canones apostolorum et conciliorum saeculorum IV, V, VI, VII (Berlin, 1839)
CYPRIAN	De eccl. unit.	De catholicae ecclesiae unitate. CSEL 3.1
	Ep.	Epistolae. CSEL 3.2

Epigrammata Bobiensia see under Section B, SPEYER.

Epistola ad Catholicos		CSEL 52
EUSEBIUS	HE	Historia ecclesiastica. GCS 9
	Laus Const.	Oratio de laudibus Constantini. GCS 7
	Praep. ev.	Praeparatio evangelica. GCS 43
Gesta Collationis Carthaginiensis		PL 11
GREGORY I	Mor.	Moralia in Job. PL 75–6
HILARIANUS		Libellus de mundi duratione sive De cursu temporum. PL 13
HIPPOLYTUS	In Daniel.	In Danielem commentarius. ed. M. Lefèvre and G. Bardy (Paris, 1947)
IRENAEUS	AH	Adversus haereses. ed. W. W. Harvey, Cambridge, 1857 [References are given according to Massuet's division of the text, PG 7]
ISIDORE OF SEVILLE	Etym.	Etymologiae. ed. W. M. Lindsay (OCT, 1911)
JEROME	Comm. in Isa. Comm. in Mich.	Commentarii in Isaiam. CC 73 Commentarii in Michaeam. PL 25
	Ep.	Epistolae. CSEL 54–6
LACTANTIUS	Div. inst.	Divinae institutiones. CSEL 19
LAWS	Cod. Theod.	Codex Theodosianus. ed. T. Mommsen and P. Meyer (Berlin, 1905)
MACROBIUS	Sat.	Saturnalia. ed. J. Willis (1963)

OPTATUS	De schism.	De schismate. CSEL 26
ORIGEN	C. Cels.	Contra Celsum. E. tr. H. Chadwick (Cambridge, 1965)
OROSIUS	Hist.	Historiarum adversus paganos libri VII. CSEL 5
OTTO OF FREISING	Chron.	Chronicon sive Historia de duabus civitatibus. ed. W. Lammers. See Section B, LAMMERS
PLOTINUS	Enn.	Enneads. ed. E. Bréhier (Paris, 1924–38)
PROSPER	De voc.	De vocatione omnium gentium. PL 51
PRUDENTIUS	C. Symm. Perist.	Contra Symmachum. CC 126 Peristephanon. CC 126
RUFINUS	HE	Historia ecclesiastica. GCS 9
RUTILIUS NAMATIANUS	De red.	De reditu suo. ed. J. Vesserau and F. Préchac (Paris, 1933)
SULPICIUS SEVERUS	Chron.	Chronicon. CSEL 1
SYMMACHUS	Rel.	Relationes. MGH. AA. 6
TERTULLIAN	Apol. Praescr.	Apologeticum. CC 1 De praescriptione haereticorum. CC 1
TYCONIUS	Reg.	Liber regularum. ed. F. C. Burkitt (T. & S. 3.1, 1894) Commentarius in Apocalypsin. The Turin fragments of Tyconius' Commentary on Revelation, ed. F. Lo Bue (T. & S. NS 7, 1963)

Sources referred to in Appendix C (thirteenth century)

| ALBERT THE GREAT | | Opera (Paris, 1890–9) |
| | In Pol. | Commentarius in VIII libros Politicorum. Opera, vol. 8 |

ALBERT THE GREAT	*In Sent.*	*Commentarius in* II *librum Sententiarum. Opera,* vol. 27
	Sum. theol.	*Summa theologiae. Opera,* vols. 32–3
ALEXANDER OF HALES		*Glossa in IV libros Sententiarum Petri Lombardi.* (Bibl. Franciscana schol. med. aevi, 12–15, 1951–7)
BONAVENTURE	*In Sent.*	*Commentaria in* IV *libros Sententiarum Petri Lombardi* (Quaracchi, 1882–9)
GILES OF ROME	*In Sent.*	*In* II *librum Sententiarum Quaestiones* (Venice, 1581)
JAMES OF VITERBO	*De reg. chr.*	*De regimine christiano.* ed. H. X. Arquillière (Paris, 1926)
PTOLEMY OF LUCCA		*Determinatio compendiosa de iurisdictione imperii.* ed. M. Krammer (Hannover, 1909) [Continuation of *De regimine principum* of Thomas Aquinas]
RICHARD OF MIDDLETON	*In Sent.*	*Super* IV *libros Sententiarum Quaestiones* (Brixen, 1591)
Summa fratris Alexandri		ed V. Doucet *et al.* (Quaracchi, 1924)
THOMAS AQUINAS	*De reg. princ.*	*De regimine principum* [*De regno*]. ed. J. Mathis (Turin, 1948)
	In Eth.	*In X libros Ethicorum Aristotelis ad Nicomachum expositio.* ed. R. M. Spiazzi (Turin, 1949)
	In Pol.	*In libros Politicorum Aristotelis expositio.* ed. R. M. Spiazzi (Turin, 1951)

THOMAS   *In div. nom.*   *In librum* B *Dionysii De Divi-*
AQUINAS   *nis Nominibus expositio.* ed.
                         C. Pera (Turin, 1950)
       In Sent.   *Scriptum super libros Sententi-*
                        arum. ed. P. Mandonnet and
                        M.F. Moos (Paris, 1929–47)
     Sum. c. gent.   *Summa contra gentiles.* ex ed.
                        Leonina (Roma, 1934)
     Sum. theol.   *Summa theologiae.* ed.
                        P. Caramello (Turin,
                        1948)

B. SECONDARY WORKS

ALTANER, B. 'Augustinus und Irenaeus', *Theol. Quartalschr.* 129 (1949), 162–72; reprinted in *Kleine patristische Schriften* (*T. & U.* 83, Berlin, 1967), 194–203.

ARCHAMBAULT, P. 'The ages of man and the ages of the world', *REAug* 12 (1966), 193–228.

ARMSTRONG, A. H. 'Salvation, Plotinian and Christian', *Downside rev.* 75 (1957), 126–39.

ARMSTRONG, A. H. and MARKUS, R. A., *Christian faith and Greek philosophy* (London, 1960).

ARQUILLIÈRE, H. X. *L'Augustinisme politique* (Paris, 1934).

BAKHUIZEN VAN DEN BRINK, J. N. 'Tradition and authority in the early Church', *Stud. patr.* 7 (*T. & U.* 92, Berlin, 1966), 3–22.

BARKER, SIR E. ed. *From Alexander to Constantine* (Oxford, 1956).

BARTH, K. 'The Christian community and the civil community', in *Against the stream* (E. tr., London, 1954).

BATIFFOL, P. *Le catholicisme de saint Augustin* (Paris, 1920).

BAYNES, N. H. 'Eusebius and the Christian Empire', *Ann. de l'Inst. de phil. & d'hist. or.* 2 (Mélanges Bidez, 1933–4), 13–18; reprinted in *Byzantine studies and other essays* (London, 1955), 168–72.

BERKHOF, H. *Kirche und Kaiser* (Zürich, 1947).

BERLIN, SIR I. *Two concepts of liberty* (Oxford, 1958).

BONHOEFFER, D. *Ethics* (E. tr., London, 1955).

BONNER, G. 'Les origines africaines de la doctrine augustinienne sur la chute et le péché originel', *Augustinus* (1967), 97–116.

Saint Augustine of Hippo (London, 1963).

Saint Bede in the tradition of Western Apocalyptic commentary (Jarrow, 1966).

BRISSON, J. P. *Autonomisme et christianisme dans l'Afrique romaine* (Paris, 1958).

BROWN, P. R. L. *Augustine of Hippo: a biography* (London, 1967).

'Pelagius and his supporters: aims and environment', *JTS*, NS 19 (1968), 93–114.

'Religious coercion in the later Roman Empire: the case of North Africa', *History* 48 (1963), 283–305.

'Religious dissent in the later Roman Empire: the case of North Africa', *History* 46 (1961), 83–101.

'Saint Augustine', Ch. 1 in *Trends in medieval political thought*, ed. B. Smalley (Oxford, 1965), 1–21.

'Saint Augustine's attitude to religious coercion', *JRS* 54 (1964), 107–16.

BURNABY, J. *Amor Dei: a study of the religion of St Augustine* (London, 1938).

BUTLER, B. C. *The idea of the Church* (London, 1962).

CARLYLE, R. W. and A. J. *A history of medieval political thought in the West*, 6 vols. (Edinburgh, 1903–36).

CASPAR, E. *Geschichte des Papsttums*, 2 Bde. (Tübingen, 1930–3).

CHENU, M. D. *Introduction à l'étude de saint Thomas d'Aquin*, 2e éd. (Paris, 1954).

COMBÈS, G. *La doctrine politique de saint Augustin* (Paris, 1927).

CONGAR, Y. M. J. '*Civitas Dei* et *ecclesia* chez Augustin. Histoire de la recherche: son état présent', *REAug* 3 (1957), 1–14.

[Introduction to] *Œuvres de S. Augustin*, t. 28: *Traités anti-donatistes*, 1 (Bibliothèque augustinienne, Paris, 1963).

COSTELLO, C. J. 'St Augustine's concept of inspiration', *Rev. de l'Univ. d'Ottawa* (1934), 81–99.

COURCELLE, P. *Les lettres grecques en occident* (Paris, 1948).

'Propos anti-chrétiens rapportés par saint Augustin', *Rech. aug.* 1 (1958), 149–86.

COX, H. *The secular city* (London, 1965).

CRANZ, F. E. '*De Civitate Dei*, xv, 2 and Augustine's idea of a Christian society', *Speculum* 25 (1950), 215–25; in French translation also in *REAug* 3 (1957), 15–28.

'The development of Augustine's ideas on society before the Donatist controversy', *HTR* 47 (1954), 255–316.

'Kingdom and polity in Eusebius of Caesarea', *HTR* 45 (1952), 47–66.

CRESPIN, R. *Ministère et sainteté: pastorale du clergé et solution de la crise donatiste dans la vie et la doctrine de saint Augustin* (Paris, 1965).

CROSS, F. L. 'History and fiction in the African canons', *JTS*, NS 12 (1961), 227–47.

CULLMANN, O. *Salvation in history* (E. tr., London, 1967).

The state in the New Testament (E. tr., London, 1957).

DANIÉLOU, J. *Bible et liturgie* (Paris, 1951).

'La typologie millénariste de la semaine dans le christianisme primitif', *VC* 2 (1948), 1–16.

DEANE, H. A. *The political and social ideas of Saint Augustine* (New York and London, 1963).

DIESNER, H. J. *Kirche und Staat im spätrömischen Reich* (Berlin, 1963).

Studien zur Gesellschaftslehre und sozialen Haltung Augustins (Halle, 1954).

DUCHESNE, L. *The early history of the Church*, vol. 3 (E. tr., London, 1924).

DUVAL, Y. M. 'L'éloge de Théodose dans la *Cité de Dieu* (v, 26.1)', *Rech. aug.* 4 (1966), 135–79.

DVORNIK, F. *Early Christian and Byzantine political philosophy*, 2 vols. (Dumbarton Oaks, 1966).

ESCHMANN, I. T. [Introduction to] *St Thomas on Kingship*, trs. G. B. Phelan (Toronto, 1949).

FOLLIET, G. 'La typologie du sabbat chez saint Augustin: son interprétation millénariste entre 388 et 400', *REAug* 2 (1956), 371–90.

FREND, W. H. C. *The Donatist Church* (Oxford, 1952).

Martyrdom and persecution in the early Church (Oxford, 1965).

'The Roman Empire in the eyes of Western schismatics in the fourth century', *Misc. hist. eccles.* (Stockholm, 1960), 9–22.

FUCHS, H. *Augustin und der antike Friedensgedanke* (*Neue philol. Unters.* 3, Berlin, 1926).

Der geistige Widerstand gegen Rom in der antiken Welt (Berlin, 1938).

GOODENOUGH, E. *The politics of Philo Judaeus* (New Haven, 1938).

GRABOWSKI, S. *The Church: introduction to the theology of Saint Augustine* (St Louis, 1957).

GRANT, R. M. *Miracle and natural law in Greco-Roman and early Christian thought* (Amsterdam, 1952).

GRASMÜCK, E. L. *Coercitio: Staat und Kirche im Donatistenstreit* (*Bonner histor. Forsch.* 22, 1964).

GREENSLADE, S. L. *Schism in the early Church*, 2nd ed. (London, 1962).

GUY, J. C. *Unité et structure logique de la 'Cité de Dieu' de saint Augustin* (Paris, 1961).

HAHN, T. *Tyconius-Studien* (*St. z. Gesch. d. Theol. u. Kirche*, VI, 2, Leipzig, 1900).

HERMELINK, H. 'Die civitas terrena bei Augustin', *Festgabe A. v. Harnack z. 70. Geburtstag* (Tübingen, 1921), 302–24.

HOFMANN, F. *Der Kirchenbegriff des hl. Augustinus* (München, 1933).

HOLTE, R. *Béatitude et sagesse: saint Augustin et le problème de la fin de l'homme dans la philosophie ancienne* (Paris, 1962).

JOLY, R. 'Saint Augustin et l'intolérance religieuse', *Rev. belge de phil. et d'hist.* 33 (1955), 263–94.

JONES, B. V. E. 'The manuscript tradition of Augustine's De civitate Dei', *JTS*, NS 16 (1955), 142–5.

KAMLAH, W. *Christentum und Geschichtlichkeit*, 2te Aufl. (Stuttgart, 1951).

KENNY, T. *The political thought of John Henry Newman* (London, 1957).

KLINKENBERG, H. M. 'Unus Petrus — Generalitas ecclesiae bei Augustinus', *Universalismus und Partikularismus im Mittelalter*, ed. P. Wilpert (*Miscellanea medievalia*, 5; Berlin, 1968), 216–42.

KÜNG, H. *The Church* (E. tr., London, 1967).

LA BONNARDIÈRE, A. M. 'Quelques remarques sur les citations scripturaires du *De gratia et libero arbitrio*', *REAug* 9 (1963), 77–85.

LACROIX, B. *Orose et ses idées* (Montréal and Paris, 1965).

LADNER, G. B. *The idea of reform: its impact on Christian thought and action in the age of the Fathers* (Cambridge, Mass., 1959).

LAMBOT, C. 'Lettre inédite de saint Augustin relative au *De Civitate Dei*', *Revue bénédictine* 51 (1939), 109–21.

LAMMERS, W. [Introduction to] *Otto von Freising: Chronik (Ausgewählte Quellen zur deutschen Geschichte d. Mittelalters*, 16, Berlin, 1960).

LAURAS, A. 'Deux cités: Jérusalem et Babylone', *La Ciudad de Dios* 167 (1954), 117–50.

LAURAS, A. and RONDET, H. 'Le thème des deux cités dans l'œuvre de saint Augustin', *Études augustiniennes* (Paris, 1953), 97–160.

LEISEGANG, H. 'Der Ursprung der Lehre Augustins von der *civitas Dei*', *Arch. f. Kulturgesch.* 16 (1925), 127–58.

LEWIS, E. *Medieval political ideas*, 2 vols. (London, 1954).

LOHSE, B. 'Augustins Wandlung in seiner Beurteilung des Staates', *Stud. patr.* 6 (*T. & U.* 81, Berlin, 1960), 447–75.

LUNEAU, A. *L'histoire du salut chez les Pères de l'Église: la doctrine des âges du monde* (Paris, 1964).

MCCABE, H. *The new creation* (London, 1964).

MADEC, G. 'Sur la vision augustinienne du monde', *REAug* 9 (1963), 139–46.

MAIER, F. G. *Augustin und das antike Rom* (Tübingen, 1955).

MANDOUZE, A. 'Saint Augustin et la religion romaine', *Rech. aug.* I (1958), 187–223.

MARKUS, R. A. '*Alienatio*: philosophy and eschatology in the development of an Augustinian idea', *Stud. patr.* 9 (*T. & U.* 94, Berlin, 1966), 431–50.

'Augustine'; Ch. 5 in *Critical history of Western philosophy*, ed. D. J. O'Connor (New York and London, 1964), 79–97.

'Donatism: the last phase', *Studies in Church history* I (1964), 118–26.

'Marius Victorinus and Augustine'; Pt. v in *Cambridge history of later Greek and early medieval philosophy*, ed. A. H. Armstrong (Cambridge, 1967), 327–420.

'Presuppositions of the typological approach to scripture', *CQR* 158 (1957), 442–51; repr. in *The communication of the Gospel in New Testament times* (London, 1961), 75–85.

'Reflections on religious dissent in North Africa in the Byzantine period', *Studies in Church history* 3 (1967), 140–9.

'A relevant pattern of holiness: Dietrich Bonhoeffer's *Ethics*', *Hibbert J.* 55 (1957), 387–92.

'The Roman empire in early Christian historiography', *Downside rev.* 81 (1963), 340–54.

'St Augustine on signs', *Phronesis* 2 (1957), 60–83.

MARROU, H.-I. *L'ambivalence du temps de l'histoire chez saint Augustin* (Montréal, 1950).

'Civitas Dei, civitas terrena: num tertium quid?', *Stud. patr.* 2 (*T. & U.* 64, Berlin, 1957), 342–50.

'La division en chapitres des livres de la Cité de Dieu', *Mélanges J. de Ghellinck*, I (Gembloux, 1951), 235–49.

Saint Augustin et la fin de la culture antique (Paris, 1938).

'La théologie de l'histoire. Rapport', *Aug. mag.* 3, 193–204.

MILL, J. S. 'Bentham', in *Mill on Bentham and Coleridge*, ed. F. R. Leavis (London, 1950).

MOLTMANN, J. *Theology of hope* (E. tr., London, 1967).

MOMIGLIANO, A. 'Pagan and Christian historiography in the fourth century A.D.', in *The conflict between paganism and christianity in the fourth century*, ed. A. Momigliano (Oxford, 1963), 79–99.

MOMMSEN, T. E. 'Orosius and Augustine', in *Medieval and Renaissance studies* (New York, 1959), 325–48.

'St Augustine and the Christian idea of progress', *J. hist. of ideas* 12 (1951), 346–74; repr. in *Medieval and Renaissance studies*, 265–98.

MONCEAUX, P. *Histoire littéraire de l'Afrique chrétienne*, 7 vols. (Paris, 1901–23).

O'MEARA, J. J. *Porphyry's Philosophy from Oracles in Augustine* (Paris, 1959).

OPELT, I. 'Augustustheologie und Augustustypologie', *Jahrb. f. Antike u. Christentum* 4 (1961), 44–57.

PATTERSON, L. G. *God and history in early Christian thought* (London, 1967).

PETERSON, E. 'Die Kirche', in *Theologische Traktate* (München, 1951), 409–29.

Der Monotheismus als politisches Problem (München, 1935); repr. in *Theologische Traktate*, 45–147.

PINCHERLE, A. 'Da Ticonio a Sant'Agostino', *Ric. rel.* 1 (1925), 443–66.

'L'ecclesiologia nella controversia donatista', *Ric. rel.* 1 (1925), 35–55.

RAHNER, K. 'The Church and the sacraments', repr. in *Studies in modern theology* (E. tr., London, 1963), 189–300.

RATZINGER, J. 'Beobachtungen zum Kirchenbegriff des Tyconius im *Liber regularum*', *REAug* 2 (Mémorial Gustave Bardy, 1956), 173–85.

'Herkunft und Sinn der Civitas-Lehre Augustins', *Aug. mag.* 2, 965–79.

Volk und Haus Gottes in Augustins Lehre von der Kirche (*Münchener theol. stud.* II/7, 1954).

RONDET, H. 'Le symbolisme de la mer chez saint Augustin', *Aug. mag.* 2, 691–701.

SASSE, H. 'Sacra scriptura: Bemerkungen zur Inspirationslehre Augustins', *Festschr. Franz Dornseiff* (Leipzig, 1953), 262–73.

SCHILLEBEECKX, E. *Christ the sacrament of our encounter with God* (E. tr., London, 1963).

SCHILLING, O. *Die Staats- und Soziallehre des hl. Augustinus* [*SSLAug*] (Freiburg, 1910).

Die Staats- und Soziallehre des heiligen Thomas von Aquin, 2te Aufl., [*SSLThom*] (München, 1930).

SCHMIDT, R. 'Aetates mundi. Die Weltalter als Gliederungsprinzip der Geschichte', *ZKG* 67 (1955–6), 288–317.

SCHMÖLZ, F. M. 'Historia sacra et profana bei Augustin', in *Perennitas: Beiträge zur christlichen Archäologie...P. Thomas Michels zum 70. Geburtstag*, ed. H. Rahner and E. von Severus (Münster, 1963), 32–45.

SCHOLZ, H. *Glaube und Unglaube in der Weltgeschichte: ein Kommentar zu Augustins De Civitate Dei* (Leipzig, 1911).

SCHUBERT, P. A. *Augustins Lex-aeterna-Lehre nach Inhalt und Quellen* (*Beitr. z. Gesch. d. Philos. d. Mittelalters*, 24/2; Münster, 1924).

SIZOO, A. 'Augustinus de senectute', in *Ut pictura poesis: studia latina P. J. Enk* (Leiden, 1955), 184–8.

SPEYER, W. *Naucellius und sein Kreis: Studien zur Epigrammata Bobiensia* (*Zetemata* 21, München, 1959).

STRAUB, J. 'Augustins Sorge um die *regeneratio imperii*: das *Imperium Romanum* als *civitas terrena*', *Hist. Jahrb.* 73 (1954), 36–60.

'Christliche Geschichtsapologetik in der Krisis des römischen Reiches', *Historia* 1 (1950), 52–81.

Heidnische Geschichtsapologetik in der christlichen spätantike: Untersuchungen zur Zeit und Tendenz der Historia Augusta (*Antiquitas*, Reihe IV, Bd. 1, Bonn, 1963).

STRAUSS, G. *Schriftgebrauch, Schriftauslegung und Schriftbeweis bei Augustin* (*Beitr. z. Gesch. d. bibl. Hermeneutik*, 1; Tübingen, 1959).

SWAIN, J. W. 'The theory of the four monarchies', *Class. philol.* 35 (1940), 1–21.

SYME, SIR R. *Ammianus and the Historia Augusta* (Oxford, 1968).

TENGSTRÖM, E. *Donatisten und Katholiken: soziale, wirtschaftliche und politische Aspekte einer nordafrikanischen Kirchenspaltung* (*St. graeca et latina Gothoburgensia* 18, 1964).

TESTARD, M. *Saint Augustin et Cicéron*, 2 vols. (Paris, 1958).

TRIEBER, K. 'Die Idee der vier Weltreiche', *Hermes* 27 (1892), 321–44.

ULLMANN, W. *Principles of government and politics in the Middle Ages* (London, 1961).

VAN DER MEER, F. *Augustine the bishop* (E. tr., London, 1961).

VEER, A. C. DE, 'L'exploitation du schisme Maximianiste par S. Augustin dans sa lutte contre le Donatisme', *Rech. aug.* 3 (1965), 219–37.

VEREKER, C. H. *Eighteenth century optimism* (Liverpool, 1967).

VITTINGHOF, F. 'Zum geschichtlichen Selbstverständnis der Spätantike', *HZ* 198 (1964), 529–74.

VON BALTHASAR, H. U. *Man in history* (E. tr., London, 1967).

VON DEN BRINCKEN, A. D. *Studien zur lateinischen Weltchronistik bis in das Zeitalter Ottos von Freising* (Düsseldorf, 1957).

WACHTEL, A. *Beiträge zur Geschichtstheologie des Aurelius Augustinus* (*Bonner histor. Forsch.* 17, 1960).

WICKER, B. J. *First the political kingdom: a personal appraisal of the Catholic Left in Britain* (London, 1967).

WILES, M. *The making of Christian doctrine* (Cambridge, 1967).

WILKS, M. J. *The problem of sovereignty in the later Middle Ages* (Cambridge, 1963).

'Roman Empire and Christian state in the *De civitate Dei*', *Augustinus* (1967), 489–510.

'St Augustine and the general will', *Stud. patr.* 9 (*T. & U.* 94, Berlin, 1966), 487–522.

WILLIAMS, R. *The long revolution* (Penguin ed., Harmondsworth, 1965).

WILLIS, G. G. *Saint Augustine and the Donatist controversy* (London, 1950).

ZEPF, M. 'Zur Chronologie der anti-donatistischen Schriften Augustins', *ZNTW* 28 (1929), 46–61.

INDEX

INDEX

INDEX

INDEX